MAKING CONNECTIONS 3:

An Integrated Approach to Learning English

TEACHER'S EXTENDED EDITION

Carolyn Kessler

Jean Bernard-Johnston

Linda Lee

Mary Lou McCloskey

Mary Ellen Quinn

Lydia Stack

Heinle & Heinle Publishers
A Division of International Thomson Publishing, Inc.
Boston, MA 02116, U.S.A.

The publication of *Making Connections* was directed by the members of the Heinle & Heinle Secondary ESL Publishing Team:

Editorial Director:	Roseanne Mendoza
Production Services Coordinator:	Lisa McLaughlin
Developmental Editor:	Nancy Mann
Market Development Director:	Ingrid A. Greenberg

Also participating in the publication of this program were:

Publisher:	Stanley J. Galek
Director of Production:	Elizabeth Holthaus
Manufacturing Coordinator:	Mary Beth Hennebury
Project Managers:	PC&F, Inc.; Martucci Studio
Composition:	PC&F, Inc.
Interior Design:	Martucci Studio
Illustration:	Jerry Malone/Martucci Studio
Cover Design:	Martucci Studio

Manufactured in the United States of America

ISBN 0-8384-3845-8
10 9 8 7 6 5 4 3 2

Printed in the United States of America.
Heinle & Heinle Publishers is a division of International Thomson Publishing, Inc.

3 CONTENTS

TO THE TEACHER

Goals, Philosophy

Middle and High School ESOL (English for Speakers of Other Languages) students are faced with a formidable task. In the few short years of school that remain, they must learn both English and the challenging content of their academic curriculum, made more challenging because so much language acquisition is demanded. *Making Connections: An Integrated Approach to Learning English* provides resources to integrate the teaching and learning of language and academic content. Resources in the series help teachers and students develop students' ability to communicate in English as they focus on motivating themes with topics, activities, tools, and procedures that introduce the content areas of science, social studies, and literature.

We are aware of the need for materials that help us to teach to the long-term learning goals we know are most important, and to teach the ways we know students learn best. We know this from our own experiences as teachers, as well as from working and talking with many classroom teachers. *Making Connections: An Integrated Approach to Learning English* is designed to do both: to help secondary students and their teachers reach toward important, essential goals, and to facilitate their learning language and content in the way they learn best. What are the goals we reach for?

Joy—the joy in life and learning that will make our students happy, successful lifetime learners;

Literacy—the ability to use reading and writing to accomplish amazing things;

Community—the knowledge that they live in an accepting community where they have rights, responsibilities, and resources;

Access—access to whatever resources they need to accomplish their own goals, including access to technology;

Power—the power to make their lives into whatever they choose;

What are the ways of teaching and learning that work best, according to our understanding of language acquisition research? The answer, we believe, is **integrated learning.** In *Making Connections,* we include four different kinds of integration: integration of language areas, language and academic content, students with one another, and school with the larger community.

- **We integrate language areas through active learning.**

We combine reading, writing, listening, and speaking into things that students do. Through interacting with authentic and culturally relevant literature, through activities that involve genuine communication, and through student-owned process writing, students learn the "parts" or "skills" of language in meaningful "whole" contexts.

- **We integrate language with academic content and process.**

Language is best learned when it is used as a tool; when students are meaningfully engaged in something important to them. Learning the language of and participating in processes specific to academic content area subjects are essential for preparing students to move into mainstream content-area classrooms. By teaching language through content, we attempt to do several things at once: we help students to learn to use a variety of learning strategies, we introduce them to science, social studies, and literature content appropriate for their age and grade level, and we help them to use accessible language and learn new esential language in the process.

- **We integrate students with one another.**

We try to help teachers and students develop a real learning community in which students and teachers use a variety of strategies—including many cooperative learning strategies—to accomplish student-owned educational goals. We acknowledge that students are not all at the same level linguistically or academically, but recognize that each student has strengths to offer in your classroom, so we provide choices of materials and activities that accommodate a multi-level class.

- **We integrate school with home culture and with the greater community.**

We strive for materials and activities that are relevant for a culturally diverse group and that help students to develop their self-esteem by valuing their unique cultural heritages. We seek to involve students in the community, and the community with schools, by providing and encouraging activities and projects that relate to community life and that put students into interaction with community representatives. This active involvement is integral to the development of students' content-area knowledge and language.

In order to reach toward these goals and implement these four kinds of integration, we have used integrated thematic units as the organizational basis for *Making Connections*. Our themes are arrived at in a variety of ways. Some, like "Choosing Foods," have very concrete connections among the sections of the units. Others,

like "Making Waves," make more metaphorical connections among sections that treat very different aspects of the theme. In all the units, students will make connections across content areas and will revisit themes and use and re-use the language of a theme in different ways. Each unit provides multi-level information and experiences that integrate language with one or more content areas and includes the following features:

Learning Strategies

In each unit, we highlight strategies to help students with their language and content area learning. We encourage teachers and students to be aware of the applicability of these strategies in new learning situations. Our goal is to create active, capable, self-starting learners. Research has shown that students apply learning strategies while learning a second language. These strategies have been classified, and they include:

Metacognitive Strategies, through which students think about their own learning processes.

Cognitive Strategies, which relate directly to learning tasks and often involve direct manipulation or transformation of learning materials.

Social/Affective Strategies, which involve teacher and peer interaction to accomplish learning goals.

Many of these strategies can be used as **Mediation Strategies,** strategies through which learning is assisted. Transfer of learning strategies from one context to another can be enhanced by combining cognitive and metacognitive strategies. In developing *Making Connections* we have constantly sought ways to assist students in developing their own repertoire of learning strategies. Following are strategies included in the series.

1. Reading Strategies: We encourage you to use a variety of ways to guide students through the reading selections. To accommodate the varied levels of students you might choose one or a combination of these strategies for reading selections:

A. *Read Aloud:* You or an advanced student read the selection aloud to the students. Pay attention to your voice. Develop your expressiveness, varying pitch, volume, and speed of reading. Create different voices for different characters when reading literature selections. Don't read too quickly since second language learners need time to process what is read.

B. *Shared Reading:* Teacher and students read together using text on a transparency or a chart or multiple copies of the selection. During shared reading, students at a variety of language levels can all participate in different ways.

C. *Paired Reading:* Two students take turns reading aloud to each other. If they are reading prose, one student can read one paragraph, and the next student can read the following paragraph. If they are reading poetry, students can alternate lines and stanzas.

D. *Silent Reading:* Provide time during class for your students to read. Students need plenty of reading material at different reading levels, selections from text as well as other sources. Set clear expectations for your students during the silent reading time. Everyone must read; they cannot talk or write during this time.

E. *Directed Reading:* Students learning to read in English often need help with their acquisition since content-area schemata may be culturally specific and not part of the second language learner's cultural background. To make difficult material accessible, the teacher divides text into manageable "chunks" and uses strategies such as questions, outlines, or story maps to support student reading. The following activities help students acquire schema:

1. *Use questions as a "scaffolding" technique.* The use of questions helps to clarify meanings of words, develop concepts, encourage both literal and inferential comprehension, and relate the story to the students' own experiences. For multilevel classes, include questions at a variety of levels, from labeling and recall to analysis. Always include some questions that do not have just one right answer, in order to encourage students to think for themselves.

2. *Use cueing strategies.* When reading literature selections with various characters, use verbal cueing strategies, such as changes of voice for different characters, pauses to indicate changes in events and dramatic moments, and exaggerated intonation for keywords and concepts. Use non-verbal cueing strategies, such as pointing to illustrations or parts of illustrations, and using facial expressions, gestures, and actions to accompany key events in the story. Story maps or content-area charts can also serve as cues. (See graphic organizers)

F. *Independent Reading:* Encourage students to read outside of class. Take students to the school or public library, and encourage them to use this resource often. Help them select reading materials at their interest and reading levels. If possible, develop a classroom library and provide class time for independent silent reading or self-selected materials. Read yourself during this time to serve as a role model.

2. Graphic Organizers: Graphic organizers are visual aids that help students remember the content as they read and then relate that content to their own experience. Graphic organizers can be used in many stages of unit study. As pre-reading activities they prepare students for the text they will read. During a reading, graphic organizers help students understand what they are reading, and after the reading. graphic organizers help students analyze what they have read. Finally, graphic organizers can be used as pre-writing activities, to help students organize material for writing stories, essays, and reports. Many graphic organizers are used in *Making Connections*. Some of these are described below.

A. *Semantic Maps:* Semantic mapping includes a variety of ways to make graphic displays of information within categories related to a central concept. This strategy helps students to demonstrate prior knowledge and add new information. The semantic maps can show relationships among terms and concepts and help students to develop vocabulary, improve understanding, review material learned, and prepare to write.

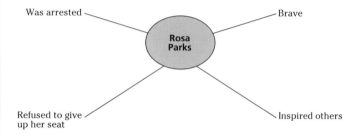

A Semantic Map

B. *Five Point Outline:* This graphic organizer helps students to generate basic information to prepare for writing by asking the basic newswriter questions. The students draw rays coming from a "sun" center and write a question word on each ray: Who, What, When, Where, Why. Then students write a phrase or two about the writing topic that answers each question.

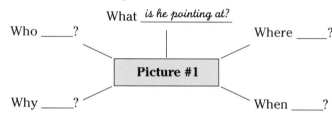

A Five Point Outline

C. *Venn Diagram:* A Venn diagram uses circles to show similarities and differences between topics or concepts. Two overlapping circles allow students to compare and contrast information. Information that is specific to one or the other of the topics or concepts is written in the circle for that topic or concept.

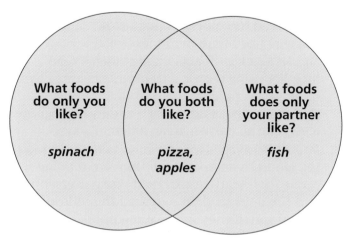

A Venn Diagram

D. *K/W/L/Chart:* The Know/ Want to Know/ Learned (K/W/L) Chart is a preparatory activity that allows students to discover what they know about a given topic and what they want to know. Before beginning to study a topic, students make a chart with two columns. At the top of one column, they write "Know" and at the top of the other column they write

Know	Want to know	Learned
What do you know about the story from the pictures?	What do you want to know?	What did you learn?
Younde lives in a village.	*Where is the village?*	

A K/W/L Chart

"Want to Know." Students meet in small groups and talk about the topic. They also brainstorm questions they want answered about the topic. In the first column students write things they know about the subject, and in the second column they write questions they want answered about the topic. After studying a topic, you may want to add a third column to the chart "Learned," and have students work in groups or with you to write information they have learned while studying this topic.

E. *Graphs:* Graphs are visual displays of data or information that help students' understanding of the information presented. A graph allows students to compare data or information.

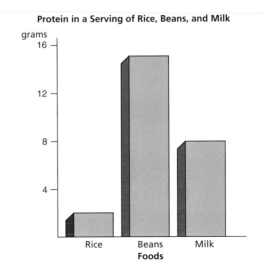

A Graph

F. *Timelines:* Timelines allow students to organize information chronologically, and often to gain an historical perspective. If events happen over time, a timeline can help students match dates to events.

A Timeline

3. Cooperative Learning:
Cooperative learning has been shown to be effective in facilitating both student learning and successful cross-cultural, multi-level student integration. Each unit uses a variety of cooperative groups and activities to achieve these goals. Some of the cooperative learning techniques used in *Making Connections* are:

A. *Jigsaw:* Divide up a task as if it were a jigsaw puzzle. The members of the home group can each become an expert in a small part of the task. Then, when they fit the pieces together, everyone understands the whole. For a reading selection:

1. Divide the reading selection into one part for each group member (4–6 students per group).
2. Each person becomes an expert on one part. To become an expert, students study the reading selection closely.
3. Then each person retells his or her part of the reading selection to the group and the home group can ask questions of the expert.
4. Either groups or individuals then answer questions on the entire reading.

B. *Think–Pair–Share:*
1. Students think about an experience they have had that is related to the topic they are studying.
2. In pairs, students tell their experience to each other. Students take notes as they listen to their partners to prepare to retell their partners' experiences.
3. Two pairs of students get together and each student tells his/her partner's experience to the group.

C. *Choral Reading.* Two or more students read a poem, a story, or a play out loud in unison.

Divide the selection and students into high voice parts, medium voice parts, and low voice parts. Students practice reading in their groups until they can read their parts in unison; then the three groups come together to read their parts of the selection in the correct order.

Language Focus

Language is learned best in a meaningful, useful contexts. From meaningful contexts, many opportunities arise to teach language concepts as they are needed. In *Making Connections,* we have provided suggestions both in the student texts and in the teacher editions for teaching language features as opportunities arise in the text materials or in the language students are using.

Although learners of English are not yet proficient in using English, they are proficient users of another language or languages, have had many academic and non-academic experiences, and are capable of high-level thinking. Language educators are challenged to provide appropriate materials for these students, materials that challenge them intellectually without frustrating them linguistically. The carefully-chosen reading selections in *Making Connections* provide students models of high-quality language, with the sophistication and complexity appropriate to the students' age levels. Readings offer new vocabulary in context and serve as a source for learning about the mechanics of language in authentic contexts. Reading selections provide a common text that students can use to negotiate meaning and to participate in lively discussions about the topics.

Each unit of *Making Connections* includes a number of *Language Focus* boxes that use content and context as opportunities to suggest practice in using particular language forms and functions. We encourage you to use these to inspire contextualized practice—drills, conversations, dialogues, and chants, for example—to build your students' language abilities.

Content-area experiences in science, social studies, and literature

We have chosen three content areas for focus in *Making Connections* because of their importance to student success and because of the importance of language to success in these areas. In science, we introduce the language of science (and frequently mathematics language as well) through offering authentic scientific experiences using materials that are accessible to an ESOL teacher. In social studies, we take advantage of the multicultural nature of ESOL classes to introduce the processes of the social sciences. We have provided literature in a variety of genres to enhance content-area learning. As students begin to learn the language, they need to talk about and create their own literary works.

Writing

Making Connections applies a process approach to writing: it offers students opportunities to select topics and experiment with writing activities using themes and forms inspired by the science, social science, and literature content. We have included activities at all stages of the writing process including Prewriting, Drafting, Responding to One Another's Writing, Revising, Editing, and Publishing. We want students to see the writing process as something they can do and we want them to see authors as real people.

Choices for teachers and students in multicultural, multilevel classrooms

Every ESOL class is a multilevel, multicultural class. In order to meet the needs of these diverse groups and in order to empower both teachers and students, *Making Connections* offers many choices. Teachers can choose among the many activities in the units to provide experiences most appropriate to their classes and can sequence these activities as needed. They can also individualize by choosing different activities for different students within the class. Each unit includes an activity menu of experiences and projects that will help students to integrate and apply the material from the unit. Both teacher and students can make choices among these culminating events to suit them to student interests, level of ability, and needs.

COMPONENTS OF THE MAKING CONNECTIONS PROGRAM

Student Text

Making Connections: An Integrated Approach to Learning English integrates the teraching and learning of language and academic content. The student text provides students opportunities to develop their ability to communicate in English as they focus on motivating themes with topics, activities, tools, and procedures that introduce the content areas of science, social studies, and literature.

The Activity Menu at the end of each unit provides opportunities to help students relate their learnings around the unit theme to one another and to review and explore further concepts developed in the unit. Following each unit is a collection of supplemental readings related to the unit topics. We have included these readings in response to requests from pilot teachers for more literary selections related to unit topics.

Teacher's Extended Edition

The Teacher's Extended Edition provides:

- an introduction to the thematic, integrated teaching approach
- a description of several approaches to presenting literature selections
- a guide to the study strategies that appear in the student book

- detailed teaching suggestions for each activity
- suggestions for extension activities
- listening scripts

Workbooks

Workbooks provide additional practice in using the vocabulary, language functions, language structures, and study strategies introduced in each of the thematic units. Workbook activities can be used in class or assigned as homework.

CD-ROM

This lively, fun, user-friendly program is available for Macintosh and Windows. The three-level program provides practice in study strategies, writing strategies, and language through context-rich environments. For example, in a National Park environment, students can practice map reading, learn about history (Native American inhabitants), and practice asking for and giving directions.

Assessment Program

The assessment program consists of several components and accommodates a range of assessment philosophies and formats. Included are:

- a portfolio assessment kit, complete with a teacher's guide to using portfolios and forms for student and teacher evaluation
- two "progress checks" per unit
- end-of-unit assessments

Transparencies

Transparencies provide enlargements of visuals from the student texts. Many teachers find it helpful to view visuals with the students as they point out details. They may also write on pages using blank overlay transparencies.

Activity Masters

Reproducible activity masters support activities from the student book by providing write-on forms and graphic organizers for students' use. Activities for use with these masters consistently promote actoive student roles in engaging experiences.

Tape Program

Audio tapes provide opportunities for group and individual extended practice with the series materials. The tapes contain all the listening activities included in the student texts. Scripts of the recorded material are included in the Teacher's Extended Edition.

ABOUT THE AUTHORS

Carolyn Kessler

Carolyn Kessler is Professor of English as a Second Language/Applied Linguistics at the University of Texas at San Antonio where she teaches graduate courses for the master's degree in ESL. She serves extensively as a consultant to school districts for ESL programs and has published widely on bilingualism, second language learning, and literacy. She has taught ESL both in the United States and abroad and is a former secondary language and science teacher.

Linda Lee

Linda Lee is an ESL/EFL teacher and writer. She has taught in the United States, Italy, China, and Iran.

Mary Lou McCloskey

Mary Lou McCloskey coordinates the Atlanta Satellite of the University of Oklahoma Bilingual Education Center. She has developed integrated curriculum and consulted with school districts across the United States. She is past second vice president of International TESOL.

Mary Ellen Quinn

Mary Ellen Quinn is Visiting Professor of Mathematics at Our Lady of the Lake University. As a consultant in science and ESL to school districts throughout the country, she has presented many papers on bilingualism and science education both nationally and internationally and has published in those areas. She has been curriculum director for elementary and secondary schools as well as a secondary school teacher of ESL, science, and mathematics.

Lydia Stack

Lydia Stack is resource teacher for the Mentor Teacher and New Teacher programs for the San Francisco Unified School District. She was formerly the ESL Department Head at Newcomer High School in San Francisco, and has consulted widely with school districts across the United States in the areas of curriculum development and teacher training. She is past president of International TESOL.

Jean Bernard-Johnston

Jean Bernard-Johnston is currently a consultant and writer of ESL materials. She has taught in Thailand, Vietnam, Lebanon, and the Sultanate of Oman, as well as in the United States. She has designed curriculum and materials aimed toward the successful integration of science, language, and learning strategies for ESL students at the middle school and high school levels. She is a member of the ESL Certification Panel for the Massachusetts Board of Education, and is a life-long student of Southeast Asian languages and performance arts.

MAKING CONNECTIONS 3:

An Integrated Approach to Learning English

Carolyn Kessler

Jean Bernard-Johnston

Linda Lee

Mary Lou McCloskey

Mary Ellen Quinn

Lydia Stack

Heinle & Heinle Publishers
A Division of International Thomson Publishing, Inc.
Boston, MA 02116, U.S.A.

I(T)P

Study Strategies	Reading Selections

Quickwriting
Predicting
Taking Notes
Previewing
Using Context
Making a Time Line
Classifying
Listening for Specific
   Information
	The Waves of Matsuyama (Japanese *tanka* by Saigyo)
	Excerpt from The Sea Around Us (by Rachel Carson)
	Earth Shaker, Wave Maker (a Greek myth)
	Letter from a Dutch Immigrant, 1846
	An Oral History (by Saverio Rizzo)
	Could We Ever Forget? (a poem by Ok Kork)
	My Name is Monique . . . (excerpt from personal essay
	   by Monique Rubio)
	How Everything Happens (a poem by May Swenson)
	At the Beach (a poem by Kemal Ozer)
	The Education of Berenice Belizaire (from a magazine article
	   by Joe Klein)
	Song for Smooth Waters (a Native American poem)
	West Side (a poem by Naomi Shihab Nye)

Brainstorming
Previewing
Making a Tree Diagram
Using Context
Predicting
Making a Story Map
Using Context
Brainstorming
	Who's Hu? (a short story by Lensey Namioka)
	Nicholasa Mohr (an autobiographical account)
	The Underground Railroad (a magazine article by
	   Robert W. Peterson)
	The Douglass "Station" of the Underground Railroad (a play by
	   Glennette Tilley Turner)
	The Road Not Taken (a poem by Robert Frost)
	Jessica Berg (a poem by Mel Glenn)
	Footpath (a poem by Stella Ngatho)
	Harriet Tubman (a poem by Eloise Greenfield)

Classifying Previewing Using Context Using Context Brainstorming Quickwriting Taking Notes in a Chart Brainstorming Previewing	Zoo (a short story by Edward Hoch) Breaking Mental Barriers (a magazine article) A Shameful Chapter (a book excerpt by Barbara Rogasky) In Reponse to Executive Order 9066 (a poem by Dwight Okita) Aiming for Peace (a magazine article by Scott Brodeur) As I Grew Older (a poem by Langston Hughes) Those Who Don't (a poem by Sandra Cisneros)

Brainstorming
Listening for Specific
   Information
Making a Web Diagram
Taking Notes in a Chart
	Far, Far Away She Was Going (excerpt from the *Kim Van Kieu*)
	The Old Man at the Bridge (a short story by Ernest Hemingway)
	I Felt Like a Queen (a memoir by Suzanne Flores)
	You've Got a Friend (a song by Carole King)
	Letter to My Sister Who Lives in a Foreign Land (a poem
	   by Daisy Zamora)
	Across Ages (a magazine article by Scott Brodeur)
	August 2002: Night Meeting (from *The Martian Chronicles*,
	   by Ray Bradbury)
	The Eighth Wonder of the World (historical overview)
	Poetry of Friendship (a poem by José Marti)

${\mathcal A}$CKNOWLEDGMENTS

The authors want to thank colleagues, students, and teachers from whom we have learned much and who have offered strong and encouraging support for this project. We thank Chris Foley, Roseanne Mendoza, Nancy Mann, Elaine Leary, and Lisa McLaughlin for their support in the development and production of this project and for weathering with us the storms and challenges of doing something so new. We also want to thank family members—Erin, Dierdre, and Jim Stack; Kevin and Sean O'Brien, and Joel and Tom Reed; Alysoun, Eliot, and Mike Johnston—for their love and support during this project.

The publisher and authors wish to thank the following teachers who pilot tested the *Making Connections* program. Their valuable feedback on teaching with these materials greatly improved the final product. We are grateful to all of them for their dedication and commitment to teaching with the program in a prepublication format.

Elias S. Andrade and Gudrun Draper
James Monroe High School
North Hills, CA

Nadine Bagel
Benjamin Franklin Middle School
San Francisco, CA

Kate Bamberg
Newcomer High School
San Francisco, CA

David Barker and Carolyn Bohlman
Maine Township High School East
Park Ridge, IL

Kate Charles
Sycamore Junior High School
Anaheim, CA

Efrain Diaz
Collier County Public Schools
Naples, FL

Anne Elmkies, Irene Killian, and Kay Stark
Hartford Public Schools
Hartford, CT

Genoveva Goss
Alhambra High School
Alhambra, CA

Margaret Hartman
Lewisville High School
Lewisville, TX

Carmen N. Jimenez
Intermediate School 184
New York, NY

Rob Lamont and Judith D. Clark
Trimble Technical High School
Fort Worth, TX

Judi Levin
Northridge Middle School
Northridge, CA

Ligita Longo
Spring Woods High School
Houston, TX

Mary Makena
Rancho Alamitas High School
Garden Grove, CA

Alexandra M. McHugh
Granby, CT

Beatrice W. Miranda
Leal Middle School
San Antonio, TX

Doris Partan
Longfellow School
Cambridge, MA

Jane Pierce
Douglas MacArthur High School
San Antonio, TX

Cynthia Prindle
Thomas Jefferson High School
San Antonio, TX

Sydney Rodrigues
Doig Intermediate School
Garden Grove, CA

Cecelia Ryan
Monte Vista High School
Spring Valley, CA

Patsy Thompson
Gwinnett Vocational Center
Lawrenceville, GA

Fran Venezia
North Dallas High School
Dallas, TX

The publisher and authors would also like to thank the following people who reviewed the *Making Connections* program at various stages of development. Their insights and suggestions are much appreciated.

Irene Papoulis
Institute for Writing and Thinking
Bard College
Annandale-on-Hudson, NY

Suzanne Barton
Fort Worth Independent School District
Fort Worth, TX

Keith Buchanan
Fairfax County Public Schools
Fairfax, VA

Carlos Byfield
San Diego City College
San Diego, CA

MAKING CONNECTIONS 3:
An Integrated Approach to Learning English
TEACHER'S EXTENDED EDITION

Unit 1:

MAKING WAVES

Activity 1: Share a Poem

1. *Part a.* If feasible, play a tape with sounds of waves breaking. Ask students to close their eyes and listen.

2. *Part b.* Read the poem aloud in English and ask students to guess the original language. If there is a Japanese speaker in the class, ask this student to read it in both Japanese and English.

3. *Part c.* Encourage students to speculate about the author's reason for writing the poem. Elicit various possibilities. You may want to ask some of the following questions: *How does the poem make you feel? Who is "my lord"? In what way is he different from the waves?*

4. Where appropriate, offer the historical information that the poem was written to pay respect to the memory of the Emperor Suhoko (d. 1164); the poem contrasts the limited span of human life with the continuing, repetitive nature of the waves.

Chapter 1: What Makes Waves?

1. Share a Poem

a. Classwork. Look at the picture. Imagine yourself alone here. What sounds would you hear as you look at the waves? How would you feel?

b. Read the poem. What does it say about waves?

c. Why do you think the poet Saigyo wrote this poem?

The waves	*Matsuyamano*
of Matsuyama[1]	*nami nokeshiki wa*
Their aspect[2] is unchanged	*kawaraji o*
but of you, my lord[3]	*kaka naku kimi was*
no trace remains	*narimashinikeri*

Saigyo (1118-1190)

[1]Matsuyama   a city in northeastern Japan
[2]aspect   the way something looks
[3]my lord   the Emperor Suhoko

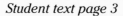

2. Explore

a. Look up the word "wave" in a dictionary. How many meanings does it have? Write the definition that fits the meaning of "waves" in the picture and the poem.

b. Read the other definitions. Which ones are new for you?

c. What do all waves have in common? Write a sentence that describes all of the different kinds of waves. Share your sentence with the class.

All waves _____

Activity 2: Explore

1. *Part a.* Have students work in pairs to do the dictionary exercise. Elicit and write the definition of an ocean wave on the board. (Possible definition: *a moving ridge of water*)

2. *Part b.* Elicit and list kinds of waves on the board. (*Possible answers:* radio waves, light waves, waves of sadness, joy or other feelings, waves in the hair, waves of the hand, heat waves and cold waves as in the weather, crime waves, waves of immigration.)

3. *Part c.* Sketch an ocean wave and a graph showing a heat wave or a crime wave. Ask students, *How are these similar?* Elicit several sentences and write them on the board. (Possible sentences: *All waves move up and down. All waves have a pattern that shows increase and decrease.*)

Activity 3 : Quickwrite

1. Direct students' attention to the picture on page 2, and ask volunteers to describe it. Elicit descriptive terms for waves from students and supply others as appropriate (for example, *wild, stormy, whitecaps, choppy, smooth, calm, rolling*). If feasible, bring in pictures of a storm at sea or on a lake as a stimulus for writing. If you provided an audiotape of ocean waves, you may want to play it again.

2. If necessary, introduce quickwriting. Tell students to write without stopping, and not to worry about correctness. The point of quickwriting is to capture ideas. If they don't know an English word, they can use the word in their native language. Model quickwriting on the board or write with your students.

3. *Optional:* Help students develop these pieces of writing and then publish them on a bulletin board along with the pictures that stimulated them. Students may also enjoy writing their own short poem like the *tanka* by Saigyo.

Activity 4: Measure a Wave

Materials

For each pair of students: six-foot length of cotton rope; ruler with centimeter markings; watch with second hand; piece of brightly colored string or small colored paper clip

---

1. Clear space on the floor for students to work. Sketch a wave pattern on the board and label *crests* and *wavelength*. Model the pronunciation of these terms and have students repeat after you.

2. On the board, copy the chart from AM 1/1. Pronounce *frequency* for the students and have them practice saying it. Explain or elicit that *frequency* means how often something is repeated in a particular period of time.

(Continued on page 5.)

Study Strategy:
Quickwriting
See page 168.

3. Quickwrite

Imagine a lake or ocean in a storm. Think about a place you have been or have seen in a movie or photograph. Quickwrite about the scene for five minutes. What do the waves look like? What do they sound like? How do they make you feel?

4. Measure a Wave

Materials: *cotton rope, ruler, watch, piece of string*

Pairwork. Ask your partner to hold one end of the rope while you hold the other close to the floor. Pull the rope out tight close to the floor. While your partner holds his or her end of the rope still, shake your end back and forth. Experiment until you can make a regular pattern of waves with the rope on the floor. Then follow these steps to learn the speed of your wave.

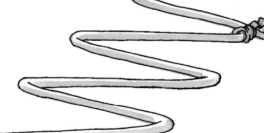
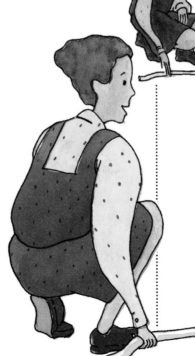

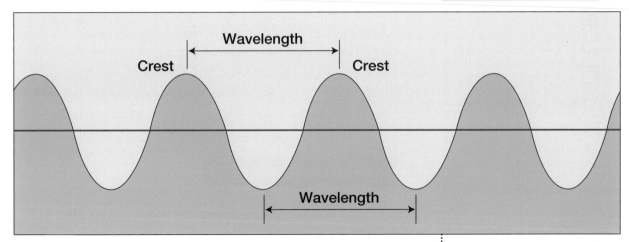

Step 1: Ask a classmate to use the ruler to measure the length of one of your waves. The **wavelength** is the distance between two high points (**crests**). Write the measurement of this wave in **centimeters (cm)** under Wave #1 in the chart.

Step 2: Tie a ribbon or piece of string around the middle of the rope. Invite a classmate to count how many waves pass the fixed point (where the string is) in ten seconds. Try it several times before you record the number.

Step 3: Divide the number you got in Step 2 by 10. This is the **frequency** of your wave. Write the frequency of Wave #1 in a chart like the one below.

Step 4: Use the following equation to find the speed of your wave: $speed = wavelength \times frequency.$

Write the speed of Wave #1 in **centimeters per second (cm/s)** on the chart.

	Wave #1	Wave #2
Wavelength		
Frequency		
Speed		

Step 5: What is the fastest wave you can make with the rope? Predict the speed.

> **Study Strategy:**
> **Predicting**
> See page 168.

3. Go through the process of measuring a wave for the students to observe before they do it themselves: Make the wave pattern and ask students to estimate the wavelength (the distance between the crests). Write some estimates in the chart on the board. Then tie a string or attach a paper clip to the rope and make the pattern for ten seconds. Ask students to estimate how many crests pass the point in ten seconds. Write some of these estimates on the board. Tell students, *This is the number of crests in ten seconds. How many are there in one second?* As students divide the estimates by ten, write the estimated frequencies in the chart.

4. Have pairs of students practice making the wave pattern together. This activity works best on an uncarpeted floor. Distribute AM 1/1 and tell students to complete the steps of the activity. Circulate to help them as they work. For each step, elicit some measurements and write them on the board.

Step 1. Tell students to stop the motion of a wave and measure a wave from crest to crest on the floor. *Step 2.* Explain that *fixed* means *not moving*. *Step 3.* Have some students divide the frequencies on the board by 10, and record their answers in the chart on the board or transparency. *Step 4.* Pronounce *centimeters per second* and have the students practice saying it. With the students, calculate the speed of some of the waves, and write the values on the board. *Step 5.* Elicit predictions from students and write some predicted speeds on the board. *Step 6.* Have students repeat steps 1–4 on their own while you circulate. When they finish, ask several pairs of students, *How accurate were your predictions?*

Activity 5: What's Missing?

1. Distribute AM 1/2 and write the chart on the board. Next to the chart, write the formula for calculating the speed of a wavelength. Point out that the ocean waves are measured in meters, while the waves the class made were measured in centimeters.

2. Demonstrate or elicit how to substitute values from the chart into the equation in order to calculate the missing values. Then circulate to help pairs of students as they work.

3. Have several students go to the board to complete the chart. (*Answers:* (1) 1.1 m; (2) 132 hz; (3) 5 m; (4) 40 hz; (5) 5 m.)

4. Supply or elicit appropriate adjectives to describe the waves (fast or slow; long or short; high or low frequency.)

Activity 6: Share Ideas

On the board, write some expressions for stating opinions, for example, *In my opinion; I agree; I don't agree with that; I think so too.* Elicit opinions from some volunteers and encourage them to frame their ideas using some of these expressions. Then have students work in pairs to exchange ideas. Circulate and encourage students to give reasons for their opinions. After pairwork, have the whole class pool ideas.

Step 6: Use the rope to make the fastest possible wave. Then repeat steps 1 through 4 and add the information to the chart under Wave #2.

How close was your prediction about the speed of the wave?

Tell the class how you measured the rope waves and describe the results.

5. **What's Missing?**

Pairwork. Use the formula for the speed of a wave on page 5 to complete a chart like this.

speed (v) in centimeters (cm)/second(s)	wavelength (l) in centimeters (cm)	frequency (f) in hertz (hz)
330 cm/s		300 hz
330 cm/s	2.5 cm	
50 cm/s		10 hz
100 cm/s	2.5 cm	
25 cm/s		5 hz

v = velocity   rate of motion in a specific direction
hz = hertz   a unit of frequency equal to one cycle per second

Describe each of the waves in this chart (fast, long, etc.)

6. **Share Ideas**

Pairwork. What causes ocean waves? Think about each of the possible causes on the next list. Check (✓) the ones you think really can make waves. Add others if you wish. Discuss your choices with a partner. Feel free to agree or disagree.

▲▲▲

A: I think the moon causes ocean waves.

B: Well, I don't think so. In my opinion, earthquakes are the main cause.

CAUSE	EFFECT
_____ earthquakes	
_____ wind	
_____ rain	OCEAN WAVES
_____ the moon	
_____ lightning	

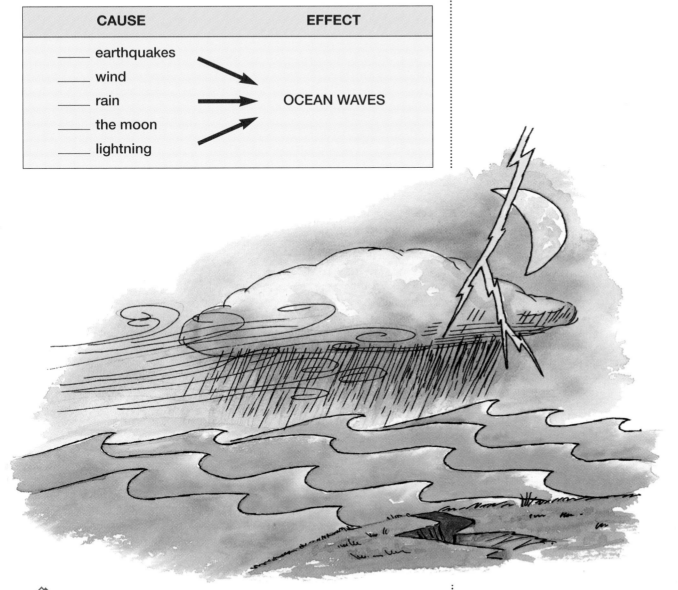

Activity 7: Shared Reading

1. Bring students' attention to the picture of Rachel Carson. Have a volunteer read aloud the biographical information about her on page 9. Tell them that Carson was one of the first people to write about the dangers of polluting the environment.

2. Have the students look at the pictures that accompany the text and to predict what the text explains. (Possible predictions: *what causes waves, how big they get, what happens to them when they reach shore.*)

3. To give students a reading goal the first time they read the selection, write focus questions on the board. Have students look for the answers to these questions as they read. (Some possible focus questions: Para. 1: *Was your prediction about the causes of ocean waves correct?* Para. 2: *What kind of a history are you going to read about?* (An imaginary life history of a wave.) Para. 3: *Does the water in a wave move across the sea?* (No, it doesn't.) Para. 4: *Where is this imaginary wave born?* (Far out in the Atlantic.) *What two phases of its life are described in this paragraph?* (Sea and swell.) Para. 5: *Where does the wave end its life?* (On the shore.)

4. When students finish reading the article, read the article aloud to model pronunciation, and then have each student read several sentences.

5. Elicit the answers to the focus questions. Help students with vocabulary as needed, using the diagrams, pictures, the glossed words, and the context of the reading to explain.

6. *Optional:* Have students work in pairs and take turns reading paragraphs to each other.

7. **Shared Reading**

On your own. Read the article and study the diagrams. Look for information about the causes of ocean waves.

from
THE SEA AROUND US
by Rachel Carson

Wind is the great maker of waves. There are exceptions, such as the tidal waves sometimes produced by earthquakes under the sea. But the waves most of us know are produced by winds blowing over the sea.

Now, before constructing[1] an imaginary life history of a typical[2] wave, we need to know certain physical things about it. A wave has height, from trough to crest. It has length—the distance from its crest to that of the following wave. The period of the wave means the time it takes for succeeding[3] crests to pass a fixed point.

None of these things stays the same—for all depend upon the wind, upon the the depth of the water, and many other matters.

The water that makes up a wave does not advance[4] with it across the sea. Each particle of water turns around in a little circle or ellipse[5] with the passing of the wave, but returns very nearly to its original position. And it is fortunate that this is so. For if the huge masses of water that make up a wave actually moved across the sea, navigation[6] would be impossible.

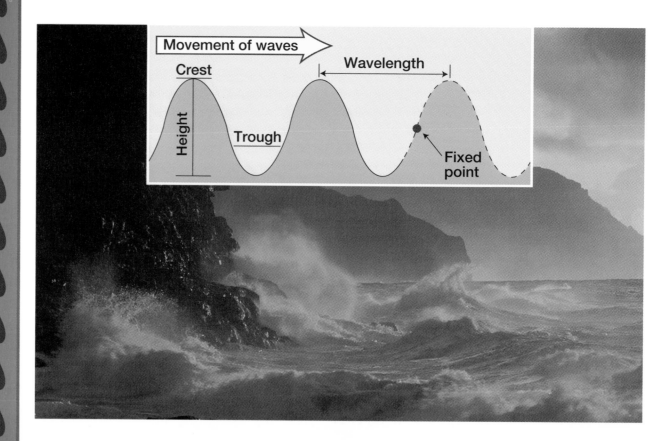

Let us look at a typical wave, born of wind and water far out in the Atlantic Ocean. Let us assume[7] that the wind is not so strong as to blow the top off and that the wave has merely grown to its full height. With its fellow waves it forms a confused, irregular pattern known as a "sea." Gradually as the waves pass out of the storm area, they lose height. The distance between crest and crest increases. The "sea" becomes a "swell," moving at an average speed of about 15 miles an hour.

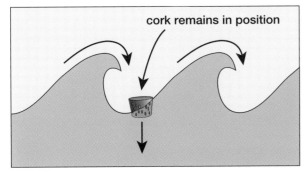

cork remains in position

This cork will remain as the waves pass by.

Near the coast, the pattern becomes more orderly—a series of long, evenly spaced ridges.[8] But as the swell enters shallow water, a startling transformation takes place. For the first time in its life, the wave feels the drag of shoaling bottom.[9] Its speed slackens. Crests of following waves crowd in toward it. Abruptly[10] its height increases and the wave form steepens.[11] Then with a spilling, tumbling rush of water falling down into its trough, the wave dissolves in a seething[12] confusion of foam.

[1]**constructing**	building
[2]**typical**	normal
[3]**succeeding**	following, coming after
[4]**advance**	move ahead
[5]**ellipse**	a flattened circle
[6]**navigation**	to make a ship move in a certain direction

[7]**assume**	agree to be true
[8]**ridge**	long, narrow crest
[9]**a shoaling bottom**	a shallow area
[10]**abruptly**	suddenly
[11]**steepens**	gets higher
[12]**seething**	moving quickly, angrily

Rachel Carson (1907-1964)

After graduating from Johns Hopkins University, Rachel Carson began a long career as a marine biologist and writer. *The Sea Around Us* was published in 1951 and won the National Book Award.

She was especially concerned about the dangers of environmental pollution. Her best known book, *The Silent Spring* (1962), helped raise awareness of this issue among readers around the world.

Activity 8: Take Notes in a Chart

1. Distribute AM 1/3 and copy the chart on the board. To identify the topics, suggest that students read aloud the first sentence of each paragraph to each other. Circulate and help students as they work. When they are finished, elicit their responses and write them in the chart on the board.

(*Answers:* Para. 2—Details: height, length, and periodicity; Para. 3—Details: elliptical; water does not move forward with the wave; Para. 4— Topic: Change from sea to swell—Details: Sea [in a storm area; irregular pattern] Swell [away from storm area; greater wavelengths, regular movement at 15 mph.] Para. 5—Topic: Death of a wave— Details: wave enters shallow water, hits bottom, slows down, height increases, wave breaks.)

Activity 9: Test Your Knowledge

1. On the board, write the sentences from the *Language Focus* box. Review pattern for passive voice (be + past participle). Ask students to find the example of the passive voice in the first paragraph of the reading. Point out that using the passive keeps the focus of the sentence on *waves*, which is the topic of the paragraph.

2. *Part a.* Brainstorm possible questions with students, and write sample questions for each paragraph on the board. (Possible questions: *What are ocean waves caused by? Does water move along with waves? What is an ellipse? What does a sea look like? How fast does a swell move? What happens when a wave reaches the coast?*)

3. *Part b.* Have groups or partners make notes about what they learned and what they would like to know. Collect the information on the board in a K-W-L chart. Help students find information that interests them.

> **Study Strategy:**
> **Taking Notes**
> See page 169.

8. Take Notes in a Chart

Pairwork. Look back at the reading and take notes in a chart like this one.

Paragraph	Topic What's the paragraph about?	Details and Examples
1	causes of ocean waves	-wind (main cause) -earthquakes (tidal waves)
2	physical characteristics	-height -
3	movement	
4		
5		

> **Language Focus:**
> **Active and Passive Voice**
> Wind causes waves to form. Waves are caused by wind.

9. Test Your Knowledge

a. Pairwork. Get together with another pair. Take turns asking and answering questions about the information in your chart.

Example: Q: What causes waves?
A: Most waves are caused by wind blowing over the sea.

b. Discuss the information about waves in the reading. Here are some questions to think about.

What did you already know?
What new information surprised you?
What more would you like to learn?

10. Define

a. On your own. The following terms are used to describe waves. Use information from the reading and the diagrams to write a short definition of each one.

| crest | length | period |
| trough | height | speed |

b. Pairwork. Make a sketch that illustrates at least three of the terms you defined. Present your sketch to the class.

11. Analyze

Classwork. What effects do the following conditions have on the size and movement of a wave? List your ideas.

CAUSE	EFFECT
A storm blows up in the open sea.	_____ _____
The waves pass out of the storm area.	_____ _____
The swell enters shallow water near the shore.	_____ _____

12. Apply

Groupwork. Imagine you are the crew of a small sailboat on the open sea. You learn by radio that a storm with 15 ft. (4.6 m) waves is approaching your position at a speed of 10 miles (1.6 km) per hour. At this rate, you estimate that the storm will reach you in two hours. You are not certain you can get to the shore in that amount of time. You can already feel the wind blowing stronger and the sea beginning to swell. Choose one of these options (A or B) or suggest one of your own (C).

A. try to make it in to shore

B. stay out at sea and "ride out" the storm

C. _____

Discuss the possible dangers of each choice and reach a group decision. Explain your decision to the class.

Activity 10: Define

1. *Part a.* Tell students that they can find all of the words in the text and illustrations. Elicit definitions and write them on the board. Ask students where in the text or illustrations they found the information. (Definitions: <u>crest:</u> *the highest point of a wave;* <u>trough:</u> *the lowest point of a wave;* <u>height:</u> *the distance from crest to trough;* <u>wavelength:</u> *the distance between the crests of two waves;* <u>speed:</u> *how fast waves move past a fixed point (the product of wavelength times frequency);* <u>period:</u> *the time it takes for one complete wave to pass a fixed point.*)

2. *Part b.* Display finished sketches on a bulletin board.

Activity 11: Analyze

Distribute AM 1/4 and copy the chart on the board. Point out to students that they will be looking for an effect on the size and movement of a wave. Have students work individually to find the information in the text. (*Answers:* 1. A wave is born; waves move in irregular patterns. 2. Height decreases and wavelength increases; waves form a regular pattern; speed averages 15 mph. 3. Waves form orderly pattern and slow down; height increases abruptly; form steepens; wave falls into its own trough.)

Activity 12: Apply

1. Let each group establish whether they are in an open or closed sailboat, how far they are from shore, etc.

2. Review useful language. a. modals: *We've got to stay in the boat. It must be a very big storm.* b. conditionals: *If we leave now, we might reach shore before the storm.*

3. *Optional:* Have each group write a news report about their rescue and read the report to the class.

Activity 1: Quickwrite

1. *Part a.* Introduce the activity by having students talk about the picture of the surfer. Ask the more proficient students, *Where is this person? What is he doing? What emotions is he feeling?*

2. Share your own experience of a time when you felt some strong emotion. Then elicit some situations from students, for example, winning an award or an important game, or coming to North America.

3. *Part b.* After students share their stories with partners, have them form small groups and tell their partners' stories to the group.

4. *Optional:* As homework, students write a short paragraph relating their own or a partner's story.

Chapter 2: Ups and Downs

𝓦aves can be relaxing, beautiful, exciting, or terrifying. Perhaps that is why people have often connected strong emotions such as love, joy, anger, or excitement with images of waves. In this section, you will read about some of these connections.

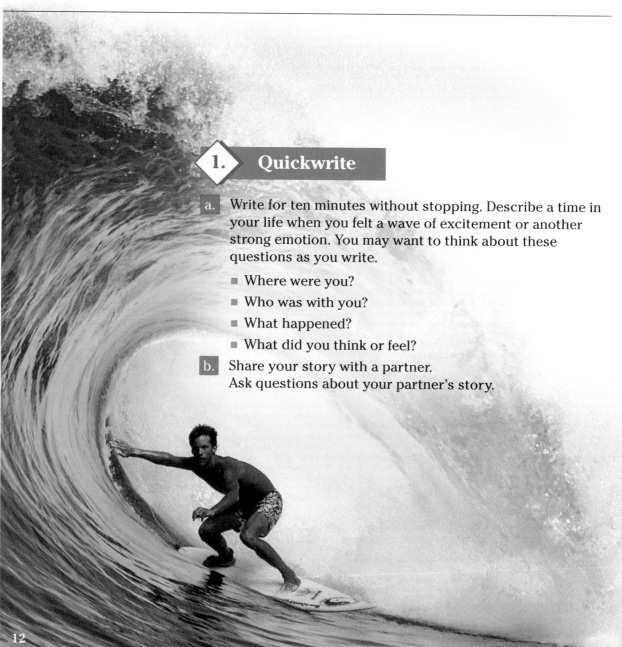

1. **Quickwrite**

a. Write for ten minutes without stopping. Describe a time in your life when you felt a wave of excitement or another strong emotion. You may want to think about these questions as you write.

- Where were you?
- Who was with you?
- What happened?
- What did you think or feel?

b. Share your story with a partner. Ask questions about your partner's story.

Activity 2: Preview

1. Ask students to find Waimea on the map. Elicit their knowledge about surfing in Hawaii. Draw the compass points on the board and elicit the direction of a southeast wind. Draw a picture to illustrate the meaning of *horizon*.

2. Next, draw students' attention to the picture of the surfer near Waimea. Note that everyone has selftalk, or an "inner voice." Elicit the kinds of selftalk students use when they face a big challenge. Ask, *What do you say to yourself when you're afraid? When you're excited by a challenge?*

3. Distribute AM 1/5 and have students work in pairs to fill out the left column. Elicit students' ideas about what the surfer is saying. Write some of the statements on the board in speech bubbles.

Activity 3: Listening

1. Before you play the cassette, tell students to listen for what the surfer says to himself. Tell them they don't have to understand everything. Play the cassette and replay as needed.

2. Elicit the surfer's two statements and write them on the board as column heads. (*Okay, you better paddle for the horizon. Okay, you want a big wave, here it is.*) Elicit students' similar positive and negative statements and write them on the board under the correct column. Ask students, *Which voice was stronger?*

---

2. Preview

> ***Study Strategy:***
> ***Previewing***
> See page 167.

Pairwork. Look at the photograph. Imagine how the surfer feels at this moment. What do you think he is saying to himself? Write down as many ideas as you can in a chart like the one below.

What we think the surfer is saying to himself	Did he really say this to himself?

3. Listening

Pairwork. Listen as a surfer describes his experience riding waves near Waimea, Hawaii. Check things on your list from #2 that are the same as or similar to things the surfer says. Which things were different?

Activity 4: Use Context

1. After students complete the exercise, go over the answers with the class. (*Answers:* series of waves; desire to live; paddled fast; falls.)

2. Play the tape and ask students to listen for the words as they hear the story again.

Activity 5: Role Play

1. Play the tape again and then brainstorm questions with the class. Write possible questions on the board, for example, *What did you say to yourself? When did you stand up on your board? How did it feel while you were riding the wave in? Was it worth the risk?*

2. After students interview each other, ask several pairs of students to role play their interview for the class.

Activity 6: Evaluate

Write *Cool* and *Crazy* on the blackboard as column heads, and take a class opinion poll. How many think surfboarding is cool? How many think it's crazy? Ask students if they have tried, or are willing to try surfing. If there are students who have surfed, ask them to describe their experiences. Have they ever had an experience like Richard Schmidt's? Do they recommend surfing?

14

---

4. Use Context

On your own. Guess the meaning of the italicized words from the story you just heard. Use the words and ideas in the sentence to help you decide.

You could see this *set* coming from way outside.	surfboard/series of waves
When you're in that situation there's this little voice inside you that's probably just a *vital instinct* talking saying, "okay, you better paddle for the horizon,"	desire to live/memory
So on about the fifth one I just *took some strokes* and hopped to my feet.	paddled fast/got sick
I could have taken one of the worst *wipeouts* of my life, but it turned out to be one of the best rides.	falls/prizes

> ***Study Strategy:***
> ***Using Context***
> See page 169.

5. Role Play

Pairwork. Pretend you are a newspaper reporter while your partner takes the role of Richard Schmidt, the surfer whose story you just heard. You are on the beach just after Richard's ride on the "big one." Listen to the story again. Ask questions about his experience.

Reporter: How did you feel when you saw the set coming?
Richard: I felt really scared.

6. Evaluate

Classwork. Some people think that surfers like Richard Schmidt are cool, and other people think they are crazy. What do you think? State your opinion to the class. How many of the students in your class have tried surfing or would like to try it?

7. Write

a. On your own. Look back at your quickwriting from Step #1. See if you can remember more details about the experience. Make as many notes as you can in the observation chart.

b. Pairwork. Read your quickwriting aloud and show your chart to a partner. Invite your partner to ask questions about the experience. See if your partner can help you add more details to your observation chart.

c. On your own. Write a first draft about your experience. Use ideas from your quickwriting and your observation chart. For more suggestions about writing a first draft, see the Writer's Guide, page 173.

Groupwork. Read your story aloud to a small group of classmates. Ask your listeners to repeat their favorite sentences from your story and tell you what more they would like to know about your experience.

> **Language Focus:**
> **Sensory Verbs**
> It looked funny.
> I felt tired.

Observation Chart: Remembering an Experience				
Sight	Sound	Feel	Taste	Smell

Activity 7: Write

1. Distribute AM 1/6 and draw a similar chart on the board. Model the activity by referring to Richard Schmidt's story. Ask students questions, and write their answers in the chart. Tell them to use their imaginations to answer questions that are not answered in the story. (Possible questions: *How did the waves look? What did they sound like? How did the ride feel? How did the ocean breeze smell?*)

2. Circulate and talk to students about their experiences as they fill in their charts. Supply adjectives for sensory details.

3. Write the sentences from the *Language Focus* box on the board. Point out that there are two patterns that students can use. Pattern 1: Adjective after the verb: The wave looked huge. I felt scared. The water tasted salty. The southeast wind smelled fresh. Pattern 2: Comparison (with *like*) after the verb: The waves looked like mountains. They sounded like thunder. I felt like an insect next to them.

4. *Part c.* Tell students to write about their experience.

5. Write pointers for listeners on the board. (a. Give positive feedback; b. Listen carefully. Ask the reader to repeat if necessary; c. Use the newswriter's questions—who, what when, where, how, why—to think of questions.) Model appropriate positive feedback.

Activity 8: Preview

Ask students to look at the map and to describe ancient Greece. Ask them, *What are the landforms?* (islands, peninsulas). *How did people from Crete and other islands get to Athens? In what ways did the sea help ancient Greeks? In what ways could it hurt them?* Encourage students to speculate, and write their ideas on the board.

Activity 9: Shared Reading

1.   Bring to class pictures and stories from other mythologies. As students look through this material, point out or elicit that each culture has myths which explain natural phenomena such as the wind, the sky, and changes in the moon. Ask students to tell myths from their own cultures.

Note that in stories from Greek mythology, the Greek gods often had very distinct personalities and faults. Ask students to notice the characters' personalities as they listen and read.

2.   Have students read and listen to just the opening paragraph by the Bard. Then ask for their ideas about what kind of story they are going to hear (elicit or explain the meaning of *courtship*). Then have them find words that describe Poseidon's personality (*anger, jealousy, vengeance*). Ask students to predict what kind of conflict the story might tell about. Write their ideas on the board.

3.   Play the tape and ask students to listen to and read the story.

(Continued on page 17.)

8.   Preview

Classwork. Look at the map of ancient Greece. Why do you think the sea was important to the Greeks? What did their ships look like? How did the sailors feel about wind and waves? Explain what led you to your answers.

9.   Shared Reading

Classwork. The ancient Greeks believed that waves and earthquakes were caused by Poseidon,[1] god of the sea. This story, based on the myth of Poseidon, is in the form of a play. Listen and read along.

[1]**Poseidon**   Neptune in Roman mythology

Earth Shaker, Wave Maker
The Myth of Poseidon

SCENE 1

(*sound of lute music*)

Bard: This story I will tell, of the all-powerful Poseidon, blue-haired lord of the sea, before whom all mortals tremble. You have heard many tales of his anger, his jealousy, his vengeance—how he stirs up a raging sea, how he shakes the earth when it pleases him—(*sound of waves*) but listeners—this is not a night for such fearful tales. Observe the dazzling stars, feel the gentle sea breeze. Tonight I will please you with a much more delightful story of the mighty Poseidon's gentler side; of his courtship of the delicate and beautiful Queen Amphritite. How did it begin?

(*sound of waves, water increases, then subsides*)

Poseidon: She has stolen my heart. I can think of nothing else. Observe, Dolphin! I am weak. I am no longer able to frighten sailors or terrify land dwellers. I must marry Amphritite!

Dolphin: But my Lord, she is terrified of you. She has run away.

Poseidon: (*beginning to anger*) She dares to flee mighty Poseidon? If she is within my watery realm, Dolphin, find her! Bring her here immediately!

Dolphin: I'm sorry, my lord. She has fled to the mountains, to the realm of Atlas for protection. He has granted her refuge in a lonely cave, with only birds for companions. She cannot be forced to do anything against her will, but perhaps she can be persuaded.

Poseidon: Then go to her, Dolphin. You are a creature of both water and air. Tell her of the glittering beauty of this undersea world. Tell her I will share this beautiful golden palace, and all of my power with her.

Dolphin: But, my lord. It is you and your power she fears.

Poseidon: Then convince her! Tell her of my incredible wealth, but not only that. Impress her with my generosity and deep respect for all creatures of the sea. After all, it is only outsiders who enrage me.

Dolphin: As you wish. But I can make no promises. She has a mind of her own, as you well know.

4. After students listen to and read the story for the first time, write the following categories on the board and elicit information about each one:

<u>characters:</u> Poseidon (angry, controlling); Dolphin (wise, obedient); Amphritite (independent, beautiful)

<u>setting:</u> 1. Poseidon's palace 2. A cave in the mountains

<u>conflict:</u> Poseidon wants to marry Amphritite; she doesn't want to marry him.

<u>action:</u> Dolphin finds Amphritite and persuades her to return with him and try to share her life with Poseidon.

<u>resolution:</u> Amphritite returns with Dolphin; she becomes Poseidon's queen.

5. Ask students whether they think that the language of the play is formal or informal. Elicit that the style is formal. Ask students to list words that are unfamiliar to them and then have them work with partners to use context clues to figure out the approximate meanings of the words on their lists. Circulate and help students as they work. When they finish, elicit any words that students could not figure out, and provide context-rich examples to help students infer the meaning. For example, *When Poseidon couldn't control his temper, he unleashed his anger and caused an earthquake or a great storm.*

SCENE 2

(lute music)

Bard: And so the faithful Dolphin traveled to the realm of Atlas, ruler of a distant, mountainous region on earth. There he found Amphritite hiding in a dark cave, far from the wind and waves. At first, she refused to see him (*sound of sobbing*). Only when he shed giant salt tears did she agree to hear what he had to say.

Amphritite: An interesting offer, Dolphin, but I can't imagine living with Poseidon. He's violent, unpredictable, and unreasonable. Look at the way he terrifies innocent sailors. Besides that, he's so ugly! That terrible scowl, and that awful blue hair. . .

Dolphin: Beneath his harsh appearance, my lady, there lies a heart of gold. I beg you to listen to one who knows him well. To all of us who live in his realm, he is a wise and gentle ruler. He would never harm the tiniest crab nor cross the majestic whale. His golden palace is beautiful beyond words. All of this he would share with you.

Amphritite: Why is it then, gentle Dolphin, that he shakes the earth and causes the sea to rage, causing untold agony to so many unfortunate mortals?

Dolphin: Well, he does have a temper, but his anger is only unleashed against those who fail to honor and treat him fairly.

Amphritite: Dolphin, I believe you are honest and intelligent. Do you think. . .

Dolphin: I *know* he is very much in love with you. He mourns because you will not even give him a chance.

Amphritite: This cave *is* getting depressing. Did you say a golden palace?

Dolphin: Just come with me and see, my lady. I'll give you a ride on my back. If you don't like him, you will not be forced to stay.

Amphritite: Promise?

Dolphin: Promise. You have my word.

(lute music)

Bard: And the loyal Dolphin sped back to Poseidon's realm of the sea with the lovely Amphritite on his back. When he saw her, Poseidon had to stop himself from shaking the earth for joy.

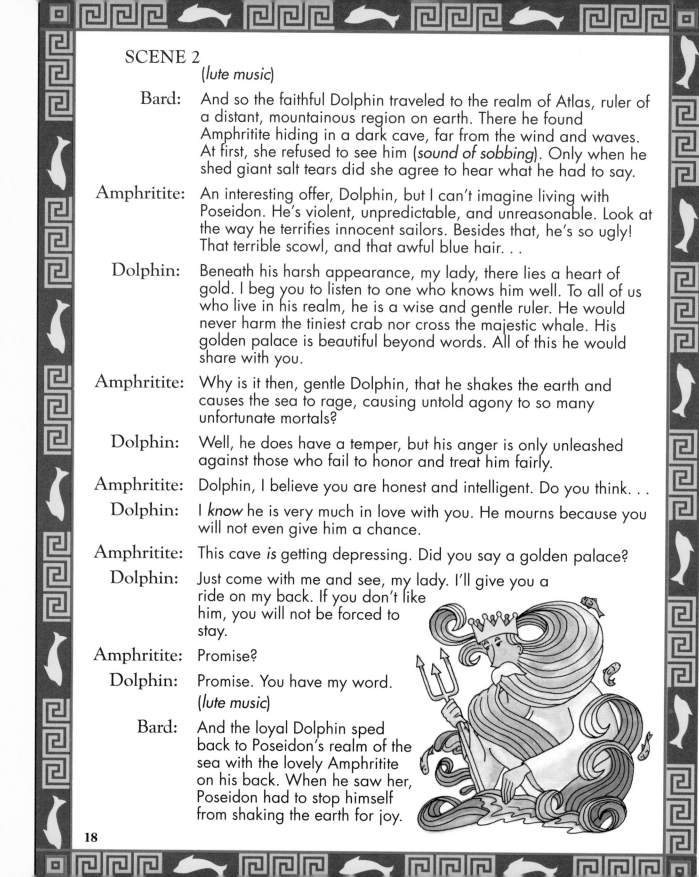

With the Dolphin's wise counsel, he persuaded her to become his queen. In time, Amphritite gave birth to a child whose name was Triton. Thereafter, Poseidon was contented to remain in the calm depths of the ocean, occasionally sending Triton to the surface on a golden sea horse to blow up a storm or calm the waves with a mighty blast on his shell.

(*conch shell sound*)

And with Triton was born an era of peace and prosperity for Greece, in which sailors and land dwellers did not need to fear Poseidon's wrath as long as they remembered to honor him. As for the Dolphin, the sea god did not forget him. Look up at the sky. Poseidon named the constellation "Delphinus" in eternal gratitude, and so that we mortals might be reminded of the creature's intelligence and loyalty.

The constellation Delphinus is located in the Northern hemisphere near Pegasus.

10. Reader's Theater

Work in groups. Act out *Earth Shaker, Wave Maker.* Use instruments or your voices to create the music and sound effects.

11. Write

Pairwork. Imagine your own scene in which one character is angry or afraid of something. Have another character persuade the first character to calm down. Discuss each of these points before you begin to write.

a. The setting. Where and when does the action take place?

b. The characters. Who are they? What are they like?

c. The situation. What does the first character want to persuade the second character to do?

d. The action. What happens?

Write the dialogue for your scene (about 10 lines) and give it a title. Practice reading your scene, then act it out for the whole class.

Language Focus

Persuasion

A: I'm not so sure.
B: Come on, at least give it a try.

Activity 10: Reader's Theater

1. Have volunteers read the play aloud. Encourage students to act out their ideas of the personalities and feelings of the characters. Model any difficult words and have students repeat them after you. Brainstorm ways to produce sound effects.

2. Divide the class into groups of four or more students to rehearse the play. Circulate and help students with pronunciation and expressiveness.

3. Have groups act out their plays for the whole class. If feasible, record the performances on video- or audiocassette. Students will enjoy reviewing this record of their work during the semester. The tapes will also serve as a resource as students work on subsequent Reader's Theater activities.

Activity 11: Write

1. If students have trouble coming up with ideas for their scene, have them review their own writing from Activity 1.

2. Write the dialogue from the *Language Focus* box on the board, and add other expressions.

> Well, I don't know . . .
> Why don't you think about it?
> It's true that he lost his temper, but he did apologize.

3. Have students perform their scenes for the class.

Activity 1: Preview

1. On the board, draw the two axes of a graph like the one in the student text on pages 20–21. Elicit that the horizontal axis measures the time in decades; the vertical axis measures the number of immigrants in millions. Ask students: *How many immigrants came to the United States in 1914, at the start of World War I?* (Around 1.2 million) *How many came in 1830?* (Around 0.1 million)

2. Ask students to compare waves of immigration to ocean waves. (*Possible answers:* Groups of immigrants are like waves because their numbers have periodic highs and lows. They are different because their patterns of crests and troughs are very irregular.)

3. You may wish to wait until students do the next activity, and have them infer the meanings of unfamiliar words from the explanations in the time line. Alternatively, introduce this vocabulary with example sentences as the class discusses the graph. Words that might need explanation include *instability,* a condition of frequent, unpredictable change; *famine,* widespread starvation; *panic,* extreme fear that often causes irrational behavior; *quota,* a limit; *The Depression,* a period of severe economic slowdown; *amnesty,* a law that forgives people who have broken the law.

4. Ask volunteers for their ideas about the four questions. Point to peaks after economic panics, and help students infer that prosperity in the United States also increased immigration. (*Answers:* (1) waves of immigration to the United States. (2) from 1820 to 1990. (3) Famine at home, economic prosperity in the United States, and the end of wars. (4) Economic panic and the beginning of wars.)

Chapter 3: People Around Us

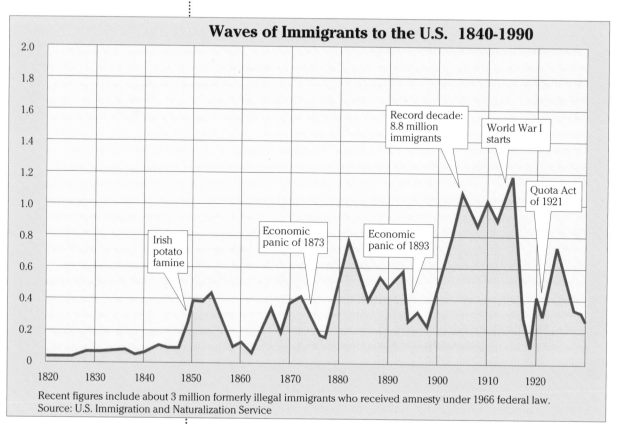

⟨**1.**⟩ **Preview**

Study Strategy

Making a Time Line

See page 164.

Classwork. How are groups of immigrants like ocean waves? How are they different? Look at the graph and discuss these questions.

■ What does the graph illustrate?

■ What period of American history does it cover?

■ What kinds of world events have caused people to immigrate to the United States? Give some examples.

■ What kinds of events have slowed down immigration to the United States? Give some examples.

Waves of Immigrants to the U.S.   1840-1990

Record decade: 8.8 million immigrants

World War I starts

Quota Act of 1921

Irish potato famine

Economic panic of 1873

Economic panic of 1893

Recent figures include about 3 million formerly illegal immigrants who received amnesty under 1966 federal law.
Source: U.S. Immigration and Naturalization Service

2. Match

Pairwork. Work with a partner to match each historical event in the box with its description on the time line. Check the graph to see if you were right. Add other events that have caused large numbers of people to immigrate to the United States.
One item has been done for you.

EVENTS

A. World War II
B. Quota system repealed
C. Great Depression
D. Economic Panic of 1893
E. Amnesty law
F. Irish potato famine

G. Economic panic
   of 1873
H. Quota act of 1921
I. Vietnam War ends
J. World War I starts

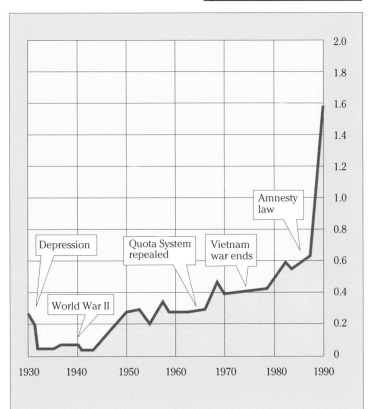

1825

1850

• Potato crop in Ireland fails, causing widespread starvation.

1875

• Period of fear follows over-expansion of business in the U.S.; money loses value, people lose jobs.

1900

• Second period of fear followed by U.S. economic depression.

• U.S. sides with England & France in European war (1914).
• U.S. Congress passes a law restricting immigration (1921).

1925

• Long period of economic slowdown follows stock market crash (1929).
• U.S. joins England, France, & Russia in war against Germany, Italy, & Japan (1944).

A

1950

• 1921 law restricting immigration is lifted by U.S. Congress.

• U.S. withdraws from Vietnam; thousands of refugees leave Southeast Asia.

1975

• New law allows many illegal immigrants to apply for permanent residence in the U.S.

2000

Activity 2: Match

1. Distribute AM 1/7. Explain that chronological order is time order. Do the first two items with the class, eliciting the connection between <u>potato crop</u> fails and Irish <u>potato famine</u>. Tell students that each historical event can be matched using similar context clues.

2. Elicit events for each year and write them on the board in a time line. Ask students to report what clues they used to match the events. (*Answers:* F/Potato crop in Ireland fails; G/Period of fear; D/Second period of fear; J/U.S. sides with England and France; H/U.S. Congress passes a law; C/Long period of economic slowdown; B/1921 law; I/U.S. withdraws from Vietnam; E/New law allows)

Activity 3: Categorize

1. Distribute AM 1/8. Do one example with students. Then have them work on their own. Circulate to help as needed. When students have finished, draw the chart on the board and elicit the causes. (*Answers:* Increase: Irish potato famine, economic prosperity, end of World War I, end of World War II, quota system repealed, end of Vietnam war, Amnesty law. Decrease: Economic panic of 1893, start of World War I, Quota Act of 1921, Depression, start of World War II.)

2. Encourage students to add more events to the graph. (Possible additions: Cuban revolution of 1956, the tearing down of the Berlin wall, dissolution of the former Soviet Union and the former Yugoslavia, famine in Somalia, civil war in Rwanda, political repression in Haiti.)

Activity 4: Listening

1. Distribute AM 1/9. Before the students listen, have them look at the pictures and read the headings under A and B. Ask them to predict the information. Introduce any vocabulary that students will need to understand the stories. For example: Story A: *novelty*, new and interesting events; *hatch,* the opening in the deck of a ship that leads to the hold; *of special note,* important or worth mentioning. Story B: *insect laden,* full of insects; *decrepit,* broken down; *magnitude,* size; *Grand Central Station,* the main train station in New York City; *shanty,* small house, often made from scrap materials; *destiny,* fate; *adapt myself to,* change myself to suit the new conditions.

2. Tell students to listen without writing as you play the cassette the first time. Play the cassette again and have them fill in the information in the Activity Master. Replay as needed.

(Continued on page 23.)

> **Study Strategy:**
> **Classifying**
> See page 163.

> **Study Strategy:**
> **Listening for Specific Information**
> See page 164.

3. Categorize

On your own. What kinds of events have caused waves of immigrants to seek better lives in the United States? What factors can cause immigration to slow down? Categorize the events mentioned on the graph into two groups: those that caused immigration to the United States to increase, and those that caused it to decrease.

Increase	Decrease
■ Irish potato famine	■ Economic panic of 1873

Classwork. Look at the time line on pages 20–21 again. Imagine what will happen in the future. Suggest some events that might happen after the year 2000. What effects will these events have on the immigration patterns of the 21st century?

4. Listening

You will hear two stories told by immigrants to America. As you listen to each story, take notes on the following information.

A

Date of immigration _____

Mode of transportation _____

Problems encountered during the trip _____

_____

_____

B

Country of origin _____

Date of immigration _____

Modes of transportation _____

Point of entry to the United States _____

Reason for disappointment _____

_____

Plan for the future _____

3. Elicit the information and write it on the board. (*Answers:* Story A: Date of immigration: 1846; Mode of transportation: sailing ship and steamboat; Problems encountered during the trip: high waves, seasickness among most of the passengers, near drowning when a wave broke through the hatch, childbirth with no doctor or nurse, death of five people. Story B: Country of origin: Italy; Date of immigration: 1903; Modes of transportation: ship and train; point of entry to the United States: Ellis Island (New York City); Reason for disappointment: the town he had imagined to be a beautiful place was a mining camp; his home was a dirty shanty; Plan for the future: adapt to the circumstances and hope for a better future.

Activity 5: Identify

1. Distribute AM 1/10 and write the information on the board. Ask students to read the information about the immigrants before they listen again. Play the tape and ask students to identify the information about each person. Replay as needed.

2. Have two students complete the chart on the board. (*Answers:* (1) both; (2) both; (3) A; (4) B; (5) both; (6) B; (7) A; (8) B.)

Activity 6: Speculate

1. Write the sentences from the *Language Focus* box on the board. Explain that we use these patterns to talk about possible occurrences in the past. Point out the two patterns:

(1) Simple past tense and an adverb such as *probably* or *maybe* (Rizzo *probably worked* all his life in the mine. *Maybe* he *married* the owner's sister and became a manager.)

(2) *Might have, may have,* or *could have* + past participle (Berendre and his wife *may have bought* a farm)

2. Have groups list possibilities.

3. *Optional:* After students listen to the possibilities, have them work individually or with a partner and write the sequel to one of the immigrant's stories. The sequel might be in the form of a letter, a diary entry, or a newspaper story.

Activity 7: Write

1. Review the information about audience in the Writer's Guide. Ask students to choose someone to write to about their own journey. Tell them to consider what that person already knows, and what he or she needs to know in order to understand the story. Give students examples of personal and formal letters and compare the salutations, information, and tone in each letter:

(Continued on page 25.)

---

5. Identify

On your own. Listen to the stories again. Write A, B, or "Both" for each statement.

A. Hendrik Berendre

B. Saverio Rizzo

_____ came from Europe.

_____ traveled to America by ship.

_____ was already married.

_____ was only 16 years old.

_____ had a difficult voyage.

_____ landed in New York City.

_____ sailed up the Mississippi River.

_____ went to work in a mine.

> **Language Focus**
>
> **Past Speculation**
>
> ■ He probably worked very hard.
> ■ He might have made a lot of money.

6. Speculate

Groupwork. Imagine what might have happened to one of the immigrants whose stories you heard. What were their lives like ten years after immigration? What happened to their children and grandchildren? Make a list of possibilities to share with the whole class.

7. Write

a. Groupwork. Think about a move or journey you have made. Why did you leave? How did you travel? What did you hope for? Tell your story to the group. Listen to your classmate's story and ask more questions.

b. On your own. Write a letter about your journey. Decide first who you want to receive your letter. For example, you may want to write to a personal friend, a relative, a teacher, or to the President of the United States. Describe the trip in as much detail as you can remember. For more information on choosing your audience, see page 174.

8. Shared Reading

Pairwork. The next two pieces were written by young people who were part of more recent waves of immigration. Choose one to read while your partner reads the other one.

A

Could We Ever Forget?

I feel restless.
My thoughts keep going back
To Cambodia,
To when I was born
Into a farmer's life.
How wonderful
Our country was then.

Now I'm far away,
So confused
About my future,
About living in another country
And becoming a citizen.
To go through with it
Would mean good-bye forever.

Ok Kork, 1991

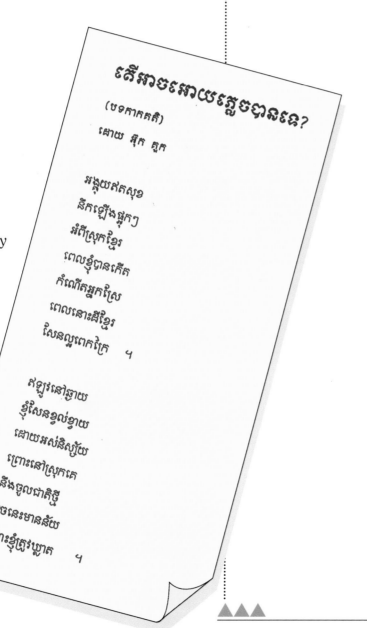

តើអាចអោយភ្លេចបានទេ?

(បទកាកគតិ)

ដោយ អុក គូក

អន្លាយអស់សុខ
នឹកថ្ពើងផ្ងួកៗ
អំពីស្រុកខ្មែរ
ពេលខ្ញុំបានកើត
កំណើតអ្នកស្រែ
ពេលនោះស៊ីខ្មែរ
សែនលួពោកក្រែ ។

សព្វូរនៅឆ្ងាយ
ខ្ញុំសែនខ្វល់ខ្វាយ
ដោយអស់និស្ស័យ
ព្រោះនៅស្រុកគេ
នឹងចូលជាតិថ្មី
ដួចនេះមានន័យ
ព្រោះខ្ញុំត្រូវឃ្លាត ។

Dear Faiza,

Well, we finally arrived! Mustapha and his wife met us at the airport. With all the delays, the trip took two days, and Sami was so tired we had to carry him off the plane . . .

Dear President Clinton:

I am an immigrant from Afghanistan. My husband, son, and I left Kabul and went to India in 1987. We just arrived in Chicago two weeks ago. I am writing to describe our journey from New Delhi to Chicago because I want you to understand what this journey meant to me and my family.

2. After they write, have students share their letters in a group. Publish the letters in a class newsletter or on a bulletin board. If students wrote to the president or another public official, they may wish to mail their letters.

Activity 8: Shared Reading

Have students work with a partner. Each partner should choose one of the selections, either the poem or the paragraph, and read it silently.

Circulate and answer any questions as students read.

My name is Monique, and I am half-Puerto Rican and half Cuban. It's easy being Puerto Rican because that's what most of my friends are, but it's not easy being Cuban. When I tell people I am half-Cuban, some act dumb and say "so you're a communist." That really gets me mad. Sometimes when I am in classes where the teacher is talking about Cuba, they expect me to know everything just because I am part Cuban. I know a few things about Cuba, but not little details like a specific poem a person made in Cuba during the Spanish-American War or the names of every town and city in Cuba.

One of the best parts of being Cuban is the stories my grandmother tells me about Cuba. Like how, when my dad was about 10 years old, he learned to drive a jeep, and how she had an orange tree in the back of her house, and how she used to go the bakery as a child with her brother to smell the bread and watch how they made it. These little stories make me want to go to Cuba more and more, especially when my grandmother tells me that the water is so blue and clear and the sandy beaches are so pretty. Someday I will go to Cuba, when I am an adult.

Monique Rubio, 1994

9. Compare

Pairwork. Take turns reading Ok Kork's poem and Monique Rubio's personal narrative aloud. Think about how the writers are similar and how they are different.

1. What do these two writers have in common? Write two sentences beginning, "They both. . ."

_____

_____

2. Now think about the differences. Make notes in a chart like this, then share ideas.

Ok Kork	Monique Rubio

10. Evaluate

Classwork. Which did you like better—the poem or the story? Explain why.

11. Journal Writing

Describe your personal reactions to either the story or the poem. Do you have anything in common with the authors? What questions would you like to ask about their experiences? What would you like to say to them?

Activity 9: Compare

1. Ask students to read their selections out loud to each other. Ask students to compare the information in their selections, and write some questions on the board to help them do so. (Possible questions: *Where was each born? What were their parents' occupations? How do they feel about living in the United States? About their native countries? What are their plans for the future?*) Encourage students to guess or make inferences if the information is not given. Then have students write a sentence about what Ok Kork and Monique Rubio have in common.

2. Write two column headings on the board: *Ok Kork* and *Monique Rubio.* Ask students to make a similar chart on a piece of paper. When students finish, elicit similarities and differences and write them on the board. (Answers will vary. Possible similarities: They are both separated from their family's native land. They both think about their native land a lot. Some differences: Monique is probably a citizen of the United States, but Ok is not yet a citizen. Ok is confused about his future; Monique has decided to visit Cuba when she becomes an adult; Ok feels he has to say goodbye forever to his native land; Monique does not.

Activity 10: Evaluate

Ask students to point to specific parts of the writing to explain what they liked or disliked.

Activity 11: Journal Writing

1. If students are willing, have them share their journal entries with another student. Each could write responses in the other's journal.

2. *Optional:* Ask students to write a poem or essay about their own experience using Ok Kork's or Monique Rubio's writing as a model.

Activity 1: Visualize

1. Introduce the chapter by pointing out the two meanings of *reflections:* images in a mirror or calm water, or deep and careful thought. Direct students' attention to the picture. Put the following questions on the board and ask students to quickwrite their responses or to talk about the questions with a partner. Tell them to use their imaginations: *Why is he there? What is he thinking about? How does he feel?*

2. *Part a.* Elicit the meaning of *visualize* (to see in one's mind). Talk about a place that is special to you, and invite students to describe their own special places. Then ask students to relax, close their eyes, and imagine themselves in that place. If feasible, play some relaxing music. After five minutes, tell students to list their thoughts. Do this activity along with your students.

3. *Part b.* Distribute a copy of AM 1/11 to each student and write the column headings *Past, Present,* and *Future* on the board. Read part of the list you made for *Part a,* and ask students for their ideas about which column each thought could be placed in. Then have students work in pairs to talk about their own lists and to transfer their thoughts to their charts. Circulate as students work, and, if necessary, review question formation with different verb tenses, for example, *Who did you go there with? Do you still write to your friend? When will you visit them?*

Chapter 4: Reflections

*W*hen the wind has died down and there are no waves, it is easier to see your reflection in the water. In periods of calm, people sometimes pause to collect their memories and dreams. In this chapter, you will read three poems that express the beauty of these moments.

1. Visualize

a. On your own. Imagine yourself in a beautiful, peaceful place. You are totally relaxed. Think for five minutes. Make a list of the thoughts that come into your mind.

b. Pairwork. Read your list to a partner. Help each other group your thoughts into three time frames. Make a chart like the one below.

Past	Present	Future

c. Choose the most interesting thing on your partner's chart. Ask your partner to tell you about it in more detail.

2. Preview

On your own. You are going to read an unusual poem. Read about the poet, May Swenson, before you begin. Then look at the whole poem on page 30 at once. What does it look like? In what way is it unusual? Where do you think it begins? Where does it end?

May Swenson (1919-1989)

May Swenson was born into a family of Swedish immigrants who had settled in Logan, Utah. After graduating from Utah State Agricultural College, she worked as a reporter, editor, and teacher. She published eight volumes of poems. She also wrote several short stories and a play, *The Floor*. She died in 1989.

3. Share a Poem

Classwork. Listen to the poem twice and read along.

29

Activity 2: Preview

After students look at the poem and think about the questions, have one or two come to the board and sketch the form. Elicit that the poem looks like a wave. Ask them to point to where the poem begins and ends. Accept all suggestions; there are no wrong answers.

Activity 3: Share a Poem

1. Ask students to read the poem silently. Then ask several volunteers to read it aloud.

2. Ask students if they see a connection between the form of some of the lines and their meaning, for example, the vertical form of the first line, which talks about stacking up, and the horizontal form of the line, *Then nothing is happening.* If appropriate, point out or elicit how verb forms help express meanings. For example, the present progressive in the first line indicates that the action is in progress at the moment. Throughout, present perfect expresses that something has just occurred.

3. Demonstrate different ways of reading the lines, with varying pitch, speed and intonation, to mimic the movement of waves. Ask several students to read the poem aloud in whatever way suits them. Practice intonation and pronunciation with the class.

4. *Optional:* Bring in poetry collections by May Swenson. After students read the biographical information about her let them look through the collection and select a poem to read for the class.

How Everything Happens

Based on a Study of the Wave by May Swenson

> happen.
> to
> up[1]
> stacking
> is
> something
> When nothing is happening
>
> When it happens
> something pulls
> back[2]
> not
> to
> happen.
>
> When   has happened.
> pulling back   stacking up
> happens
>
> has happened   stacks up.
> When it   something   nothing
> pulls back while
>
> Then nothing is happening.
> happens.
> and
> forward
> pushes
> up
> stacks
> something
> Then

[1]**stacks up** gets ready
[2]**pulls back** slows down, withdraws

4. Identify

a. Groupwork. Identify the six sentences in the poem. How do you know where each sentence begins and ends? Take turns reading each sentence aloud, moving around the group until you have read the whole poem several times.

b. Pairwork. Copy the diagram of a wave below. Mark places on the diagram where these words and phrases from the poem might fit.

nothing is happening

something is stacking up to happen

it happens

something pulls back

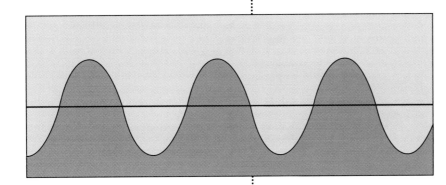

c. Get together with another pair. Compare your diagrams and discuss any differences.

5. Apply

a. Groupwork. Discuss how "something stacks up to happen." What sequence of events lead up to a larger event? Choose one of the examples below or use one of your own.

1. a soccer or football game
2. a party
3. a storm
4. a trip or major move
5. a marriage

b. Use the same example to explain how "something pulls back not to happen."

Example: When one team wins the game, the other team loses.

Activity 4: Identify

1. *Part a.* In their groups, encourage students to experiment with different ways of reading the sentences. You may want to copy the poem for each group and have them cut it into strips, one sentence or phrase per strip. Have groups arrange strips in patterns to guide pitch, intonation, and rhythm. Emphasize that there is no "right" way to do this. Encourage groups to have fun with the project, and to present a dramatic reading for the whole class when they are finished.

2. *Parts b and c.* When students finish the group work, ask several pairs with different results to come to the board to draw and label their diagram. Ask them to explain their labelling to the class.

Activity 5: Apply

1. *Part a.* Before students begin, brainstorm one of the topics with the whole class. Ask: *How does a party stack up to happen?* Elicit inviting people, planning food, arranging for music, etc. Write ideas on the board.

2. *Part b.* Write the sentence from the *Language Focus* box on the board. Tell students we use this pattern to talk about conditions and the results that almost always follow. Present tense is usually used in both clauses. Note that we also use *if* and *whenever* for this type of time clause. Give additional examples: *If you give a party on Wednesday night, a lot of people can't come. Whenever someone moves to a new country, he or she leaves behind a lot of friends.*

3. Send students to the board to write sentences that explain how something pulls back not to happen. Have them use the event that their group discussed. Examples: *When people get married, sometimes they don't keep in touch with their friends anymore. If there's a big storm, you have to cancel plans to travel.*

Activity 6: Journal Writing

1. Have students review their thoughts from Activity 1. If feasible, play relaxing music to get them into a reflective mood. Give students time to think as well as write, and do the activity along with them.

2. If students are willing, have them exchange journals to read and comment about each other's reflections.

Activity 7: Describe

Write several captions on the board. Elicit students' reactions to the picture.

Activity 8: Listen

Tell the students that they are going to hear a poem entitled "At the Beach." Ask them to look at the picture as they listen. Play the tape several times.

Activity 9: Identify

1. Have students work individually or in pairs to identify the "doers" of the three actions. Ask them to write their answers on a separate piece of paper. Play the tape again for them to check their recollections. Elicit answers and write them on the board. (*Answers:* making footprints and saying words: two people; erasing footprints: the waves; carrying away words: the wind.)

Activity 10: Read

Have students work in pairs and read the entire poem to each other. Circulate and listen to the readings.

> **Language Focus**
>
> **Time Clauses**
>
> When a storm is on the way, people don't plan to have picnics at the beach.

6. Journal Writing

On your own. Imagine yourself back in a beautiful, peaceful place. Reflect on something important that happened in your life. Explain what happened and what led up to it. How did things stack up to happen? Did anything pull back not to happen? How did you feel after it was over?

7. Describe

Pairwork. Discuss this photograph with your partner. Write two sentences that describe the scene.

8. Listen

Listen to the poem several times. Keep looking at the photograph as you listen.

9. Identify

On your own. Who or what is making things happen in the poem? Identify the "doer" of each action. Listen again if you need to.

_____ making footprints and saying words

_____ erasing footprints

_____ carrying away words

10. Read

Pairwork. Take turns reading the whole poem aloud.

AT THE BEACH
by Kemal Ozer

translated by O. Yalim, W. Fielder, and Dionis Riggs

The waves are erasing the footprints
Of those who are walking the beach.

The wind is carrying away the words
Two people are saying to each other.

But still they are walking the beach
Their feet making new footprints.

Still the two are talking together
Finding new words.

11. Share Ideas

a. Pairwork. Discuss your reactions to the poem with a partner. Here are some questions to think about.

1. Did you like this poem? Why or why not?
2. What is happening to their footprints and words?
3. Why do they go on making new footprints and saying new words?
4. What other meaning might "footprints" have?
5. What does the poem say about life? Do you agree?

b. Look back at the poem on the first page of this unit. Compare it to "At the Beach." How are the two poems alike? How are they different?

12. Share a Poem

Groupwork. Bring in a poem or song you know. It can be a poem or song written first in another language, then translated into English. Introduce it to your group and read it aloud. If you have a tape of the song or poem, you may want to play it for your group. Answer any questions your classmates may have.

Kemal Ozer

Kemal Ozer is a well known modern Turkish poet. He was born in 1935 and lives in Istanbul. "At the Beach" is part of a collection of poems entitled *This Same Sky.* All of the poems in this collection were written in languages other than English.

Activity 11: Share Ideas

1. *Part a.* Before students begin their discussion, talk about literal and symbolic meaning. Point out that often we compare small, concrete things and events with larger or more spiritual issues. Remind students about their work in Activity 5, in which they compared a complicated event to a wave stacking up.

2. Have students discuss the questions with a partner. Afterwards, partners may enjoy forming larger groups and comparing their ideas. Then discuss the poem as a whole class. (Answers will vary. Some possible answers: (1) Will vary with each student. (2) Their footprints and words are disappearing as they go. (3) Because they want to keep walking and talking together; they enjoy this communication. (4) The course of one's life or of this relationship. (5) That the process is more important than the result; it's important to keep going.)

3. After the discussion, ask one or two students to make a statement about the poem's symbolic meaning.

4. *Part b.* Ask students to work in pairs and to consider how both poems look on the page. (*At the Beach* has eight lines in four stanzas. *The Waves of Matsuyama* has 5 short lines in one stanza.) Then ask students to think about how each poem presents human life. Elicit their ideas. (*Possible responses:* Both poems show life as transitory and changing. Ozer's poem is more hopeful and shows human beings continually renewing their contact with each other. In Saigyo's poem, the lord is gone forever.)

Activity 12: Share a Poem

If students have trouble finding a poem to bring in, suggest they look in the Ozer collection *This Same Sky,* or go to the library with them to help find material. Encourage groups to give readings for the class.

Activity Menu

Read and discuss the activities with the class. Have each student select an activity. Students can work individually, in pairs, or in groups. When students complete their projects, have them present their work to the class.

Activity Menu

1. Find the Speed
A wave made with rope has a wavelength of two meters. The frequency of the wave is measured at 0.5 hertz. What is the speed of this wave? When you have an answer, ask a classmate to solve the problem too. Talk about how you found your answers and compare methods.

2. Write a Problem
Write a word problem of your own about waves. Give it to a partner to solve.

3. What's Your Idea?
Draw a picture of water wave patterns near the beach. Explain how you could make measurements of waves like this if you were at the beach. Write your ideas for a classmate.

4. Research an Author's Work
Look up Rachel Carson in an encyclopedia. Write down the titles and publication dates of the books she wrote during her lifetime. Then search in the card or on-line catalogue at your school or local library. Are any of Rachel Carson's books available? If you find a catalogue card or listing for one or more of Rachel Carson's books, write down the call number, the title, and the publication date on a slip of paper or in your notebook. If the book is in the library, find it on the shelves. Ask a librarian if you need help. Report what you found to the class.

5. Identify Ways to Express Emotion
Watch a 30-minute drama on television. Listen for the way the music and sound effects communicate emotions such as happiness, fear, anger, or humor to the television audience. Describe your observations to a partner.

6. Research an Historical Event
Find out more about one of the historical events that has caused immigration to the United States to increase or decrease.

Get the basic facts from an encyclopedia or history textbook:

What happened?

Where did it happen?

When did it happen?

How did it increase or
decrease immigration?

Ask a librarian or teacher if you need help finding information. Take notes on the basic facts, and report back to the class.

7. Debate the Issue
The United States has been called a nation of immigrants, yet today the government has strict rules about immigration. Should the United States allow unlimited immigration? Why or why not? Organize a debate in which one team (Team A) argues for an "open door" immigration policy in which all groups would be allowed to immigrate in unlimited numbers.

The second team (Team B) presents a case for restricting immigration to certain groups or numbers.

Each team gets 15 minutes to prepare a five minute presentation. In the discussion that follows, try to reach a basic principle about immigration upon which all students on both teams can agree.

8. The Power of Waves
Waves can be very destructive. In 1870, a lighthouse was built on the coast of North Carolina. At first, the lighthouse was about 2000 feet from the water. Over the years the waves have eroded[1] the beach. Today the lighthouse stands only 125 feet from the water. Design an advertisement to save this lighthouse. Include answers to these questions: How much closer to the water does the lighthouse get in a year? How many years will it take until the waves reach the lighthouse? What can people do to save the lighthouse?

[1]**eroded** worn away

Read On

The Education of Berenice Belizaire

by Joe Klein

When Berenice Belizire arrived in New York from Haiti with her mother and sister in 1987, she was not very happy. She spoke no English. The family had to live in a cramped Brooklyn apartment, a far cry from the comfortable house they'd had in Haiti. Her mother, a nurse, worked long hours. School was torture. Berenice had always been a good student, but now she was learning a new language while enduring constant taunts* from the Americans (both black and white). They cursed her in the cafeteria and threw food at her. Someone hit her sister in the head with a book. "Why can't we go home?" Berenice asked her mother.

Because home was too dangerous. The schools weren't always open anymore, and education—her mother insisted—was the most important thing. Her mother had always pushed her: memorize everything, she ordered. "I have a pretty good memory," Berenice admitted last week. Indeed, the other kids at school began to notice that Berenice always, somehow, knew the answers. "They started coming to me for help," she says. "They never called me a nerd."

Within two years Berenice was speaking English, though not well enough to get into one of New York's elite public high schools. She had to settle for the neighborhood school, James Madison—which is one of the magical American places, the alma mater[1] of Ruth Bader Ginsburg[2] among others, a school with a history of unlikely success stories. "I didn't realize what we had in Berenice at first," says math teacher Judith Khan. "She was good at math, but she was quiet. And the things she didn't know! She applied for a summer program in Buffalo[3] and asked me how to get there on the subway. But she always seemed to ask the right questions. She understood the big ideas. She could think on her feet. She could explain difficult problems so the other kids could understand them. Eventually, I realized: she wasn't just pushing for grades, she was hungry for *knowledge*. . . and you know, it never occurred to me that she also was doing it in English and history, all these other subjects that had to be much tougher for her than math."

---

*taunt   a scornful remark
[1]**alma mater** the school from which a person graduated
[2]**Ruth Bader Ginsburg** a justice on the United States Supreme Court

[3]**Buffalo** a city in New York State, 390 miles northwest from New York City

Read On

The Education of Berenice Belizaire

1. Prepare students by drawing their attention to the picture and caption. Ask: *What does "acting American" mean?*

2. Ask students to think about their first weeks in the United States. What were the biggest differences at home and at school? How did they deal with these changes? Ask students to talk about these questions with a partner. Elicit some examples from volunteers.

3. Discussion questions: (1) What did Judith Khan, Berenice's high school math teacher, realize about Berenice? (2) What ideas would an "immigrant's valedictory" stress? (3) How had Berenice changed by the time she entered MIT? (4) What are some of the characteristics that Khan admires in her immigrant students?

She moved from third in her class to first during senior year. She was selected as valedictorian,[4] an honor she almost refused (still shy, she wouldn't allow her picture in the school's yearbook). She gave the speech, after some prodding—a modest address about the importance of hard work and how it's never too late to try hard—an immigrant's valedictory.

Last week I caught up with Berenice at the Massachusetts Institute of Technology where she was jump-starting[5] her college career. I asked her what she wanted to be doing in 10 years: "I want to build a famous computer, like IBM," she said. "I want my name to be part of it."

Berenice Belizaire's story is remarkable, but not unusual. The New York City schools are bulging with overachieving immigrants. The burdens[6] they place on a creaky,[7] corroded[8] system are often cited[9] as an argument against liberal[10] immigration policies, but teachers like Judith Khan don't seem to mind. "They're why I love teaching in Brooklyn," she says. "They have a drive in them we no longer seem to have. You see these kids, who aren't prepared academically and can barely speak the language, struggling so hard. They just sop it up. They're like little sponges. You see Berenice, who had none of the usual, preconceived[11] racial barriers in her mind—you see her becoming friendly with the Russian kids, and learning chess from Po Ching (from Taiwan). It is so exciting."

from Newsweek, Aug. 9, 1993

---

[4]**valedictorian** a student, usually with very good grades, who gives the graduation speech

[5]**jump starting** started early

[6]**burdens** problems that are difficult to solve.

[7]**creaky** old and not in good working order

[8]**corroded** broken down

[9]**cited** spoken or written about, given as evidence

[10]**liberal** not strict

[11]**preconceived** an opinion formed earlier

Song for Smooth Waters

(Native American, traditional)

Ocean Spirit
calm the waves for me
get close to me, my power
my heart is tired
make the sea like milk for me
yeo
yeholo

West Side
by Naomi Shihab Nye

In certain neighborhoods
the air is paved with names.
Domingo, Monico, Francisco,
shining rivulets of sound.
Names opening wet circles
inside the mouth,
sprinkling bright vowels
across the deserts of
Bill, Bob, John.

The names are worn
on silver linked chains.
Maria lives in Pablo Alley,
Esperanza rides the Santiago bus!
They click together like charms.
O save us from the boarded-up windows,
The pistol crack in a dark backyard,
save us from the leaky roof,
the rattled textbook that never smiles.
Let the names be verses
in a city that sings!

Song for Smooth Waters

Read the poem aloud for students to appreciate. Ask students, *How does the poem make you feel?* Ask students to compare the Ocean Spirit in this poem with Poseidon, the Greek god of the oceans.

West Side

1. Explore the imagery of the poem with the students. Ask, *How is the air paved with names?* (Possibly from people calling out these names.) Elicit the picture that *rivulets* and *deserts* evokes. Ask students to look up the meanings of *charms* in a dictionary, and discuss how these meanings function in the second stanza. (Charms are (1) pieces of jewelry worn to ward off evil and (2) expressions that have the power to protect from evil.) Note that the prayer in the last six lines is a kind of charm. Ask students to compare the neighborhoods of "West Side" with the neighborhood Berenice lived in when she moved to the United States. Ask: What was Berenice's "charm" against these dangers? (Possibly her desire for education.)

2. Have groups of students practice the poem, experimenting with different combinations of voices. Encourage them to stress the open vowels of the Hispanic names, and the staccato sounds of the American names. Make a tape so that students can listen to all the different readings.

Unit 2:

CHOOSING PATHS

Activity 1: Brainstorm

1. Have students form groups; then introduce brainstorming. Tell students that they should call out any ideas that come to mind. They can edit the list later. The purpose of brainstorming, like quickwriting, is to capture ideas. Model the activity by drawing students' attention to the photographs and asking, *What decisions have the people in these pictures made?* Write ideas on the board. Have each group choose one student to record the group's ideas.

2. Note the pattern of *wh-* word + infinitive: *In college, people have to decide what to major in.*

3. When the groups have completed their lists, have students come to the board and make a master list of important decisions. Ask students to identify which decisions are most important and which ones are the hardest to make. Ask, *Have you made any of these decisions yet?*

Chapter 1: Making Difficult Decisions

In this chapter, you will think about some of the decisions people make during their lives and read a story about a young woman who has to make a difficult decision.

> **Study Strategy:**
> **Brainstorming**
>
> See page 163.

1. Brainstorm

Groupwork. What are some of the important decisions that people make during their lives? List your group's ideas on another piece of paper.

Examples: whether or not to go to college

where to go to college

whether or not to get married

who to marry

Compare ideas with the other groups in your class.

Activity 2: Think-Pair-Share

1. *Part a.* Ask students to list some of the important decisions that they have made, and then choose one to quickwrite about. You may want to model the activity by writing ideas about one of your own decisions on the board.

2. *Part b.* Remind students that they will be telling their partner's story in the next step. Tell them to listen carefully and to ask their partners to repeat when they don't understand something. Encourage partners to ask questions about each other's stories.

3. *Part c.* Participate in the groups as students tell each other's stories. Model responses by asking questions and sharing your own experiences.

Activity 3: Preview

1. *Part a.* Explain that by looking at different parts of a text, readers can predict what kinds of information the text provides. Note that previewing is a skill that students can use in many courses.

2. Your students may enjoy doing this activity as a game. Explain that this is like a scavenger hunt—a party game in which players use clues to find different items. Call each group a team, and give the teams a limited time to find the information.

3. Elicit answers from volunteers. Ask students to explain how they arrived at their answer to question 4. (Answers: 1. Who's Hu? 2. See information on page 51; 3. Emma Hu, Arthur Aldrich, Mr. Antonelli, Kim.)

4. (Answers will vary) A Chinese girl feels she's a freak and won't get a date to the senior prom because she is a math whiz.

(Continued on page 43.)

---

2. Think-Pair-Share

a. On your own. Think of a time when you had to make an important decision. What did you decide to do? Why? How do you feel about your decision today?

b. Pairwork. Get together with a partner. Tell your partner about the decision you made. Listen carefully to your partner's story.

c. Groupwork. Get together with another pair. Tell your partner's story.

Study Strategy:
Previewing
See page 167.

3. Preview

a. Groupwork. Scan the story on pages 44–45. Look for answers to these questions:

1. What's the title of the story?

2. What do you know about the author of this story?

3. Who are the main characters in this story?

4. What do you think this story is about?

Get together with your classmates and compare answers.

b. Classwork. Read the first four paragraphs of the story. Then share what you know about the main character, Emma Hu. Write your ideas on a tree diagram like this:

Study Strategy:
Making a Tree Diagram
See page 165.

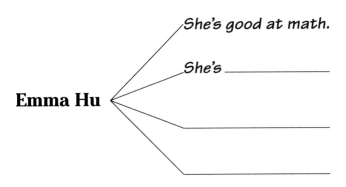

She's good at math.

She's _____

Emma Hu

_____

_____

Share ideas with your classmates and make one tree diagram on the board.

c. On your own. Reread the first four paragraphs. Choose three words that are unfamiliar to you. Try using context to guess the meaning of each word. Then look up each word in the dictionary. Choose the definition that best fits the word in this context. Take notes in a chart like this.

Example:

New words	My guess from context	Dictionary definition
nasty	unfriendly	unpleasant in manner; angry

Tell your classmates about the words in your chart.

4. **Read**

On your own. As you read the first part of the story on pages 44–45, write your thoughts and questions in your journal. Also, try using context to guess the meaning of any unfamiliar words.

> ***Study Strategy:***
> ***Using Context***
> See page 169.

5. *Part b.* Have students work individually or with a partner to make the tree diagram. Then have two students go to the board and make a comprehensive diagram as students call out their ideas. (Possible information: Her father's a professor at M.I.T. She's learning to speak English. She may be from China. She lives in the U.S. She's a high school senior. No one has asked her to the prom.)

6. Ask students to think of questions they have about Emma. Elicit the questions and have the two students at the board write them next to the tree diagram.

7. *Part c.* Distribute AM 2/1. Write several examples on the board, giving students enough time to analyze parts of the text for context clues. Encourage them to read past an unfamiliar word to find context clues. After students do the exercise individually, have them work in groups to give examples of words they worked with. Elicit the ways in which students used context to guess the meaning. Remind students that they do not have to know the exact meaning of each word; a general idea will often suffice. The math terms, for example, illustrate that this is an advanced class, but students can understand the story without knowing their exact meanings.

8. *Optional:* Divide the class into groups, and have each group work on one paragraph. Then have each group teach the rest of the class the words in their paragraphs. Tell students to supply example sentences for the words they teach.

Activity 4: Read

1. If your students have not yet written a reader response journal, introduce this activity. Tell them that their responses can take any form, including questions about vocabulary or language, about the setting, and about characters' motivations. Students should also write their own responses to the story, such as their interpretations and opinions about parts of the story, or notes about their own experiences.

(Continued on page 44.)

2. Circulate and encourage students to keep reading even when they don't understand particular words or paragraphs. Help them to use the context to guess the meanings of words.

3. When students finish reading, divide them into groups and ask them to read their journal responses to each other. Have them work in their groups to answer the questions they recorded in their journals.

4. Ask groups if there were any language problems that their groups could not resolve. Have the whole class offer ideas regarding unresolved interpretation questions, but do not offer answers since students will continue working with the text.

Who's Hu? (Part 1)

by Lensey Namioka

I was tired of being a freak.[1]

My father was a professor of mathematics at M.I.T., and whenever I got 100 on my math test (which was pretty often) my high school teachers would say, "I know where Emma Hu gets help with her homework . . . cackle[2] . . . cackle . . ." The rest of the class usually cackled along. At first I didn't see why they were so nasty about it. Later I discovered that girls in this country weren't supposed to be good in math. The teachers didn't like it when Arthur Aldrich—our self-styled math genius—corrected their mistakes in class. They hated it a lot more when I did.

In China there was nothing wrong with girls being good at math. In fact, Chinese women were supposed to keep the household or business accounts. But in America, when I opened my big mouth to correct my algebra teacher—in broken English, yet—everyone thought I was a freak. Once I thought I would cheat on my math test by deliberately making a couple of mistakes, but when it came to the point, I just couldn't do it. Mathematics was too beautiful to mess up.

On most days I wasn't too bothered by my math grades, but lately I had begun to worry. I was a senior at Evesham High, a high school in the suburbs of Boston, and the senior prom[3] was only three weeks away. Who was going to ask a Chinese girl math whiz?[4] According to my friend Katey, everybody went to the prom except freaks.

After lunch the first class I attended was math. Just being in the classroom made me feel better. I liked to look around the room at the portion of the blackboard painted with a permanent white grid for graphing equations, the hanging cardboard models of regular polyhedra we had made as a class project, and the oak shelf containing plaster models of conic sections and various surfaces. My favorite was the hyperbolic paraboloid, or saddle, with its straight lines neatly incised in the plaster.

The class was Advanced Mathematics, intended for seniors who were going into science or math and who had already taken algebra, geometry, and trig. The course covered analytic geometry, calculus, and a little probability theory. Actually, it wasn't so much the content of the course that I liked best: it was the teacher, Mr. Antonelli. He was a short man only a little taller than I, and he had a swarthy face dominated by a huge beak of a nose. Unlike my other math teachers (one of them even a woman), he didn't seem to find it bizarre that a girl should do well in his class. As for my being Chinese, I doubt if he even noticed. Mr. Antonelli didn't care if you were a Martian eunuch, as long as you did the math correctly.

Today Mr. Antonelli gave the impression of suppressed excitement. He clearly had something on his mind,[5] because for the first time I remember, he let one of the boys do a maximum-minimum problem without checking the second derivative to see if it was an inflection point. Arthur Aldrich and I

[1] **freak**   a strange or weird person
[2] **cackle**   shrill laughter
[3] **senior prom**   dance party for seniors before
                       they graduate
[4] **whiz**   genius, very smart person
[5] **had something** was thinking about
on his mind   something

beat each other to a draw[6] in pointing out the mistake. Mr. Antonelli acknowledged our reproof[7] almost absentmindedly. He certainly was preoccupied.[8]

With five minutes left of the period, Mr. Antonelli made an announcement: "Class, you remember that last fall you all took the semi-final exam for the Sterns Mathematics Prize. Today I received word of the results."

The Sterns was a mathematics prize given annually to a high school senior in Massachusetts. The award was for $200, but the prestige it carried was immeasurable. Never in the history of the Sterns Prize had it been won by a girl.

"Now," Mr. Antonelli went on, "it is an honor for our school if a student here makes it to the finals. Well, we've got not just one student, but two who are going into the finals. One is Arthur Aldrich."

Arthur was a tall, gangly[9] boy with hair so blond that it looked almost white. With his long nose and sharp chin, he reminded me of a white fox in one of the Chinese fairy tales. Arthur had very few stumbling blocks[10] in his life. His family was comfortably off,[11] he did well in every subject in school, and he was a credit to the Evasham High School track team. In spite of his successes, Arthur was too arrogant[12] to be popular.

"The other," Mr. Antonelli announced, "is Emma Hu."

The class cheered. My thoughts were in a whirl. I thought I had fallen down badly[13] on the exam the previous fall because there were two problems I hadn't been able to do. Now it seemed that my performance hadn't been so bad after all.

I have only the vaguest memories of my other classes that afternoon. I barely realized when the final bell rang. Leaving school, I almost hugged my books to my chest. It was like waking up on my birthday and finding a pile of presents outside my door.

I was so absorbed that I didn't hear footsteps coming up behind me. I jumped when Arthur's voice spoke in my ear. "I want to talk to you."

"About what?" I asked, surprised. In Arthur's ranking of animal intelligence, girls came somewhere between sheep and myna birds. Of course that made me even more of a freak in his eyes.

Arthur grinned now. In the illustrations of my Chinese fairy tale book, foxes grinned with their mouths forming a big V. Arthur's smile was just like that. "I hear you want to go to the senior prom but can't find anyone to take you. I have a simple proposition to make: I'll take you to the prom—refreshments, corsage,[14] dinner afterward, the whole works—if you'll drop out of[15] the Sterns exam."

[6]**beat each other to a draw**	tied, were even
[7]**reproof**	criticism
[8]**preoccupied**	worried
[9]**gangly**	tall, thin, and ungraceful
[10]**stumbling blocks**	barriers, difficulties
[11]**comfortably off**	without financial problems
[12]**arrogant**	proud
[13]**fallen down badly**	not done well
[14]**corsage**	flowers to pin on one's dress
[15]**drop out of**	leave; decide not to participate in

Activity 5: Distinguishing Fact and Opinion

1. Distribute AM 2/2 and draw the chart on the board. Use the examples on the chart to clarify the differences between fact and opinion. Facts can be observed and measured. Opinions are often evaluations such as *good, bad, nice, ugly.* Point out that the distinction between the two is not always clear.

2. After groups complete their work, have students come to the board and combine ideas from the whole class into a chart on the board. Clarify which information states a fact and which states an opinion. Ask students to use material from the text to support the opinions.

Activity 6: Speculate

1. *Language Focus.* Write the sentences from the Language Focus box on the board. Point out that the verb in the *if*-clause is in the simple present tense, while the verb in the main clause is in the future. Provide more *if*-clauses and elicit additional examples, such as,

If Emma doesn't get a date for the senior prom, she will feel . . .

If Mr. Antonelli finds out about Arthur's proposition, he'll probably . . .

2. Have students work individually or with a partner to make a list of possible consequences on a piece of paper. Then write the two *if*-clauses on the board, and have a student list the consequences as the class calls them out. Students can then take turns reading the complete sentences aloud, checking for grammatical accuracy.

5. Distinguishing Fact and Opinion

Groupwork. Share ideas about these characters from the story. Add information to a chart like this.

Emma Hu	Mr. Antonelli	Arthur Aldrich
Her father teaches math. (F)	He's a good teacher. (O)	He's tall. (F)

Language Focus:

Expressing Possible Consequences

- If Emma accepts Arthur's proposition, Mr. Antonelli will be disappointed.
- If she accepts Arthur's proposition, she won't _____.
- If she rejects his proposition, she will probably feel _____.

Look back over the information on your chart. Put an (F) next to the facts. Put an (O) next to any opinions. Then compare charts with the other groups in your class.

6. Speculate

Classwork. In the story, Arthur makes a proposition.

I have a simple proposition to make: I'll take you to the prom if you drop out of the Sterns exam.

If Emma accepts Arthur's proposition, what will the consequences be? If she rejects his proposition, what will happen? List your ideas on the board.

If she accepts his proposition,. . .

_____

_____

_____

If she rejects his proposition,. . .

_____

_____

_____

Study Strategy:
Predicting
See page 167.

7. ▶ **Predict**

a. Pairwork. How do you think Emma will respond to Arthur's proposition? Write your prediction.

b. Pairwork. Role play the conversation between Emma and Arthur on page 45. Add your own ideas to continue their conversation.

8. ▶ **Read**

On your own. Read the rest of the story to check your prediction from Activity 7.

Activity 7: Predict

1. *Part a.* Note or elicit that predictions about Emma will be based on what the reader already knows about her. Tell students to look over the information about Emma in the chart from *Activity 5.* Elicit Emma's conflict: She loves math, but she's tired of being a "freak." She wants to go to the prom. Ask students: *Which do you think will be more important to Emma, her math talent or her need to belong?*

2. Elicit several responses and write them on the board in speech bubbles.

3. *Part b.* Have two students model the conversation on page 45. Encourage them to exaggerate characters and reactions. Circulate and help students as they work. Have several pairs act out their role play for the class.

Activity 8: Read

1. Have students read the first paragraph of Part 2 of the story, and compare their predictions to Emma's reaction. Have them consider what will happen next and make a prediction about how the story will end. Then have them finish reading the story on their own, using their reading journals to record questions and responses. Provide several inference questions for them to consider as they read. (Possible questions: *Why was Emma grateful for Kim's words? What was Emma's state of mind when she went to take the exam? What was Arthur's reaction to Emma's state of mind? How did Emma come to make her decision about the exam?*)

2. Circulate and answer students' questions as they read. Help them infer the meanings of words from context.

(Continued on page 48.)

3. *Optional:* Ask two students to read aloud the next part of the story, Emma's conversation with Kim. Encourage them to read expressively, and act out Emma's and Kim's feelings. Elicit other students' reaction to the reading: Ask, *Is this how Emma and Kim feel?* Then have students complete the reading on their own.

4. When students finish the reading, have them work in groups. Ask them to read their journals to each other and to exchange ideas about the inference questions and their own questions from their journals.

Who's Hu? (Part 2)

The sheer gall[1] of Arthur's proposition took my breath away, and for a moment I was too astounded even to be angry. In the end my main reaction turned out to be triumph. "So you're really afraid I might do better than you on the exam!" I said, unable to hide my satisfaction.

Two spots of color appeared on Arthur's pale cheeks, but he kept his foxy grin. "I can do better than you any day, don't you worry! But I know you're desperate to go to the prom. Every red-blooded, normal high school senior goes to the prom, right?"

I said nothing. The price of being a red-blooded, normal high school senior was pretty high.

"Well?" demanded Arthur.

I was determined to be equally curt. "No," I said.

He stormed away[2] without another word.

"I'm terribly sorry. I couldn't help overhearing."

I turned around and saw it was Kim. He was a Korean boy who was one of my mother's music students.

It was almost a relief not to have to pretend. "It doesn't matter," I said. To my fury, my lips were beginning to quiver.[3] "There isn't a person in school who doesn't already know I haven't been able to find a date for the prom. It's been a joke for so long that I don't even feel humiliated about it anymore."

But that was a lie.

Kim looked as if he were trying not to laugh. "I don't even try to understand all these American customs anymore. But this prom sounds like some sort of native ritual or tribal dance."

He was a foreigner in America and not bothered by it at all. He was even inviting me to join him in enjoying the amusing antics[4] of the natives.

"Don't you feel lonely sometimes?" I asked, remembering my loneliness the first day of school on discovering I was to be the only Chinese there. That loneliness I suffered until Katey and her friends took me in.[5]

[1]**gall**	nerve; rudeness
[2]**stormed away**	left angrily
[3]**quiver**	tremble; shake
[4]**antics**	strange behavior
[5]**took me in**	accepted me; made me part of their group

Kim only smiled and shook his head. "I'm too busy. Schoolwork is hard for me because of my poor English, and after school all my time is taken up with practicing. Even if I had the money, I wouldn't go." He looked at me curiously. "You are devoted to mathematics the way I am to music, aren't you? I think I heard your mother say so."

I nodded, grateful for these words. He considered our situations to be comparable, and he didn't think that a girl being interested in math was any stranger than a boy being interested in music.

As Kim got on his bus, he said, "You should try to do the best you can on the exam. You owe it to yourself."

• • •

On the appointed afternoon, I entered the Boston University classroom where the Sterns examination was being held. The monitor checked my name against his list and nodded. "Good. All fifty of you are now here."

It seemed I was the last one to arrive. For a while I had considered not coming at all.

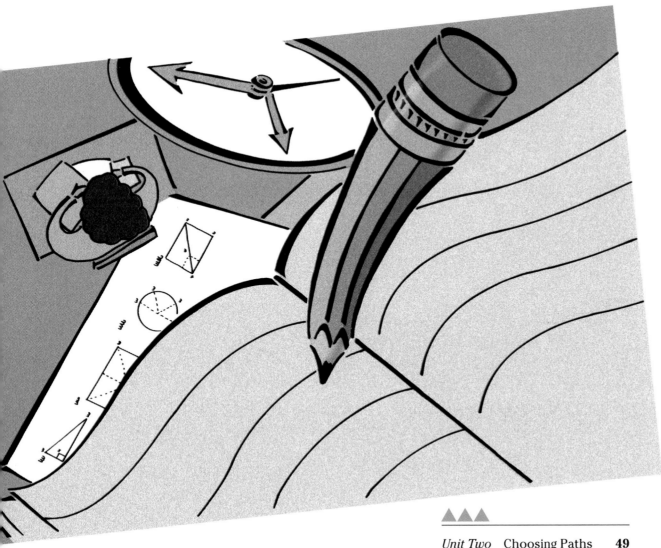

What was the point? I was in no condition to do mathematics. I suppose I came because it would have been too much trouble to tell Mr. Antonelli I was planning to drop out.

We all sat down and arranged our pencils and bluebooks[6] on the desks in front of us. When the monitor passed out the exams, heads bent eagerly over the papers. I looked at the first page with dull despair. There were some diagrams with circles, but nothing made sense to me. In my present state I hardly knew the difference between an ellipse and a circle. An ellipse was just a tired circle.

All around me pencils scratched busily in bluebooks. On my left, Arthur glanced up at me. He looked different, and I realized he had applied a pomade on his hair to stick it down. He flashed his foxy grin, and the smugness in

it told me I looked a mess. I had not slept at all the night before, and my eyes were red and puffy—not all from sleeplessness.

My watch showed that almost an hour had passed. Already half the time allotted for the exam was gone and I hadn't started a single problem.

I glanced at Arthur again and found his eyes fastened on me eagerly. How many times had he looked this way? He must have noticed that I hadn't done a thing, because when his eyes met mine, his grin widened triumphantly.

I picked up the exam paper and looked at it once more. The writing might as well have been in Greek. Only I could read Greek a little, since I already knew all the Greek letters from seeing them used in mathematics. No, the writing here might as well be in Korean for all I could understand.

Kim entered my mind. He could not afford to give up classical music, for he owed it to himself not to squander[7] his talent.

It was the thought of Kim that finally opened my eyes. I should not try to be something I was not. And I was not, nor could ever be, a normal American teenager. I was going to be a mathematician. This was the Sterns exam, my first opportunity to show my mettle.[8] I could not afford to squander my talent. As Kim had said, I owed it to myself. I had to stop frittering[9] away the precious minutes and get down to work. Having made the decision, I felt a weight lift from my chest.

[6]**bluebooks**   booklets in which students write examination answers
[7]**squander**   waste; use foolishly
[8]**mettle**   courage
[9]**frittering**   wasting

About the Author

Lensey Namioka is a Chinese American writer who is known for her historical and fantasy stories. The story "Who's Hu?" is an excerpt from a novel of the same name.

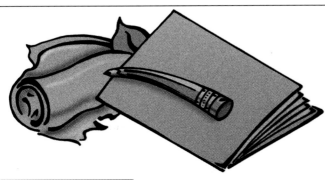

9. **Share Ideas**

a. Groupwork. Write three opinion-questions based on the story *Who's Hu?* (Opinion-questions do not have a right or wrong answer.)

Examples: Why do you think going to the senior prom was important to Emma?

b. Write your group's questions on the board. Look over the other groups' questions on the board and choose one question to discuss in your group. Let one person record your group's ideas.

c. Tell the class which question your group chose. Report any differences of opinion among the members of your group and identify any conclusions your group reached.

d. Choose another question from the list on the board and repeat the process.

Language Focus:

Asking for and Stating Opinions

We think that going to the prom was important to Emma because her friends were going and she didn't want to be left out.

Activity 9: Share Ideas

1. *Language Focus.* Write the question and answer from the *Language Focus* box on the board, and underline the gerund subject and the verb in each: <u>going</u> to the prom <u>was</u> important

Point out that the *-ing* form of the verb can be used as a subject and always takes a singular verb. Give other examples:

Subject *Verb*
<u>Remembering</u> Kim's words <u>helped</u> Emma make her decision.

Subject *Verb*
<u>Seeing</u> Arthur's foxy grin <u>depressed</u> her more.

Subject *Verb*
<u>Trying</u> to be a typical American teenager <u>was</u> a waste of time.

2. *Part a.* Ask each group to choose one person to record the group's ideas. If feasible, keep students in the same groups that they worked in for *Activity 8*, and ask them to write opinion-based questions for other groups to consider. These questions may arise from their reading journals and group discussion in *Activity 8*.

3. *Part b.* When groups begin their discussions, remind them that there are no right or wrong answers to opinion questions.

4. *Part c.* If groups finish their discussion at different times, put two groups together for *Part c,* and have them report to each other about their part b discussion. Let other groups continue to work at their own pace.

Activity 10: Make a Story Map

1. *Part a.* Distribute AM 2/3. Introduce story mapping or review it with your students. Remind them that the map includes the main characters, the story's setting (where and when), and the major events. Have students work in pairs on their maps.

2. When students finish retelling the story in pairs, have several students complete a story map on the board as the class gives the information.

(Answers: <u>Title</u>: Who's Hu; <u>Author</u>: Lensey Namioka; <u>Setting</u>: <u>Time</u>—During and after math class; during the Sterns Examination <u>Place</u>—Evesham High; Boston University; <u>Characters</u>: Emma [personality: intelligent, sensitive; behavior: confused at first, then decisive] Arthur [personality: intelligent, arrogant; behavior: dishonest] Kim [personality: devoted to music, emotionally detached; behavior: friendly, straightforward]; <u>Plot</u>: <u>1st Event</u>—Mr. Antonelli announced that Arthur and Emma are both semifinalists in the Sterns Examination; <u>2nd Event</u>—Arthur proposed to Emma that he take her to the prom in exchange for her dropping out of the exam; <u>Third Event</u>—Kim overheard their conversation and told her to do her best; <u>Fourth Event</u>—Emma went to the exam, but couldn't concentrate; <u>Fifth Event</u>—Emma made her decision to do her best, and started to work on the exam.)

10. Make a Story Map

a. Pairwork. What happened in the story *Who's Hu?* Organize your ideas on a story map like this:

b. Get together with another pair. Use your story map to retell the story *Who's Hu?* Take turns giving information.

Study Stategy:

Making a Story Map

See page 164.

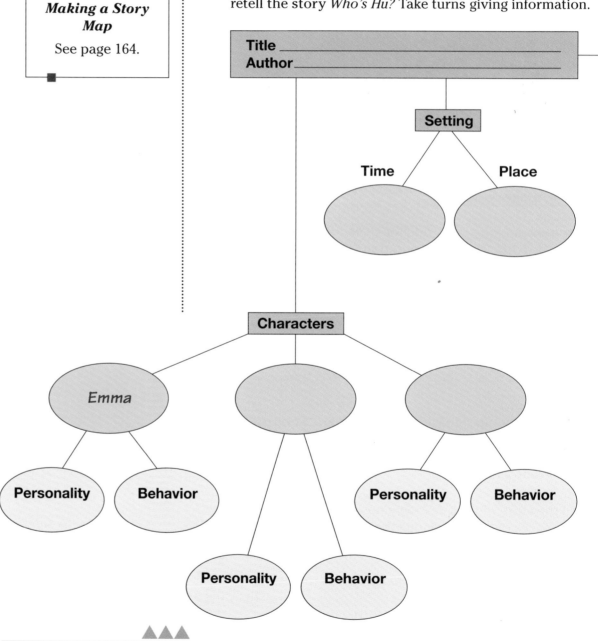

11. Reflect

On your own. What choices does Emma make in the story? Do you think she makes good choices? Why or why not? How would you have acted in this situation? Why? Write your response in your journal.

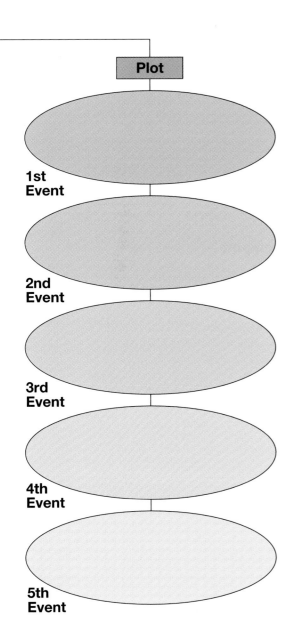

Plot

1st Event

2nd Event

3rd Event

4th Event

5th Event

Activity 11: Reflect

1. Remind students that *reflect* means *think deeply*. Give them time to think and write in their journals.

2. Students can share ideas in small groups. If feasible, collect your class's reading journals and write your own short response to each student.

Activity 1: List

1. *Part a.* Draw students' attention to the pictures on page 55. Elicit the names of the careers and write them on the board. Ask students, *Would you like to work in this field? Why? Why not?* Ask students to identify their preferences and tell what they know about different jobs.

2. Bring to class several career books for young adults. Distribute the books to groups of students and give them time to look them over. Distribute one copy of AM 2/4 to each group and ask groups to list some careers in each category. Then ask students to think about people they know who work in these fields, and add their careers to the list.

3. Draw the chart on the board. Have a student from each group go to the board and list careers in categories they have just discussed. As an expansion activity, have pairs of students choose one career from the chart and list what people in this career do. Have pairs report back to the class.

4. *Part b.* Brainstorm some questions partners can ask each other, and write the questions on the board. Then have partners ask and answer questions. When partners finish, have them form groups of four with other pairs of students. Write the following sentence frame on the board:

I'd like to be _____ because _____.

(Name) would like to be _____ because _____.

Ask students to explain their own or their partners' preferences.

Chapter 2: Career Paths

*W*hat career path do you think you will follow? What choices will you probably make along the way? In this chapter you will look at the career path of a well-known writer and then research the career path of another person.

1. **List**

a. Classwork. Study the chart below. Then think of different careers in each area of work. Add your ideas to a chart on the board.

Work Areas	Careers	
Health	Doctor Hospital Administrator Nurse Physical Therapist	Dietician Pharmacist
Education		
Arts		
Science/Technology		
Sports		
Business		
Travel		
_____		

b. Pairwork. Which of these careers might interest you? Why? Tell a partner.

Activity 2: Preview

1. If feasible, bring in some of Ms. Mohr's books for students to look over briefly. Direct their attention to the photograph of Mohr on page 58. Then ask them to read the instruction line.

2. Copy the diagram on the board. Have each group choose one person to record the group's questions and then add them to the diagram on the board. (Possible questions: *When did you start writing/decide to become a writer? When do you write? Why did you become a writer? Where do you write? Who do you write about? Who reads your first drafts? Who encouraged you to write?*)

Activity 3: Read

To give the students a purpose for reading, have them look for the answers to the questions on the board as they read the article. Circulate and answer questions as needed. Encourage students to use context to guess the meaning of unfamiliar words.

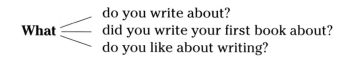

Groupwork. In the reading on page 57, Nicholasa Mohr tells about the path she followed to become a writer. Imagine that you are going to interview Ms. Mohr. What questions would you ask? List your group's questions on another piece of paper.

What do you write about?
did you write your first book about?
do you like about writing?

When

Why

Where

Who

Write your group's questions on the board.
Look over the other groups' questions.

3. Read

On your own. Read pages 57–58 to look for answers to your questions from Activity 2.

Nicholasa Mohr

From the moment my mother handed me some scrap paper, a pencil, and a few crayons, I decided that by making pictures and writing letters I could create my own world, like "magic." In the small, crowded apartment I shared with my large family (six older brothers, parents, aunt, and a boy cousin), "making magic" permitted me all the space and freedom my imagination could handle.

I was born in the urban village in the heart of New York City's Manhattan known as "El Barrio," meaning "the neighborhood." Also known as Spanish Harlem, it is the oldest Spanish-speaking community in the city. My parents had migrated with four small children from the island of Puerto Rico before the Second World War. Like many other strangers preceding them, they hoped that with hard work and opportunity they too could offer their children that good life known as the American Dream. Subsequently three more children were born, of which I was the youngest and only daughter.

We moved to the Bronx, where I spent most of my formative[1] years. Through the loss of my parents and separation from my family in my early teens, I continued to rely on my ability to draw and to tell stories. After high school, I enrolled in the Art Students League and pursued my career as a fine artist. I studied in the Taller de Graficos in Mexico City, returned, and continued to study at the Brooklyn Museum Art School, the New School for Social Research, and the Pratt Center for Printmaking. I got married and had two sons, David and Jason. All of this time I worked and exhibited my prints and paintings in New York City galleries. In 1972 when I was asked to do a book jacket for Harper and Row[2] I showed them fifty pages of vignettes[3] I had written dealing with my childhood. The result was a contract and my first book. *Nilda* was published in 1973. I also did the book jacket and eight illustrations for *Nilda*.

What I thought would have been a temporary diversion[4] (I assumed I'd return to visual art and be done with this business of writing!) turned out to be my new focus[5] in life. Writing satisfied and fulfilled my needs to communicate in a way I had not

---

[1]**formative years**   years in which a person develops
[2]**Harper and Row**   a publishing company in New York
[3]**vignettes**   short written descriptions
[4]**diversion**   turning point
[5]**focus**   centering activity

experienced as a visual artist. *Nilda* is the most autobiographical of my books, not so much in fact (it takes place during the Second World War) but in feeling and circumstances. This was followed by *El Bronx Remembered*, a collection of short stories and a novella dealing with the decade of the promised future for Puerto Rican immigrants, 1946-1956. My next book was *In Nueva York*, a collection of interrelated stories about the Hispanic community in New York City's Lower East Side, during the end of the Vietnam War. *Felita*, a novel for younger children, is about contemporary times. It shows how a family is forced out of an all-white neighborhood and back to their barrio, and how in spite of this setback and humiliation, they pull together and continue to build a future for themselves. *Rituals of Survival*, an adult book, is a collection of stories about the struggles and courage of Puerto Rican women. This was followed by *Going Home*, a sequel to *Felita*. In this novel, Felita visits Puerto Rico to discover that she is seen as an outsider, a gringa, and she must deal with her identity. I have recently completed two plays and an original fairy tale. In celebration of my work, the State University of New York at Albany has awarded me an honorary Doctor of Letters degree.

Growing up, I had never seen or read any book that included Puerto Ricans (or Hispanics, for that matter) as citizens who worked hard and contributed to this nation. In American letters,[6] we were *invisible*. Writing has given me the opportunity to establish my own sense of history and existence as a Puerto Rican woman in the literature of these United States. I know that even if I had been born rich, and white Anglo-Saxon Protestant, I would still be doing creative work . . . i.e., visual art and writing. However, because of who I am, I feel blessed by the work I do, for it permits me to use my imagination and continue to "make magic." With this magic, I can recreate those deepest of personal memories as well as validate[7] and celebrate my heritage and my future.

[6]**letters**   literature
[7]**validate**   confirm; see as worthwhile and acceptable

4. Share Information

a. Pairwork. Share any answers you found to your questions from Activity 2.

b. What do you learn about Nicholasa Mohr from her autobiographical account? Add information to each category in a chart like this:

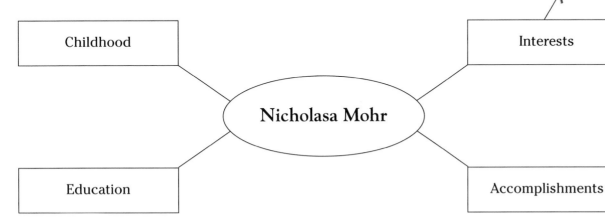

Childhood

Interds

painting

Interests

Nicholasa Mohr

Education

Accomplishments

Get together with another pair and share information.

c. Identify important events in Mohr's career path. Collect information in a diagram like this:

drew and told stories when she was a child → →

Get together with another pair. Use your diagram to tell about Mohr's career path. Take turns giving information.

d. On your own. Use your diagram to write a one-paragraph summary of Mohr's career path. Include only the most important information in your summary.

Language Focus:

Using Time Words

When she was a child, she liked to draw.

While she was in high school, ____.

After high school, she ____.

Following high school, ____.

Activity 4: Share Information

1. Tell pairs of students to make a chart on a separate piece of paper and to work together to add information to their chart.

(Possible information: <u>Childhood</u>: lived in El Barrio and the Bronx; had a large family, lost her parents and was separated from her family <u>Interests</u>: drawing and telling stories. <u>Education</u>: Art Students League, Taller des Graficos, other art schools. <u>Accomplishments</u>: exhibited prints and paintings in New York; wrote *Nilda, El Bronx Remembered, In Nueva York, Felita, Rituals of Survival,* and *Going Home.*)

2. *Part b.* Circulate and check students' charts as they work in groups.

3. *Part c.* Have students work in pairs to map Mohr's career path. Remind them to concentrate on the most important steps in her path to becoming a professional writer. Have several pairs put their diagrams on the board. Compare diagrams. Then have pairs get together with other pairs of students to take turns giving information about Mohr.

4. *Language Focus.* Write the Language Focus sentences on the board. Together, think of ways to complete the sentences. Note that the time words help to connect the steps of a summary. Point out that writers put time phrases and clauses both at the beginning and end of sentences. For example, *While she was raising her children, she continued to paint.* OR *She continued to paint while she was raising her children.* Note that a comma follows the time phrase only when it appears at the beginning of the sentence.

5. *Part d.* When students finish, have them work in pairs and groups and read each other's summaries. Have them discuss the information each writer chose to include.

Have students underline sentences with time words in their own summaries and with a partner, check the sentences for accuracy. Have volunteers write sentences on the board.

Activity 5: Listen

1. *Part a.* Elicit that Herrera has been both a bicycle racer and a business person, as well as any other information about Herrera that your students already know.

2. *Part b.* Have students read the instruction line and look over the chart. Tell them to make a similar chart on a piece of paper. Play the tape or read the report once while students just listen. Then tell students to make notes on their charts about Herrera's career path as they listen again. Replay the report as needed.

3. *Optional:* If students need additional help, write important time expressions from the report on the board to help students pick out information as they listen. (Important phrases: *In his early years/ By the age of thirteen/The next four years/When he was seventeen/Besides these events/Three years ago*)

4. *Part c.* After students work in pairs, have several pairs copy their charts of Herrera's career path on the board. Compare the information that different pairs chose to include. (Possible career path: 1. *In his early years, Herrera used his bicycle to deliver flowers and to ride in the mountains near his home.* 2. *He won his first race at 13, and then won many awards as an amateur cyclist.* 3. *He turned professional at seventeen.* 4. *As a professional, he won many international competitions and became famous.* 5. *Three years ago, he became a businessman. He owns cyclist schools and factories and exports flowers.*)

Activity 6: Investigate

1. *Part a–c.* To help students select a subject, have them browse through this textbook, history textbooks, and biographies which you have in the classroom or that you bring in.

2. *Part d.* Distribute AM 2/5. Tell students to fill it in as they research the person they have chosen.

(Continued on page 61.)

5. Listen

a. Classwork. The photographs below give information about Luis Herrera. What can you guess about his career path from these pictures? Share ideas with your classmates.

b. On your own. The report you are going to hear was written by Jaime Chavez, a student at Jersey City State College. In his report, Chavez tells about the career path of Luis Herrera. As you listen to the report, take notes in a chart like this:

c. Pairwork. Use your diagram to tell about Luis Herrera's career path. Take turns giving information.

6. Investigate

Find out about the career path of someone who interests you. This might be a well-known person or someone you know personally. In writing, tell your classmates about the important events in this person's career. Here are some suggestions to help you get started:

▲▲▲

a. With a group of classmates, make a list of people you might want to research. Look through textbooks and library books for possible subjects.

b. Think of people you know personally. What career paths have they followed? List the name of anyone you might want to write about.

c. Choose one person to find out about. Be sure to choose someone who really interests you. If you want to write about someone you know personally, make sure you have a good source of information (someone to get information from).

d. What do you want to find out about this person's career path? Make a list of questions. Write your questions in a chart like this:

Person's Name:		
Questions	**Answers**	**Sources** (where you found the answers)

e. Look in the library for several sources of information. Read about the person you chose and take notes in your chart. Be sure to write down your source of information. If you are collecting information about someone you know personally, interview that person and take notes.

f. Tell a classmate about this person's career path. Answer any questions your classmate has. If you need to do more research, go back to the library.

g. Look back over your notes and circle the information you want to include in your writing.

h. Write a first draft of your paper.

i. Refer to the Writer's Guide on pages 174–175 for suggestions on how to revise your first draft.

Activity 6: Investigate *(continued)*

3. *Part e–f.* After students have chosen a subject and started their list of questions, arrange with the school librarian for an orientation tour of the library. On the tour, bring students' attention to reference books such as *Newsmakers* and *Current Biography.* Also show them how to find biographical information in the computer or card catalog and in newspaper and magazine indexes.

4. *Part g.* When students complete their research, have them make a career path diagram about their subject with the information that they want to use. Tell them to arrange information logically within each step of the career path. Ask students to describe the career path to a partner, using the diagram to guide them as they talk. Listeners should ask for more information or clarification as needed.

Have students use the diagram as an outline from which to write their first draft.

5. Divide students into groups to read their first drafts to each other. Have them ask each other questions about things they don't understand or would like more information about.

6. Tell students to work with their group's feedback and the suggestions on page 174 of the Writer's Guide to revise their drafts.

7. Publish the reports for the class and/or post them on a bulletin board.

8. If feasible, ask a speaker to come to your class to talk about his or her career path. With students, make a list of questions before the speaker comes to class, and let students interview him or her after the presentation. The speaker could be from the community, or a parent, a teacher, or another professional from the school.

Activity 1: Preview

1. Have students read the questions and then look over the pictures and map on pages 64–65. Then ask them to read the first two paragraphs. Ask them to work with a partner to answer the questions on a separate piece of paper. Elicit the answers and write them on the board.

(*Answers:* 1. A secret network that helped slaves flee to freedom. 2. Escaping slaves. 3. Before the Civil War (1861–1865). 4. Not answered in the first two paragraphs.)

2. Have students share what they already know about the Underground Railroad and slavery in the United States. As appropriate, supply additional background information that will help students understand the article. Bring in a map of the United States and point out the Jamestown Colony in Virginia, the first permanent English settlement in North America. Point out that plantations were very large farms that grew cash crops such as cotton, tobacco, and sugar. Slaves provided unpaid agricultural labor that made these plantations profitable. Point out the border states of Maryland, Virginia, and Kentucky, from which many slaves, including Harriet Tubman, escaped to the free states.

Activity 2: Read

Encourage students to make notes about their questions as they read. Circulate and assist students. Help them to use context to figure out unfamiliar vocabulary.

Chapter 3: The Underground Railroad

*T*he Underground Railroad was a secret network of people who helped runaway slaves escape to freedom. In this chapter, you will find out how the Underground Railroad worked and read a play about a group of people who used the Undergound Railroad to escape from slavery.

1. **Preview**

Classwork. Read the questions below. Then look over the pictures on pages 63–65 and read the first two paragraphs of the passage. On another piece of paper, write any answers you find.

Questions	Answers
1. What was the Underground Railroad?	
2. Who used the Underground Railroad?	
3. When did the Underground Railroad exist?	
4. How did the Underground Railroad help people to escape?	

2. **Read**

On your own. As you read pages 63–65, look for answers to the questions in Activity 1.

The Underground Railroad

The Underground Railroad wasn't underground and it wasn't a railroad. But it was real just the same. And it was one of the brightest chapters in American history.

The Underground Railroad was a secret network of people who helped slaves flee[1] to freedom before the Civil War (1861–65). The slaves were black people from families who had been brought from Africa in chains. They were owned by their white masters and forced to work without pay.

The first slaves arrived in Jamestown, Virginia in 1619. Two hundred years later, there were nearly four million slaves in the United States. Most worked on large plantations in the South. By then, slavery had been outlawed[2] in most northern states.

Many slaves were treated cruelly. Some were not. All could be bought and sold. Some slaves bought their own freedom by earning money during time off from work at the plantation. There were free black people in both the North and South during slavery days.

Thousands of slaves ran away each year. Some fled to get away from harsh masters. Others wanted to enjoy liberty. The Underground Railroad was started to help them.

The "stations" of the Underground Railroad were homes, shops, and churches where runaway slaves were hidden and fed. The "agents" or "stationmasters" were people— both black and white—who hated slavery. They wanted to help slaves get free.

"Conductors" on the Underground Railroad led or transported fugitives[3] from station to station on their way to free states. They had to watch for slave catchers, who were paid to capture runaways and return them. Some conductors guided slaves all the way to Canada.

[1]**flee**　　　　run away
[2]**outlawed**　　declared against the law
[3]**fugitives**　　people who are running away from something

The most famous conductor was Harriet Tubman. She was a strong, determined woman. Before she became a conductor, Mrs. Tubman had been a passenger on a dangerous journey on the Underground Railroad.

She lived as a slave on a plantation in Maryland. One day in 1849, Mrs. Tubman heard that she was going to be sold. She decided to escape instead.

Harriet Tubman walked away from the plantation that night. She followed the North Star toward the free state of Pennsylvania 90 miles away. Sometimes she hiked all night, from station to station on the Underground Railroad. Once she was hidden under blankets and vegetables in a farm wagon, and she rode through the night. Another time she was carried in a rowboat for miles.

She got to Pennsylvania one morning just at sunrise. Years later she recalled that moment:

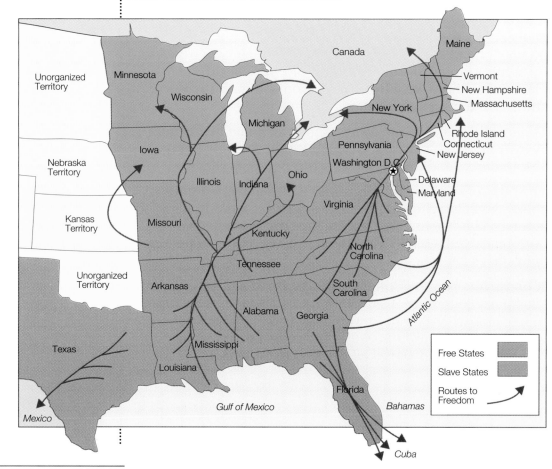

"I looked at my hands to see if I was the same person now I was free. There was such a glory over everything, the sun came like gold through the trees and over the fields, and I felt like I was in heaven."

Soon Harriet Tubman became a conductor on the Underground Railroad. Over the next 10 years, she made 19 trips into the slave states and guided 300 slaves to freedom.

We can only guess how many slaves used the Underground Railroad. Historians estimate the total at between 40,000 and 100,000 by the time the Civil War began in 1861. The war was fought in large part over the slavery issue.

In 1863, President Abrahm Lincoln declared slaves free. That was the end of the Underground Railroad. There were no ceremonies and no celebrations. The invisible railroad ended as it began—quietly and without fanfare.[4]

Robert W. Peterson

[4]**fanfare**   noisy celebration

Activity 3: Define

1. Distribute AM 2/6. Remind students that context will often supply an explanation of unfamiliar vocabulary. After students find the information in the text, elicit the definitions and write them on the board. (*Answers:* <u>station</u>: a place where runaway slaves were hidden and fed; <u>stationmaster</u>: a person who wanted to help slaves get free; <u>conductor</u>: someone who led or transported fugitives from station to station on their way to free states; <u>passenger</u>: a slave escaping to freedom.)

2. If feasible, bring in a tape of songs such as "Follow the Drinking Gourd" that contained coded information for escaping slaves. Play it for your students after they have explored possible reasons for using secret terms. Point out that most fugitives were illiterate since it was illegal to teach a slave to read or write, and many had never left the plantation. Encourage students to speculate about what it must have felt like to be a fugitive under these circumstances.

Activity 4: Share Ideas

1. *Parts a–b.* Ask students to read aloud to their groups the questions that they wrote down as they read.

2. Bring in material or accompany your class to the library to look up additional information that they have expressed interest in. Help them to locate information in encyclopedias, biographies, magazines, and other sources. Read your students accounts of Harriet Tubman and Frederick Douglass, the escaped slave and abolitionist. Have students find information about the Fugitive Slave Act of 1850, which empowered slave catchers to pursue fugitives into free territory and re-enslave them.

3. *Parts c–d.* After students read more about this topic, discuss the choices made and risks taken by Harriet Tubman and other conductors.

Study Strategy:
Using Context
See page 169.

3. Define

Pairwork. In the reading on pages 63–65, the terms listed below have a special meaning. Look back over the reading to help you define these words as they relate to the Underground Railroad.

Terms	Railroad	Underground Railroad
station	place where trains stop to pick up and drop off passengers	
stationmaster	person who runs the train station	
conductor	person who takes care of passengers on the train	
passenger	person who rides in a train	

Why do you think people used these words when they talked about the Underground Railroad? Share ideas with your classmates.

4. Share Ideas

Groupwork. Share ideas about the passage. Here are some questions you can discuss in your group:

a. What interested you about the Underground Railroad? Why?

b. What else would you like to find out about the Underground Railroad? Where could you find the answers to your questions?

c. What choices did Harriet Tubman make? What risks did she take?

d. Why do you think some people chose to become conductors on the Underground Railroad? What risks did they take?

5. Read

a. Classwork. The following play is about a group of fugitives on the Underground Railroad. Look over the play quickly. What do you know about the characters in the play?

b. Imagine that you are one of the characters in this play. As you read the play, think about the choices this person makes. After you finish reading the play, share ideas with your classmate.

The Douglass "Station" of the Underground Railroad
by Glennette Tilley Turner

Cast: *Frederick Douglass*   *First Son*   *Harriet Tubman*   *First Narrator*
           Anna Douglass   *Second son*   *Eight Fugitive Slaves*   *Second Narrator*

First Narrator:	It is late one night in early November, sometime after the 1850 Fugitive Slave Act[1] has become law. Harriet Tubman and a party of eight fugitive slaves have just arrived outside the Douglass home in Rochester, New York.
Second Narrator:	Harriet Tubman goes from a wooded area to the back door, trying to stay in the shadows of the house. Her knock is so quiet it can hardly be heard.
Harriet:	(*Knock, knock. Pause. Knock, knock.*)
First Narrator:	One of Douglass' sons looks out the window and whispers:
First son:	It's Moses.
Second Narrator:	Frederick Douglass turns the lamplight off and goes to the door—just barely opening it.

[1]**Fugitive Slave Act**   law requiring that slaves who had escaped to states where slavery was outlawed be captured and returned to their owners.

Unit Two   Choosing Paths   **67**

---

1. *Part a.* Have students look over the title and the cast of characters of the play. Ask them to share what they have already learned about Anna and Frederick Douglass and Harriet Tubman. Elicit predictions about the play from this information. Then ask students to check their ideas by silently reading the First Narrator's introduction to the play.

2. Point out Rochester, New York on a map. Ask students, *Where is the party of fugitives going?* Elicit students' ideas.

3. *Part b.* Have students read the instruction line. Ask several students who they have chosen to be.

4. Ask students to read the play silently, and to look for examples of choices that their character must make. They may want to make notes of these examples as they read.

5. Ask students to identify the choices that the characters make in the play, including Tubman's decision to follow her hunch and leave the same night, the Douglass's decision to help the fugitives, and the fugitives' decision to keep going in spite of the dangers. Ask students, *What risks did each character take when he or she made this choice? What benefits did each hope for?*

6. Write the following questions on the board and ask students to think about them as they read the play a second time.

- What was Tubman's code name and why? (Like Moses, she led her people out of slavery.)

- Why was Tubman still nervous after reaching Rochester, in the free states? (According to the Fugitive Slave Act, slave catchers could pursue fugitives into free territory.)

Frederick Douglass:	Come in, Moses.
First narrator:	Harriet Tubman steps inside, and whispers . . .
Harriet Tubman:	I have eight. I had them wait in the woods 'til I knew it was safe to come in.
Frederick Douglass:	One of my sons is the lookout.[2] He let us know you were nearby and that the coast is clear.[3]
Anna Douglass:	Welcome, Harriet. Have them come in.
Second Narrator:	Harriet Tubman signals to her company of slaves. One at a time they approach the house just as she had done.
First Narrator:	Douglass barely opens the door and admits the slaves. Once they are inside, they gather near the fireplace to warm themselves after their long journey. Some are barefooted; others are wearing summer-weight clothes.
Frederick Douglass:	Congratulations. Moses has brought you to the doorstep of freedom. The land of Canada is just across the lake. You'll be there by this time tomorrow night.
Anna Douglass:	Meanwhile, here's food and some blankets so you can eat and then rest.
First Narrator:	She gestures to an iron pot in the fireplace and blankets in the corner.
Frederick Douglass:	I know from experience what it's like to escape. You really can't relax until you get to the Promised Land.
Second Narrator:	The Douglass' second son appears at the door with a huge ladle and dishes up stew for everyone. In the meantime the first son has gone to take his turn as the lookout.
Anna Douglass to Harriet Tubman:	How was your trip?
Harriet Tubman:	(*eating like she's really hungry, but in a hurry to get through—talks between mouthfuls*) We had lots of close calls, but made it safely this far. Main thing was trying to race the snow. Didn't want that to catch us. Can't take the chance of leaving tracks.[4]
Frederick Douglass to Harriet Tubman:	Which route did you take this time?

[2]**lookout**   person who keeps watch
[3]**the coast is clear** no enemies are nearby
[4]**tracks**   footprints; marks

Harriet Tubman:	(*obviously worried about something as she talks*) Eastern Shore to Wilmington in Delaware. Some of the young ones got scared when they heard the slave catchers' dogs. We had to wade in water so the dogs would lose our scent.
Frederick Douglass:	It must have been a relief to reach Thomas Garrett's house in Wilmington, wasn't it?
Harriet Tubman:	(*trying to answer Douglass' question, although it is more and more obvious she has something else on her mind*) Yes, he gave us dry clothes and we slept a while. He had a former friend take us to Philadelphia in a wagon with a false bottom.
Frederick Douglass:	Where William Still met you—right?
Harriet Tubman:	Yes. (*then, putting her dish down abruptly*) Excuse me, Frederick, but what's the plan for us going from here to Canada?
Frederick Douglass:	I've arranged for a friend to get you and your party on the morning train. You'll have to board before daylight, so you won't be seen. Hope you don't mind having to travel in the baggage car. It's getting harder and harder to cross the border.
Harriet Tubman:	Let me stop you, Frederick. I thank you for what you're planning, but I won't feel safe 'til we get on the Canadian side. Can you possibly get somebody to take us across the lake tonight? All of a sudden I had this strange feeling the slave catchers are on our trail.
Anna Douglass:	Can't you wait until morning? As tired as you all are, a good night's sleep would do you some good.
Harriet Tubman:	Thank you, Anna. I am bone tired and the others are too, but I can't chance waiting. Morning may be too late.
Frederick Douglass:	What makes you so sure slave catchers are trailing you?
Harriet Tubman:	There's a $40,000 reward on my head and lots of people want to cash in. I don't know what gave me this feeling, but my hunches[5] have been right too many times before to ignore them.
First Narrator:	Douglass' second son has made an inconspicuous exit while his parents talked with Harriet Tubman. That son now reappears and announces,
Second Son:	Excuse me for interrupting, but my brother and I have arranged to take you across the lake.

[5]**hunches**   suspicions; feelings

▲▲▲

Activity 6: Role Play

1. *Part a and b.* Have students work in groups and choose roles that they wish to play. Tell them to reread the play to establish the setting (e.g., the door, window, fireplace, furnishings), and to determine where characters are at different points. Encourage students to act out the fear, suspicion, or relief that their characters feel.

2. *Part c and d.* As students practice, circulate and help with pronunciation and intonation.

3. *Part e.* Have groups perform for the class. If feasible, invite a history or other class from your school to the performance of one of the groups.

Harriet Tubman:	Oh, thank you. (*turning to Frederick and Anna*) You certainly raised your sons well. Thank you all!
Second Narrator:	Harriet gathers her things and wakens the fugitives in her group.
Harriet Tubman:	Hurry now. It's time to go.
Frederick Douglass:	(*shaking Harriet's hand*) Have a safe journey, Moses.
Anna Douglass:	(*giving Harriet a hug*) God be with you.
First Son:	(*in an urgent whisper*) The coast is clear. Let's go.
First Narrator:	Harriet and the fugitives walk in the shadows as the Douglass' first son leads the way to the shores of Lake Ontario.
Second Narrator:	There the second son is waiting to help them into a boat and they all set out for the Canadian shore.

6. **Role Play**

Work in groups of eight. Follow the suggestions below to act out *The Douglass Station of the Underground Railroad.*

a. Assign a role to each person in your group.

b. Think about the setting of the play. Where are the characters when the play begins? Where is the door of the Douglass house? What is inside the house?

c. Practice reading the play. Consider what your character is thinking and feeling as you read the lines. Use appropriate body language when you speak.

d. Change roles and read the play again.

e. Perform your version of the play for your classmates or for another class.

7. Trace a Route

Groupwork. In the play, Harriet Tubman mentions three places that she and the eight fugitives travel through. Find these places on a U.S. map. Then answer the questions below:

a. How did they get to Wilmington, Delaware? What problems did they have along the way?

b. How did they get from Wilmington to Philadelphia? How long do you think it took?

c. How did they get from Rochester to Canada? How long do you think it took?

8. Write

a. On your own. Imagine that you are a stationmaster, a conductor, or a fugitive on the Underground Railroad. Write a diary entry telling about a day on the Railroad. You can use the questions below to help you get started.

  ▪ What happened on this day?

  ▪ What difficulties did you encounter?

  ▪ What choices did you make?

b. Get together with several classmates. Take turns reading your diary entries aloud.

Activity 7: Trace a Route

1. Distribute maps to groups of students and have them find the three places. Then tell them to find where the places are mentioned in the text, and to answer the questions. (*Answers:* (a) They followed the Eastern Shore to Wilmington. They were followed by slave catchers with dogs. (b) They traveled to Philadelphia in a wagon with a false bottom. The trip may have taken two days. (c) They traveled from Rochester to Canada by boat. It probably took the whole night to cross lake Ontario.)

2. If feasible, read your students some narratives of escaped slaves, such as *The Narrative of the Life of Frederick Douglass* to give them some ideas of the risks and problems fugitives faced.

Activity 8: Write

1. *Part a.* Before they write, tell students to look at the map and decide where they are on the route, and what time of year it is. Elicit ideas from several volunteers and brainstorm with the class about possible difficulties and encounters.

2. *Part b. Optional:* Create a bulletin board display with the diary entries. Use a map showing the routes of the Underground Railroad, and post the entries at different parts of the routes.

Activity 1: Predict

1. *Part a.* With students, review the paths they have read about in this unit: Emma Hu's decision to pursue mathematics, the career paths of Nicolasa Mohr and Luis Herrera, and the choice for freedom of Tubman, Douglass, and other fugitive slaves. Then ask them to think about things they want to do. Tell students to look at the diagram on page 72 and make a similar one on a separate piece of paper.

2. *Language Focus.* Write the example sentences from the Language Focus box on the board. Elicit endings for the last two sentences, such as:

> I plan to *major in biology.*
> I intend to *work part time while*
> *I'm in school.*

Point out that we also express possibilities with <u>might</u> and <u>may</u> plus base form of the verb. For example, *I may live at home while I'm in college. Merla might start her own business after a few years.*

3. *Part b. Optional:* After students work with a partner, have pairs of students form larger groups. Students can talk about their partner's plans, for example, *Rigoberta intends to work in her family's business.*

Activity 2: Shared Reading

1. *Part a.* Ask students to silently read the instruction line. Then have one student read the three points aloud. Remind students of the symbolic meanings they found in Kemal Ozer's poem in Unit 1, Chapter 4. Ask them to consider the symbolic meaning that the journey in *The Road Not Taken* has for each of them.

2. *Part b.* Have students work in groups of four, with students taking turns reading stanzas of the poem. Circulate among the groups and help out as needed with meaning or pronunciation.

(Continued on page 73.)

Chapter 4: Choosing a Path

*W*hat path will you take in the future? What choices will you make? In this chapter, you will find out how two poets answer these questions.

1. Predict

a. On your own. What path will you take in the future? Think of some of the things you hope to do. Write your ideas on a diagram like this:

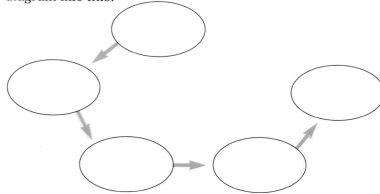

b. Tell a partner about the things on your path.

Language Focus:

Future Plans and Possiblities

- I hope to go to college.
- I plan to ___.
- I intend to ___.

---

2. Shared Reading

a. On your own. Read the poem on page 73 several times. Keep these thoughts in mind as you read.

- A poem can mean different things to different people.
- There is no one correct interpretation of a poem.
- Each time you read a poem, you may see and hear different things.

b. Groupwork. Choose one stanza from the poem. Together, practice reading your group's stanza aloud. Then read your stanza aloud to the class.

THE ROAD NOT TAKEN

Two roads diverged[1] in a yellow wood,
And sorry I could not travel both
And be one traveler, long I stood
And looked down one as far as I could
To where it bent in the undergrowth;[2]

Then took the other, as just as fair,[3]
And having perhaps the better claim,
Because it was grassy and wanted wear;[4]
Though as for that the passing there
Had worn them really about the same,

And both that morning equally lay
In leaves no step had trodden black.
Oh, I kept the first for another day!
Yet knowing how way leads on to way,
I doubted if I should ever come back.

I shall be telling this with a sigh
Somewhere ages and ages hence:[5]
Two roads diverged in a wood, and I—
I took the one less traveled by,
And that has made all the difference.

Robert Frost

[1]**diverged**	went in different directions
[2]**undergrowth**	plants growing around trees
[3]**fair**	beautiful
[4]**wanted wear**	had not been used much
[5]**hence**	after now; in the future

About the Author

Robert Frost is one of America's favorite poets. He was born in 1874 in San Francisco, but lived much of his life in New England. Many of his poems have New England settings. Frost read one of his poems at the inauguration of President John F. Kennedy in 1961. He died in 1963.

3. Go over the poem line by line with your class. Elicit and write on the board a prose translation of the literal meaning of the poem, especially such poetic inversions as *long I stood* (=I stood for a long time).

Activity 3: Share Ideas

1. Ask students to imagine that they have just taken a walk with the narrator. Have them quickwrite an account of what happened on their walk. Ask them to describe the woods, their companion the narrator, and how they and their companion came to their decision about which road to walk down. Then have students work in groups and share ideas about the questions.

2. After students share their ideas in groups, compare answers to the four questions. For Question d, give an example of a time when you had to make a difficult decision, and relate your steps in making a decision to some lines of the poem. For example, *I wanted to stay at home with my parents and go away to school at the same time. Like Frost, I was sorry I could not travel both/And be one traveler.*

3. Ask students to choose two or three lines of the poem that they find personally meaningful. Have them copy the lines on a piece of paper and then quickwrite by starting off, *This reminds me of a time when . . .*

Activity 4: Write

1. Ask students to review the diagram they made for *Activity 1* of this chapter and to imagine that they are now 80 years old. Tell them to quickwrite about where they live, who they are living with, how they feel now, how they spend their time, etc. Ask for a volunteer to be interviewed by the class. Students can ask, *What's it like to be eighty years old? How do you feel?*

2. Have students list some of their imagined accomplishments in the past 65 years. Volunteers can write their lists on the board. Their classmates can ask questions to get more detailed information.

(Continued on page 75.)

---

 3. **Share Ideas**

Groupwork. Get together with your classmates and share ideas about the poem. Choose one or more of these questions to discuss in your group.

a. What do you see as you read the poem?

b. How would you describe the narrator of this poem? What do you know about this person?

c. Describe the two roads in the poem. How are they different?

d. How might you connect the poem to your life?

 4. **Write**

On your own. In the last stanza of the poem, the poet says "I shall be telling this with a sigh/Somewhere ages and ages hence." Imagine that you are 80 years old. Describe the road you took in life. Are you happy with this road? Why or why not? What do you wish you had done differently?

 5. **Preview**

a. Classwork. Do you ever choose the easiest way to do something, even if it is not the best way? This is sometimes called "taking the easy way out." Look at the choices below and identify "the easy way out."

or

do your own homework — copy a friend's homework

revise a paper several times — revise it just once

volunteer to make a presentation — say you are too nervous to make a presentation

quit school because it's too hard — stay in school even though it is hard

What are some other examples of "taking the easy way out"?

b. Classwork. Read the title of the poem below and study the photograph. Why is graduation an important time in a person's life?

c. Classwork. Look over the poem below. How does it look different from the poem on page 73?

6. ▷ Read

Classwork. Read the poem aloud in different ways. For example, you might take turns reading a line aloud.

Jessica Berg
(Graduation)

It's too easy to
    Walk away,
    Sit down,
    Get over.
It's too easy to be
    Cynical,[1]
    Cool,
    Miserable.
It's too easy to turn
    A deaf ear,[2]
    A cold heart,[3]
    A silent voice.
It's too easy to doubt
    Your chances,
    Your future,
    Yourself.
And I never liked nor took the easy way out
So, in a few minutes when they call my name
To come up for the diploma I earned,
I will walk with pride up to the stage.
Easily.

Mel Glenn

[1] **cynical**   negative; seeing only the bad in people and things
[2] **turn a deaf ear**   refuse to listen
[3] **a cold heart**   refuse to feel

About the Author
Mel Glenn is a teacher and poet. Many of his poems are written from the point of view of high school students in the United States.

Activity 4: Write (continued)

3. *Language Focus.* Write the sentences from the Language Focus box on the board, and point out that the past perfect is used after <u>wish</u> to express regrets about something that happened in the past. Ask students to think about the accomplishments they just listed, and to write some sentences about things they wished they had or hadn't done. Have them share ideas with a partner; then elicit examples and write them on the board, for example,

> *Ning wishes she had learned how to drive sooner.*
> *I wish I hadn't dropped out of school.*

4. Give students time to quickwrite about the path that they took in life. Then have them tell a partner about it and answer the partner's questions. They should use the questions to collect more details, and then write a first draft.

5. *Optional:* When students finish writing, have them share their accounts with a partner and then form a group with another pair, and tell about their partner's path.

Activity 5: Preview

1. *Part a.* With the class, brainstorm some other examples of taking the easy way out. Have a volunteer write them on the board.

2. *Part b.* Ask students what happens at a graduation ceremony. Compare customs in different cultures.

Activity 6: Read

Have groups of students experiment with different combinations of voices for reading the poem. For example, students may do a choral reading of the first line, and then have single voices reading each of the three short lines of each stanza. They may also enjoy acting out the three short lines. Have each group do a dramatic reading of the poem and compare the effects of the different readings.

Activity 7: Write-Pair-Share

Encourage students to give examples from their own lives or their observations of others when they write about what particular lines mean to them.

Activity 8: Brainstorm

1. Prepare students for writing by looking closely at the poem. Ask students, *What does each stanza talk about?* (Some possible categories: first stanza, actions; second stanza, attitudes; third stanza, ways we treat others; fourth stanza, our faith in the future and ourselves.) Suggest to students that they think about categories as they brainstorm things to write about.

2. Some students may be interested in the repetitions in the poem. If so, encourage them to come up with their own patterns. They may enjoy working with lists of phrasal verbs or idioms to create patterns.

3. *Optional:* Bring in stacks of magazines and have groups choose pictures to illustrate their poem. Create a bulletin board display of poems and pictures.

Activity 9: Journal Writing

If students are willing, have them share their journal entries with a partner. Ask partners to write responses in each other's journals.

7. Write-Pair-Share

a. On your own. Choose one or more lines in the poem that interest you. In writing, tell what these lines mean to you.

b. Get together with a partner. Tell your partner what you wrote about. Listen carefully to your partner's ideas.

c. Get together with another pair. Tell them what your partner wrote about.

> ***Study Strategy:***
> ***Brainstorming***
> See page 163.

8. Brainstorm

Groupwork. Think of different ways to complete the sentence below. Write your ideas on another piece of paper.

It's too easy to _____.

Examples: It's too easy to watch TV instead of doing your homework.

It's too easy to pretend you are sick on the day you must make a presentation.

It's too easy to be lazy.

Read your group's ideas to the class. Together write your own version of the poem.

9. Journal Writing

On your own. Think of a time when you had to choose between taking the easy path and the difficult path. Which path did you choose? Why? What were the consequences of your decision?

Activity Menu

Choose one of the following activities to do.

1. Reader's Theater

Write a Reader's Theater version of the story *Who's Hu?* Assign roles to different classmates and act it out for another class.

2. Read a Novel

Find the novel *Who's Hu?* in a library and read it. Tell your classmates about another event in Emma Hu's life.

3. Make a Career Chart

Choose a career of interest to you. Find out more about this career by looking for information in the library. Try to find answers to these questions:

- What training or education do you need to get a job in this field?

- What special skills does a person in this job need to have?

- Is the number of jobs in this field increasing or decreasing?

Tell your classmates what you learned.

4. Read a Story

Read a story by Nicholasa Mohr. If you like the story, recommend it to your classmates. Tell them why you think they should read it.

5. Interview Your School Guidance Counselor

What does a guidance counselor do? How can this person help you? Invite your school guidance counselor to speak to your class.

6. Explore Careers

Invite someone to your class to talk about his or her career. Before your guest arrives, prepare a list of questions to ask.

7. Find Out More about the Underground Railroad

Think of three things your would like to find out about the Underground Railroad. Then look in the library to find the answers to your questions. Share what you learned with your classmates.

8. Read a Poem

Read another poem by one of the poets in this unit. Recommend one of the poems to your classmates.

Activity Menu

Read and discuss the activities with the class. Have each student select an activity. Students can work individually, in pairs, or in groups. When students complete their projects, have them present their work to the class.

Read On

Footpath

1. Have students work with a partner and take turns reading parts of the poem to each other. Then have pairs of student combine into groups of four and experiment with ways to do a group reading. Have groups read for the class.

2. Ask students to stay in their groups and to choose one of the following activities: (a) Quickwrite from the narrator's point of view, and tell a story that led up to the poem. (b) Find the words that describe the path; then draw a map showing where the path leads. (c) Write from the mother's point of view explaining where she is and when she is coming home.

Ask students to share their work with their group when they have finished.

Read On

Footpath

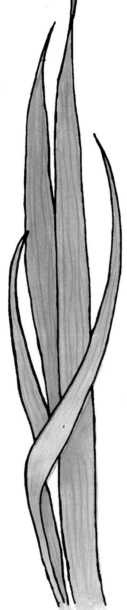

Path-let . . . leaving home, leading out,
Return my mother to me.
The sun is sinking and darkness coming,
Hens and cocks are already inside and babies drowsing,
Return my mother to me.
We do not have fire-wood and I have not seen the lantern,
There is no more food and the water has run out.
Path-let I pray you, return my mother to me.
Path of the hillocks, path of the small stones,
Path of slipperiness, path of the mud,
Return my mother to me.
Path of the papyrus, path of the rivers,
Path of the small forests, path of the reeds,
Return my mother to me.
Path that winds, path of the short-cut,
Over-trodden path, newly-made path,
Return my mother to me.
Path, I implore you, return my mother to me.
Path of the crossways, path that branches off,
Path of the stinging shrubs, path of the bridge,
Return my mother to me.
Path of the open, path of the valley,
Path of the steep climb, path of the downward slope,
Return my mother to me.
Children are drowsing about to sleep,
Darkness is coming and there is no fire-wood,
And I have not yet found the lantern:
Return my mother to me.

Stella Ngatho
Kenya

▲▲▲

Harriet Tubman

Harriet Tubman didn't take no stuff
Wasn't scared of nothing neither
Didn't come in this world to be no slave
And wasn't going to stay one either

"Farewell!" she sang to her friends one night
She was mighty sad to leave 'em
But she ran away that dark, hot night
Ran looking for her freedom

She ran to the woods and she ran through the woods
With the slave catchers right behind her
And she kept on going till she got to the North
Where those mean men couldn't find her

Nineteen times she went back South
To get three hundred others
She ran for her freedom nineteen times
To save black sisters and brothers
Harriet Tubman didn't take no stuff
Wasn't scared of nothing neither
Didn't come in this world to be no slave
And didn't stay one either

And didn't stay one either

Eloise Greenfield

Harriet Tubman

Have students silently read the poem. Then ask several volunteers to read a stanza aloud.

Unit 3:

Have lectures in public schools about understanding different cultures; maybe if someone really knew about someone else's culture then they would know why that person acts different.

11th-grader
Middletown High School
Middletown, R.I.

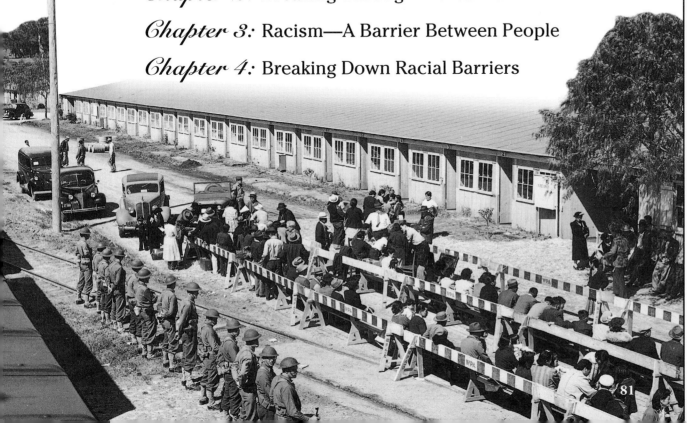

BREAKING DOWN BARRIERS

Activity 1: Define

1. To prepare students for the activity, draw their attention to the pictures and elicit the names of the barriers. Write the names on the board. Ask for students' ideas about the functions of these barriers. Accept all ideas offered.

2. *Part a.* Ask a volunteer to read the instruction line. Introduce the task: to find what these barriers have in common and to write a definition that includes this common characteristic. Write on the board, *A barrier is something that* _____. Put the class in groups and have each group select one person to write down the definition the group decides on.

3. *Part b.* Ask a representative from each group to write the group's definition on the board. Ask students to compare the definitions.

4. *Part c.* As volunteers read dictionary definitions, write them on the board. Talk about any differences.

Chapter 1: Why Do We Build Barriers?

*W*hat is a barrier? What purpose do barriers serve? These are two of the questions you will think about in this chapter.

1. **Define**

> **Study Strategy:**
> **Classifying**
> See pages 163–164.

a. Groupwork. These pictures show different kinds of barriers. Use the pictures to help you define the word *barrier*. Write your group's definition on another piece of paper.

b. Compare definitions with the other groups in your class.

c. Look up the word *barrier* in a dictionary and check your definition.

Activity 2: Classify

1. *Part a.* On the board, make a chart with the column headings "Natural barriers" and "Barriers made by people." With students' help, add some other common examples, such as *river* and *window*. Then have students work in groups to classify the barriers in the pictures. Have each group make a group chart. Ask students to pass paper and pen around and have members take turns adding ideas. If possible, have some magazine pictures at hand to stimulate ideas for other examples.

2. *Part b.* Erase the list for "Natural barriers" from the board and add the column heading "Purpose." With suggestions from students, give other examples, such as *fence/keeps people or animals from entering or leaving an area.* Have groups separate into pairs to describe the purposes of the boundaries made by people that they listed in their charts. Groups can then get back together to compare the purposes that they described.

Activity 3: Preview

1. *Part a.* Elicit the meaning of *zoo,* and encourage students to talk about their own visits to zoos. Ask them what particularly interested them on their visits. Invite students to describe the types of barriers between the animals and the visitors, and whether the animals appeared interested in the visitors. Then ask volunteers to describe the pictures on pages 86–88.

2. Ask students to predict what the story is about, and write predictions on the board. Accept all ideas.

3. *Part b.* Ask a volunteer to read the instructions. On the board, copy the chart from the student text, with the three questions about picture one. Ask students for possible answers. Encourage them to speculate and use their imaginations. Then distribute AM 3/1 and have students work in pairs to write questions for the other pictures.

(Continued on page 85.)

---

2. Classify

a. Groupwork. Classify the barriers in Activity 1. Group them in a chart like this:

Natural barriers	Barriers made by people
mountains	dam

Think of other examples to add to your chart. Then read your ideas to the class.

b. Pairwork. Write your examples of barriers made by people on a chart like this. Then identify the purpose of each barrier.

Barriers made by people

Barrier	Purpose
shower curtain	▪ keeps the water in the shower ▪ prevents the water from getting the floor wet

Get together with another pair. Take turns telling about a barrier on your chart.

Study Strategy:
Previewing
See page 167.

3. Preview

a. Classwork. Look over the short story on pages 86–88. Based on the title and the illustrations, what do you think the story is about?

b. Pairwork. Choose one of the pictures on pages 86–88. What questions could you ask to get more information about the picture? List your ideas in a chart like this:

Example: Picture #1

Questions	Possible Answers
Who is inside the spaceship?	
Where is the spaceship from?	
Why is the spaceship coming to Earth?	

Read your questions to the class. Together think of possible answers to your questions.

4. Using Context

a. Classwork. When you read a story, you may come across unfamiliar words. You can make good guesses about the meaning of these words by looking at the context—the words and sentences that come before and after the unfamiliar word. To see how this works, read the paragaph in the box. Use the ideas in the paragraph to help you think of a word or words to write on the line.

Which words and ideas in the paragraph helped you to complete the last sentence?

b. Read the first paragraph of the story "Zoo." What do you think the words *settled down* mean? Which words and ideas in the paragraph helped you guess?

5. Predict

Classwork. The story on pages 86–88 takes place in the distant future when it is possible to travel from one planet to another. The name of the zoo in the story is "Professor Hugo's Interplanetary Zoo." What do you think this zoo might be like? How might it be different from a zoo today? List your ideas on the board.

> ### *Study Strategy:*
> ### *Using Context*
> See page 169–170.

> The children were always good during the month of August, especially when it began to get near the twenty-third. It was on this day that the great silver spaceship carrying Professor Hugo's Interplanetary Zoo
> _____ for its annual six-hour visit to the Chicago area.

> ### *Language Focus:*
> ### *Speculating*
> ■ Professor Hugo's zoo might travel to different planets.
> ■ It might ____.
> ■ It could ____.

Activity 3: Preview (continued)

4.   When students finish, have each pair add questions to a chart on the board. As an extension, have students work in groups. Each group chooses three questions and adds possible answers to the chart on the board.

Activity 4: Using Context

1.   *Part a.* Have one student read aloud the explanation of using context and the instructions for the activity. Ask another volunteer to read aloud the paragraph with the blank line. Elicit the part of speech that students need to supply (a verb). Ask students to read the paragraph again silently. Elicit possible verbs and write them on the board in their past tense forms. Write all the candidates on the board. Ask students to cite specific words and ideas that helped them guess the word.

In Part b you can examine why certain ones worked and others didn't.

2.   *Part b.* Ask students to silently read the first paragraph of *Zoo.* Ask for a definition of *settled down.* Then ask which words on the board from *Part a* correspond to the meaning. Circle them. Point out that *landed* is the most accurate synonym, but that verbs like *arrived* and *came* also work and do not change the meaning of the paragraph.

Activity 5: Predict

1.   Write the sentences from the *Language Focus* box on the board. Point out the pattern:

<u>might/could + base form of verb</u>

2.   Read the instructions aloud and ask the class to guess what Professor Hugo's zoo might be like. Write their ideas on the board. Check for grammatical accuracy.

Activity 6: Read

1. Ask students to take out their AM 3/1 charts of questions from *Activity 3* and to review them before they begin. Then have them read the story silently and look for answers to their questions as they read.

2. Circulate as students read the story, and assist them in using context to understand any unknown words.

6. Read

As you read the story, look for answers to your questions from Activity 3.

Zoo

The children were always good during the month of August, especially when it began to get near the twenty-third. It was on this day that the great silver spaceship carrying Professor Hugo's Interplanetary Zoo settled down for its annual six-hour visit to the Chicago area.

Before daybreak the crowds would form, long lines of children and adults both, each one clutching his or her dollar, and waiting with wonderment to see what race of strange creatures[1] the Professor had brought this year.

In the past they had sometimes been treated to three-legged creatures from Venus, or tall, thin men from Mars, or even snakelike horrors[2] from somewhere more distant. This year, as the great round ship settled slowly to earth in the huge tri-city parking area just outside of Chicago, they watched with awe[3] as the sides slowly slid up to reveal the familiar barred cages.

In them were some wild breed[4] of nightmare[5]—small, horselike animals that moved with quick, jerking motions and constantly chattered in a high-pitched tongue. The citizens of Earth

[1]**creatures**	animals, including people
[2]**horrors**	things causing fear; scary things
[3]**awe**	wonder mixed with fear and respect
[4]**breed**	type
[5]**nightmare**	frightening dream; something frightening

clustered around as Professor Hugo's crew quickly collected the waiting dollars, and soon the good Professor himself made an appearance, wearing his many-colored rainbow cape and top hat. "Peoples of Earth," he called into his microphone.

The crowd's noise died down and he continued. "Peoples of Earth, this year you see a real treat[6] for your single dollar—the little-known horse-spider people of Kaan—brought to you across a million miles of space at great expense. Gather around, see them, study them, listen to them, tell your friends about them. But hurry! My ship can remain here only six hours!

And the crowds slowly filed by, at once horrified and fascinated by these strange creatures that looked like horses but ran up the walls of their cages like spiders. "This is certainly worth a dollar," one man remarked, hurrying away. "I'm going home to get the wife."

All day long it went like that, until ten thousand people had filed by the barred cages set into the side of the spaceship. Then, as the six-hour limit ran out, Professor Hugo once more took microphone in hand. "We must go now, but we will return next year on this date. And if you enjoyed our zoo this year, phone your friends in other cities about it. We will land in New York tomorrow, and next week on to London, Paris, Rome, Hong Kong, and Tokyo. Then on to other worlds!"

He waved farewell to them, and as the ship rose from the ground the Earth peoples agreed that this had been the very best Zoo yet...

Some two months and three planets later, the silver ship of Professor Hugo settled at last onto the familiar jagged rocks of Kaan, and the queer horse-spider creatures filed quickly out of their cages. Professor Hugo was there to say a few parting words, and then they scurried away in a hundred different directions, seeking their homes among the rocks.

In one, the she-creature was happy to see the return of her mate[7] and offspring.[8] She babbled a greeting in the strange tongue and hurried to embrace[9] them. "It was a long time you were gone. Was it good?"

[6]**treat**   something special that gives pleasure
[7]**mate**   husband or wife, male or female of a pair
[8]**offspring** child or children
[9]**embrace** hug

▲▲▲

Activity 7: Share Ideas

1. *Part a.* Elicit the answers to questions from *Activity 3*. Resolve any differences in the answers by referring students back to the story.

2. *Part b.* Ask a volunteer to read the instruction line for *Part b.* Put students into groups and have each group select one member to take notes. Circulate and join in the discussions. If time permits, have groups choose a second question.

3. As groups report their ideas, elicit additional reactions from the rest of the class. (Answers to the questions will vary. Possible ideas: (1) Professor Hugo's zoo is different because it carries creatures from other planets. Both the creatures in the cages and the creatures who visit the zoo pay Professor Hugo. (2) Both Earth people and Kaan people thought that they were the observers, not the attractions. (3) The zoo is unusual because the Earth people and the Kaan people are each both audience and attraction. (4) The bars probably protect the Kaan people from the Earth people, as well as the Earth people from the Kaan people. (5) The story suggests that barriers work both ways: they isolate creatures as well as protect them from each other.)

About the Author
Edward Hoch has written more than 500 mystery short stories. He also writes material for TV programs.

And the he-creature nodded. "The little one enjoyed it especially. We visited eight worlds and saw many things."

The little one ran up the wall of the cave. "On the place called Earth it was the best. The creatures there wear garments over their skins, and they walk on two legs."

"But isn't it dangerous?" asked the she-creature.

"No," her mate answered. "There are bars to protect us from them. We remain right in the ship. Next time you must come with us. It is well worth the nineteen commocs it costs."

And the little one nodded.
"It was the very best Zoo ever. . . ."

Edward Hoch

 7. **Share Ideas**

a. Classwork. Share any answers you found to your questions from Activity 3.

b. Groupwork. Choose one of the questions below to discuss in your group. Ask one person in your group to take notes on your discussion.

1. Think back to your predictions from Activity 5. What do you know about Professor Hugo's zoo now? How is it different from a zoo today?

2. Both the Earth people and the Kaan people paid to go to Professor Hugo's zoo. Why?

3. What was unusual about Professor Hugo's zoo?

4. What was the purpose of the barred cages in Professor Hugo's zoo? Who do you think the bars were protecting?

5. What does this story say to you about barriers?

Report your group's ideas to the class.

8. Interpret

a. Classwork. Describe Professor Hugo's Interplanetary Zoo from two points of view. First tell what you think the Kaan people are thinking and feeling at Professor Hugo's zoo. Then tell what the Earth people might be thinking and feeling.

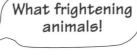

How strange. They're wearing garments!

What frightening animals!

Kaan people	Earth people

b. Pairwork. Use the ideas in your diagram to write a conversation between two people at Professor Hugo's zoo. First decide if your conversation is between two Earth people or two Kaan people. Then write your conversation.

Example:

Person A: What do you think of the zoo?

Person B: It's incredible. What weird animals!

Person A: _____

c. Pairwork. Read your conversation aloud to the class. Let your classmates guess where the two people are from.

Activity 8: Interpret

1. *Part a.* To introduce the concept of point of view, ask, *What would a Kaan creature find unusual or uncomfortable in this classroom?* Point out or elicit that our perceptions are influenced by beliefs, culture, and environment.

2. Ask a student to read the instructions. Have a volunteer at the board write ideas for the thought bubbles as students call them out.

3. *Part b.* Circulate as students write and help less proficient students express their ideas.

4. *Part c.* Have pairs of students act out their conversations. If possible, have students tape the conversations for use in *Activity 10*.

5. *Optional:* Divide the room into a Kaan section and an Earth section. After each pair of students acts out a conversation, have them go to the appropriate section. When all the students are in the proper section of the zoo, they can continue the role play.

Activity 9: Define

1. *Part a.* Ask students to copy the chart on a separate piece of paper. Write column headings on the board and then write the first word, *clutching*, in the first column. Ask a student to read Sentence Number One. Point out that this sentence provides the context for the word. Ask students to guess the meaning, and then have them identify the ideas or words that helped them guess the meaning.

2. Have students complete the chart on their own. Make sure they realize that *tongue* in Sentence Number Two means *language* in that context. Circulate and help students as they work.

3. Have volunteers read the example sentences from the *Language Focus* box. Then elicit answers and complete the chart on the board. Ask for volunteers to look up the words in a dictionary and write the definitions on the board. Compare students' guesses with the dictionary definitions. If there are differences, examine whether they change the meaning of the story.

4. *Optional:* Divide the class into groups, and assign a section of the story to each group. Have each group select several words from their section to work on. Ask each group to lead the class in working out the meaning of the words they chose by examining context and guessing.

Activity 10: Write

1. *Part a.* Read the instruction line. Remind students of the Reader's Theaters that they acted out in Units 1 and 2. Tell them that now that they've had the experience of working with two of them, they are ready to write their own Reader's Theater.

2. Ask students to read the cast of characters and elicit that the first scene takes place on Earth and the second scene takes place on Kaan.

(Continued on page 91.)

---

9. Define

a. Classwork. The sentences below are from the story "Zoo." Were you able to use context to guess the meaning of the underlined words? Read the sentences and complete a chart like this:

Word from the story	Guess from context	Helpful context clues
clutching		
chattered		
garments		

Sentences from the Story

1. Before daybreak the crowds would form, long lines of children and adults both, each one <u>clutching</u> his or her dollar . . .

2. In the cages were small, horselike animals that moved with quick, jerking motions and constantly <u>chattered</u> in a high-pitched tongue.

3. "On the place called Earth it was the best. The creatures there wear <u>garments</u> over their skins, and they walk on two legs."

b. Look up each word in a dictionary and check your guesses.

Language Focus:
Guessing

- I think the word *clutching* means "holding."
- The word *clutching* probably means something like "holding."

10. Write

a. Classwork. In Unit 2, you read a Reader's Theater about people on the Underground Railroad. Below, is the first part of a Reader's Theater based on the short story "Zoo." Look over the cast of the play. Where do the two scenes take place? What is the setting of each scene?

b. Listen to the first part of Scene 1 and read along.

The Zoo

A Reader's Theater based on the story by Edward Hoch

Cast, Scene 1
Professor Hugo
First Earth Person
Second Earth Person
First Kaan Person
Second Kaan Person
First Narrator
Second Narrator

Cast, Scene 2
She-creature of Kaan
He-creature of Kaan
Young child of Kaan
Professor Hugo
First Narrator
Second Narrator

SCENE 1

First Narrator: It's daybreak in August, sometime in the distant future. Outside the city of Chicago, a line of people is forming in a large parking area.

Second Narrator: Suddenly a large spaceship appears above the crowd of people.

First Earth Person: There it is. There's Professor Hugo's Zoo.

Second Earth Person: What do you think he brought?

First Earth Person: I can't imagine. Did you see the zoo last year?

Second Earth Person: With the three-legged creatures from Mars? They were terrifying!

First Narrator: The spaceship slowly descends to Earth and lands in the parking area.

Second Narrator: The sides of the spaceship slide up to reveal barred cages.

Second Earth Person:

---

c. Groupwork. What happens next in the play? Finish Scene 1 and write a Scene 2. Take turns recording your group's ideas.

d. Groupwork. Practice reading your play aloud. Some people in your group can take two roles.

e. Type your play into a computer or handwrite it so that your classmates can read it easily. Then make copies of your play.

f. Get together with another group. Choose roles and practice reading each group's play.

g. Tape record both versions of the play or perform your plays for the class.

▲▲▲

---

3. With several volunteers, read the first part of the play to the class. With the students, read expressively and use body language.

4. At the end of the reading, ask, *What do you think the Second Earth Person says now?* Accept all ideas.

5. Play the tape that students made for *Activity 8,* and tell them they can draw on these conversations as they write their Reader's Theater. Then go over the text and point out how the narrators provide the description and the transitions from one part of the story to the other.

6. *Parts b–e.* Have students work in groups to prepare their Reader's Theater. Students may enjoy working with a tape recorder to record their ideas. They can transcribe the script later. Circulate and help students as they work.

7. *Parts f–g.* Have groups perform the plays. Make audiotapes or videotapes of the plays to use as reviews.

Ask a volunteer to read the introduction. Elicit students' knowledge about the role of a sports counselor—someone who gives psychological support to athletes. Then ask, *How do people's ideas or feelings affect their performance?*

Elicit students' own experiences.

Activity 1: Interpret

1. Draw students' attention to the two pictures. Ask a student to read the words in the second speech bubble with feeling. Ask another volunteer to describe what the young woman is thinking about. What might she be saying to herself?

2. Have a student read the instruction line. Guide students' use of language for predicting, especially factual conditional sentences and modals *may*, *might* and *could:*
If he tells himself he can't learn, he won't be able to do it.
His ideas might make him fail.

Activity 2: Journal Writing

1. Ask students how they feel about public speaking or speaking in front of a class. If appropriate, share your own experiences, perhaps when you first began teaching or started to learn a foreign language.

2. Have a student read the instruction line and the three questions. Tell students to picture the scene as if they were watching it on television or in a movie.

3. If students feel comfortable about sharing their journal entries, have each of them read a partner's journal and respond briefly to the entry, either verbally or in writing.

Chapter 2: Breaking Through Mental Barriers

*M*ental barriers can make it difficult to give a speech, take a test, or learn to do something new. But according to sports counselor Marlin Mackenzie, you can learn how to overcome these barriers.

1. Interpret

Classwork. What are these people thinking? How might their thoughts act as a barrier? Share ideas with your classmates.

2. Journal Writing

On your own. Imagine yourself giving a speech to your classmates. Describe the picture that you see in your mind. As you write, think about the questions below.

■ What do you see yourself doing as you give your speech?

■ How do you feel?

■ How are your classmates reacting to your speech?

3. Preview

a. Pairwork. Look over the article on pages 93–94. Read the first sentence in the first four paragraphs. Then write a question based on the information in each sentence.

Example: *What was the pole-vaulter's problem?*

b. Read your questions to the class. Together think of possible answers to your questions. Then tell what you think the article is about.

4. Read

On your own. As you read the article, look for answers to your questions from Activity 3.

Breaking Mental Barriers

from *Science Digest*

1 **A** young pole-vaulter had a problem. Time after time he would sprint down the track, place his pole and leap for the crossbar. Time after time, he sailed into the bar, not over it. The harder he tried, the more his body seemed drawn into the bar, like a nail to a magnet. He knew how to vault; he just had a mental block that kept him from doing it.

2 Now he's competing successfully again, thanks to Marlin Mackenzie, head of the sports-counselor training program at Columbia University Teachers College. Mackenzie is one of a growing number of professionals being consulted by athletes whose performance problems have a psychological basis.[1] And there is a growing realization that crippling mental barriers of all sorts can be overcome, whether they involve hitting a golf ball or giving a speech, taking a test or talking to the boss.

3 "Any given goal has a strategy," says Mackenzie, "a mental 'map' of the best way to reach that goal. The map will often be largely subconscious,[2] and it is usually a complicated set of sensory images—pictures, sounds, physical

[1] **a psychological basis** come from one's mind
[2] **subconscious** in the mind but not consciously known

Activity 3: Preview

1. *Part a.* Draw students' attention to the picture on page 94 and ask them to tell you the name of the sport. Ask, *what is a pole vaulter's goal?* Ask if any students have participated in this activity, and find out what they know about the sport and its challenges.

2. Ask students to read the instruction line silently. Then have them read the first sentence of the first paragraph. Write the example question on the board. Note that this activity is a way of predicting what they are going to read in the paragraph.

3. Tell students to write their questions on a separate piece of paper, and to leave space for notes below each question. Ask them to number the questions.

4. *Part b.* Have volunteers write questions on the board. (Possible questions: Para. 2: *How did Marlin Mackenzie help the athlete?* Para. 3: *What is a mental map?* Para. 4: *Was the strategy successful?* Para. 5: *How can average people break through mental barriers?*) Ask students to speculate about answers.

Activity 4: Read

1. Tell students to read the article silently, and to take notes about the answers to their questions as they read. Circulate to assist students while they work.

2. When students finish reading, elicit the answers to their questions from *Activity 3.* Then ask them how accurate their predictions of the topic were.

sensations—mixed with emotional images." In the case of the pole-vaulter, Mackenzie elicited the images that raced through the young man's mind in the split second it took to spring from ground to crossbar. "He was talking to himself, trying to get himself through the jump by 'hearing' words of encouragement. But words are too slow. He needed an image that would distract his mind from the task. His body knew how to jump—his brain had just forgotten that he knew."

4   Mackenzie told the vaulter not to think about jumping, but to think of the sound of his pole hitting the ground as the first note of a love song. The strategy worked almost the first time he had the chance to use it.

5   Is there anything the average person can do to break through a mental barrier? According to Mackenzie, a positive mental image of the goal successfully attained[3] is crucial.[4] "If I say, 'don't think about pink elephants,' what's the first thing you think of?" he asks. "If you go into a job interview telling yourself not to stumble over your words, you picture the mistake—and often commit[5] it. But if you picture yourself speaking clearly and well, your subconscious is channeled into the right groove and you're likely to live up to[6] that picture."

---

[3]**attained**   reached, accomplished
[4]**crucial**   extremely important; of the greatest importance
[5]**commit**   make, do
[6]**live up to**   act like

5. Share Ideas

a. Pairwork. Choose one of the questions below to discuss with your partner. Take notes on your discussion.

1. How can mental barriers cause problems?
2. How did Marlin Mackenzie help the pole-vaulter compete successfully?
3. How could you use the ideas in this article?
4. According to Mackenzie, what should you picture yourself doing before you give a speech?

b. Find another pair of students in your class who discussed the same question. Exchange ideas.

c. Tell the class which question you chose and report on your discussion.

6. Use Context

a. On your own. Were you able to use context to define these words from the article? Look back at the reading to find the words and write your guesses. Then answer each question.

1. Paragraph #**1**: *mental block*

   Definition: _a barrier in your mind; a way of think-_
   ing that stops you from doing something

   What do you have a mental block against doing?

   _____

2. Paragraph #**3**: *mental map*

   Definition: _____

   What can a mental map help you to do?

   _____

> **Study Strategy:**
> **Using Context**
> See page 169–170.

Activity 5: Share Ideas

1. *Part a.* Remind students to take notes about their discussion.

2. *Parts b and c.* As pairs of students finish their discussion, have them form a group with other students to share ideas about the same question. Then ask students to share answers with the whole class. For each question, elicit answers from several students. Answers will vary. (*Possible answers:* (1) Mental barriers can prevent people from achieving even when they have the necessary skills. (2) Mackenzie helped the athlete by providing a sensory image—he told him to think of the sound of his pole hitting the ground as the first note of a love song. (3) Answers will vary—the ideas could be used in speaking or writing English or doing other school work, talking in front of a class, sports, driving a car, or using a computer. (4) You should picture yourself speaking clearly.)

Activity 6: Use Context

1. *Part a.* Have a volunteer read the instruction line. Then tell students to find the term *mental block* in the first paragraph. Ask them if they agree with the example definition. Ask, *What idea or phrase in the context explains the term?* (*kept him from doing it*). Supply an example from your own experience and write it on the board.

2. Distribute AM 3/2 and have students complete the rest of the activity. Circulate and help them as they work. After students share their answers with a partner, ask for definitions and examples from volunteers. (Definitions will vary somewhat. 2. mental map: a strategy for reaching a goal. 3. sensory image: a mental picture of a sight, sound, or physical sensation. a4. words of encouragement: words that give hope or courage.)

Activity 7: Apply

1. Before students start the activity, have them reread the last paragraph of the article. Ask, *What happens to people when they worry about making a particular mistake?* (They picture that mistake, and often commit it.)

2. Have each group choose one student to take notes as they explore advice for the three situations. Then have groups list their advice on the board and compare ideas.

3. *Optional:* Have groups role play giving advice to one group member. Have each group set up a situation, for example, giving advice to a friend, seeking advice from a sports counselor, or talking to colleagues at work.

Activity 8: Journal Writing

1. *Part a.* With students, brainstorm some questions to stimulate their writing. Write the questions on the board for students to refer to as they write. (Possible questions: 1. *What is the occasion of your speech?* 2. *What is your topic?* 3. *How are you speaking?* 4. *Who is in the audience?* 5. *How are they reacting to your speech?*)

2. After students write their descriptions or draw a picture, ask them to reread their journal entries from *Activity 1.* Have them work with a partner to compare the differences between their two journal entries.

3. Paragraph **#3:** *sensory image*

Definition: _____

Imagine yourself doing something. What sensory images come to mind?

_____

4. Paragraph **#3:** *words of encouragement*

Definition: _____

Write a sentence with words of encouragement. When might you say this sentence to yourself?

_____

b. Compare ideas with a partner. Then, share your definitions and answers with your classmates.

7. Apply

Groupwork. What advice do you think Marlin Mackenzie would give these people? Write your group's ideas on another piece of paper.

1. A student is having trouble taking tests. Before a test, she tells herself, "Don't be nervous."

2. A young man is trying to learn to swim. The night before he goes swimming, he lies in bed thinking about the next day. In his mind, he sees himself sinking in the water.

3. A businessperson has to give a speech to a large group of people, and she is worried about forgetting what to say and speaking too quickly.

Compare ideas with your classmates.

8. Journal Writing

a. On your own. Think about the information in the article "Breaking Mental Barriers." Then imagine yourself giving a speech to the whole school. Draw or describe the picture that you see in your mind. How is this picture different from the picture you described in Activity 2?

b. Think of something you have a mental block against doing. How might you use the information in the article to overcome this mental block? Write your ideas in your journal.

9. Write

On your own. Think about something difficult that you have done. How did you feel? What thoughts went through your mind? What helped you do this difficult thing? In writing, share your experience with your classmates. Here are some ideas to get started:

1. With a group of classmates, brainstorm a set of things that are difficult to do. Record your group's ideas.

   Examples: move to a new country
   learn to play a new sport
   walk away from a fight
   say that you made a mistake

Look over your group's ideas. Which of these ideas makes you think of something from your experience? Is it something you want to write about?

2. Complete these sentences in different ways.

   Examples:

   I had a difficult time _making new friends when I moved here._

   It was hard for me to _understand the language when I_

   came here.

Look over the ideas you wrote down.
Is there something you want to write about?

3. Look over your notes for #1 and #2 and choose an experience to write about. Be sure to choose something that you feel comfortable sharing with your classmates.
4. Think about the experience you chose and quickwrite in your journal for five minutes.
5. Read your quickwriting aloud to a classmate. Find out what your classmate would like to know more about.
6. Write a first draft of your paper.
7. Refer to the Writer's Guide on pages 174–175 for ideas about revising your paper.

> **Study Strategy:**
> **Brainstorming**
> See page 163.

> **Study Strategy:**
> **Quickwriting**
> See page 168.

Activity 9: Write

1.   To get students started, refer to Section 1 ("Think") on page 172 of the Writer's Guide. Ask students to identify the prewriting strategies that they have found most useful so far. Then give them ample time to explore the three methods (brainstorming, completing the sentences, and quickwriting) suggested in this activity. Remind students to choose a topic that they can comfortably share with their classmates.

2.   Have students read Section 2 of the Writer's Guide about writing a first draft. Suggest that they select their classmates as an audience. Then have them work in pairs to identify their purpose for writing and plan an outline of their first draft.

3.   When students finish their first draft, have them read their drafts to each other in small groups, and then revise, taking their audience's comments into account.

4.   *Optional:* Distribute copies of finished writing and ask students to write responses to some of their classmates' stories.

Have students silently read the introductory paragraph. Ask for definitions of the term *racism*, and then ask students to look up the word in their dictionaries and to report the definitions (*the belief that one's own race is superior; social, political, and economic policies based on that belief*)

Activity 1: Listen

1. *Part a.* Direct students' attention to the picture and ask a volunteer to describe it. Elicit students' own knowledge about anti-Japanese racism in the United States. Then have a student read the instruction line.

2. Tell students to take notes as they listen to the tapescript. Play the tape as many times as needed.

3. *Part b.* As students call out examples, make a list on the blackboard. (Examples: Those born in Japan could not buy land, and were never allowed citizenship. Japanese Americans were stoned; restaurants would not serve them, barbers wouldn't cut their hair, and homeowners wouldn't sell or rent to them. Racist signs were displayed.)

Chapter 3: Racism—A Barrier Between People

*R*acism is a barrier because it prevents people from getting to know each other; it causes people to fear and hate those who are different.

1. Listen

a. Classwork. The article on pages 100–101 deals with the treatment of Japanese Americans before and during the Second World War. According to the article, racism against Japanese Americans had a long history in the United States. Listen for the examples of racism in this paragraph from the reading. List them on another piece of paper.

b. Listen again and then compare notes with your classmates.

▲▲▲

2. Predict

Classwork. In 1942, the U.S. government forced nearly 120,000 people to leave their homes and businesses and to move to internment camps. These internment camps were really prisons. All of the people forced to move were of Japanese ancestry. What reasons can you think of to explain the government's action?

 Japanese detainees await barracks assignments.

3. Read

On your own. Read to check your predictions from Activity 2.

Activity 2: Predict

1. Have a student read aloud the introduction to the activity. Ask students, *What was happening in the world in 1942?* Elicit that World War II was being fought, and that the United States was just entering the war. Ask, *Which countries opposed the United States and its allies?* Elicit Germany, Italy, and Japan.

2. Tell students that they are going to read about the internment camps where Japanese Americans were forced to live during the war. Ask them to predict the reasons for the U.S. government's actions against the Japanese Americans. Tell them to write their predictions on a piece of paper. Then ask volunteers to write predictions on the board.

Activity 3: Read

Ask students to keep their predictions at hand, and to look for information to check their predictions as they read the article. Have students read silently and circulate to assist them as needed.

A Shameful Chapter

(Part 1)

by Barbara Rogasky

1   **O**n December 7, 1941, Japanese planes bombed the Pearl Harbor Naval Base in the Hawaiian Islands and destroyed most of the U.S. Pacific fleet.[1] In a few days America was at war with Japan and her allies, Germany and Italy.

2   The lives of most people with German and Italian backgrounds who lived in America did not change much because of the war. The Japanese were not so lucky.

3   Nearly all 120,000 Japanese living on the West Coast spent the war years locked up behind barbed wire[2] and under armed guard. Two thirds of them were American citizens.

4   The real reason seems simple. German Americans and Italian Americans were Caucasian. They were white. But the Japanese were not. That was enough to suspect each and every one of being a spy.[3]

5   Racism against the Japanese had a long history here. The *Issei*, those born in Japan but living in the United States, were not allowed to own land. Nor were they ever permitted to become American citizens, no matter how long they lived here. They, and their American-born children, called *Nisei*, were stoned[4] in the streets. Many restaurants refused to serve them, barbers would not cut their hair, homeowners would not sell or rent to them. Hand painted signs announced JAPS KEEP MOVING—THIS IS A WHITE MAN'S NEIGHBORHOOD.

[1]**fleet**   group of warships
[2]**barbed wire**   wire with sharp points attached to it
[3]**spy**   person employed by a country to find secret
                     information about another country
[4]**stoned**   hit by stones thrown at them

6   When the war started, rumors[5] flew. Japanese were said to be radioing war planes about to bomb the coast. Japanese farmers burning brush were accused of lighting "arrows of fire," directing enemy aircraft to important targets. Japanese even were blamed for sabotaging[6] power lines that were actually broken by cows scratching their backs on poles.

7   No evidence[7] of spying or sabotage was ever found, then or at any time during the war. Yet, on February 19, 1942, President Franklin Roosevelt signed Executive Order 9066. It allowed the army to call sections of the country "military areas." Any person or group could be kept out of those areas if the army thought it necessary.

8   The West Coast was already officially a war zone. Lieutenant General John L. DeWitt, chief of the Western Defense Command, issued the first "Civilian Exclusion Orders." He intended to move out anyone he believed threatened the region's security.[8] Soon all people of Japanese ancestry were forced to leave their homes.

9   The Japanese were given as little as one week's notice. They had to leave everything behind and sell what they could for whatever they could get. They were cheated in countless[9] ways—by those who paid twenty-five dollars for a new car and three hundred dollars for a house, and by the U.S. Government, which promised to protect Japanese property but used it or disposed of it without offering compensation[10] of any kind. The government promised to keep cars owned by the Japanese until the end of the war, and then took them for its own use without paying a penny.

[5]**rumors**   information, often false, spread from person to person
[6]**sabotaging**   damaging on purpose
[7]**evidence**   proof
[8]**security**   safety
[9]**countless**   more than can be counted; very many
[10]**compensation**   payment

Activity 4: Review

1. *Part a.* Look again at the predictions that are on the board from *Activity 2.* Have students refer to specific parts of the text as they decide whether the predictions match information in the article. Then have the students talk about their own predictions with a partner.

2. *Part b.* Have students stay with the same partners. Ask a volunteer to read the instruction line. Write the column headings on the board, and ask a student to read the first paragraph out loud. Write the example question in the second column and elicit the answer. Work together to list other questions that are answered in the first paragraph.

Distribute AM 3/3 and have students work in pairs. Tell them to take turns reading paragraphs aloud to each other, to identify the kind of information in the paragraph, and then to write a question. The question should focus on an important idea in each paragraph. Circulate to assist students as they work.

3. *Part c.* Have volunteers ask and answer questions from their charts. Discuss any differences in the questions students wrote. For additional practice, have students work in groups and take turns asking and answering questions. Answers will vary. (Para. 2: *What happened to people of German and Italian backgrounds during the war?*/Their lives did not change much. Para. 3: *What happened to people of Japanese background?*/Nearly 120,000 Japanese were locked up. Para. 4: *Why were the two groups treated so differently?*/The Japanese were not white. Para. 5: *Was there anti-Japanese racism in the United States before the war?*/Yes; there were many forms of discrimination against them. Para. 6: *What were some rumors about Japanese-Americans when the war started?*/That they spied and sabotaged for the Japanese. Para. 7: *What did Roosevelt do on Feb. 19, 1942?*/He signed Executive Order 9066.

(Continued on page 103.)

4. **Review**

a. Classwork. Look back at your predictions from Activity 2. Do any of your ideas match the information given in the reading?

b. Pairwork. Check your understanding of the passage. Look back at each paragraph. What questions does the paragraph answer? For each paragraph, write one question. Then write the answer to the question.

Example:

Paragraph #	Question	Answer
1	What happened on December 7, 1941?	Japan bombed U.S. ships in Hawaii.

c. Classwork. Take turns asking and answering questions about the information in the passage.

d. Classwork. Did you find this activity helpful? If so, how did it help you?

5. **Read**

Classwork. Think of three things you would like to find out in the next part of the reading. On the board, list your ideas as questions. Then look for answers to your questions as you read Part 2.

A Shameful Chapter
(Part 2)

10   **N**o one told the Japanese where they were going. Loaded onto trains and buses, they were taken to "assembly centers." These were sometimes stockyards[1] or stables,[2] stinking and dirty. Each family was given a table, a chair, cots, and mattresses and straw to stuff them with. Everyone was kept under armed guard at all times.

11   In a few months the Japanese were moved again—this time to Camp Jerome in Arkansas, Camp Manzanar in the California desert, Camp Poston in Arizona, and to seven more camps miles from the West Coast. These were terrible places. It could get as hot as 120 degrees and as cold as below zero. The wind- and sand-storms were severe.[3]

12   The Japanese found unfinished wooden barracks[4] at the camps. Each barrack was divided into four or six rooms. Here, each family was given one twenty-by-twenty foot space, which contained a potbellied stove, one bare bulb hanging from the ceiling, cots, and blankets. That was all.

13   These places were called internment camps. They were really prisons. The Japanese were fenced in, the gates were locked, and they were watched twenty-four hours a day. According to American law, people may not be arrested and imprisoned unless there is some evidence of a crime. They are then considered innocent until proven guilty by a judge or jury using the evidence as proof. Then—and only then—may a resident or citizen be sentenced to a period of time under lock and

¹**stockyards**   places where large groups of cattle or other animals are kept for a short time
²**stables**   places where horses are kept
³**severe**   hard, harsh
⁴**barracks**   buildings designed to house soldiers

Activity 4: Review *(continued)*

Para. 8: *How was the order carried out on the West Coast?*/Japanese-Americans were forced out of their homes. Para. 9: *What happened to the Japanese who were forced to leave?*/They were cheated out of their belongings.)

4.   *Part d.* Ask students how they can apply this type of activity to reading in their other courses. As an extension activity, have each student choose a short passage from a social studies or science text and analyze it by asking and answering questions about an important idea in each paragraph.

Activity 5: Read

1.   Have volunteers write their questions on the board. Ask students to look for the answers to these questions as they read.

2.   *Optional:* Have students make notes in their reading journals about thoughts and questions that come to mind as they read.

key. The Japanese were denied[5] these rights. The American government had broken its own law.

14   Ironically, in February 1943, the *Nisei* were allowed to be drafted into the army. Many eventually formed the 442nd Regimental Combat team. By the end of the war in Europe, this group of thirty-three thousand men had won more military honors than any other unit in the entire U.S. armed forces. Their families remained imprisoned.

15   The Japanese began to be released from the camps in January 1945. The war ended for good[6] in August 1945, but the last internment camp was not closed until March 1946.

16   Gradually, several groups and individuals began pressuring the government to admit that it had violated the Constitution by interning the Japanese. In 1983, a government committee published a report called *Personal Justice Denied*. It admitted that the law had been broken and called for the government to apologize and make some payment to the Japanese who had been forced into camps.

17   Five years later, the government agreed. It would pay twenty thousand dollars to each person from the camps who was still alive. Every payment would come with a letter of apology from the president. By then, it was forty-six years after the camps had opened, and half of the original 120,000 had died.

18   The first payments were made on October 9, 1990. A personal letter of apology from President George Bush came with each check.

19   But are the money and the apology enough? No apology or payment can make what happened less wrong. Only one thing can begin to right[7] this shameful chapter in our history. We must remember it. Because nothing like it must ever happen again.

▲ *Former President George Bush*

[5]**denied**   not allowed to have
[6]**for good**   forever
[7]**right**   correct

6. Share Ideas

Groupwork. Here are some questions you can discuss in your group.

1. What thoughts and questions came to mind as you read the article? Point to specific lines in the article and explain your reaction.

2. Why do you think this article is titled "A Shameful Chapter"? What does the title mean to you?

3. Reread the last paragraph of the article. Do you agree with the writer? Why or why not?

4. How did racism against Japanese Americans act as a barrier?

7. Take Notes

a. Classwork. Share any answers you found to your questions from Activity 5. Show where in the passage you found the answers.

b. Pairwork. Look back over Parts 1 and 2 of the reading to find information about each topic listed in the chart below. Identify the paragraph with information about each topic. In your own words, note the important details about each topic.

Topic	Paragraphs	Details
■ rumors against Japanese	6, 7	rumors said Japanese Americans were helping Japan—directing Japanese planes, sabotaging power lines; rumors were untrue
■ Executive Order 9066		
■ how the Japanese were cheated		
■ internment camps		
■ the 442nd Regimental Combat team		
■ apologizing to the Japanese		

c. Get together with a partner and compare charts. Then share information from your chart with the class.

> **Study Strategy:**
> **Taking Notes in a Chart**
> See page 169.

Activity 6: Share ideas

1. Have volunteers read the instruction line and the four questions. If students wrote in their reading journals for *Activity 5*, ask them to read their journal entries to their group and work out questions that have arisen in their reading. To check students' comprehension of paragraph 13, ask, *How did the U.S. Government break its own laws when it imprisoned Japanese Americans?* Make sure students understand the legal process necessary before a resident or citizen can be deprived of liberty or property.

2. Circulate and participate in the discussions. When groups have finished, have them pool their ideas with the whole class. For question 4, answers should include the idea that Japanese Americans were barred from their rights as citizens and residents, as well as physically restricted.

Activity 7: Take Notes

1. *Part a.* Ask volunteers to share questions and answers. Have them refer to specific parts of the text for the answers.

2. *Part b.* Write the column headings for the chart on the board. Ask a volunteer to read the instructions. Then distribute AM 3/4. Have students find the paragraphs in the article that discuss rumors against the Japanese. (Para. 6 and 7). Then ask a student to read the notes under "Details" in the chart. Point out that students should write the notes in their own words. Suggest that after they read the relevant paragraph, they shut their books and write the information as they remember it. (Wording of details will vary; paragraph numbers are:

Executive Order 9066: 7, 8;

how the Japanese were cheated: 9;
internment camps: 10-13;

the 442nd Regimental Combat team: 14;

apologizing to the Japanese: 16-19)

(Continued on page 106.)

Activity 7: Take Notes *(continued)*

3. *Part c.* When partners complete their charts, have them join another pair and compare charts. Have students then come to the front and complete the chart on the overhead or the board.

4. *Optional:* Do the activity as a jigsaw: Have each pair of students prepare one topic. When they finish, they can join other pairs who have done the same topic and compare charts. When all the groups have completed their topic, have each group appoint members to go to the board and introduce the material, pointing out where in the text the topic appears, and summarizing the details about the topic.

Activity 8: Give Examples

1. *Part a.* Have students continue to work with their partners from *Activity 7.* Distribute AM 3/5 and read the instructions. Have a volunteer read the first statement. Ask, *Is this true?* When they respond, tell students to place a check in the *False* column. Then ask them to find in the text the information that supports their ideas. When they find the information, tell them to make a note about it in the last column.

2. Circulate to help as students complete the chart. (Wording of answers will vary : (1) False. No evidence of spying was ever found. (2) True. People paid $25 for a new car, $300 for a house; the U.S. government took property and never paid for it or returned it. (3) False. The climate was very severe. Each family had a small space in a barracks with only a stove, a bare bulb, cots, and blankets. (4) False. The Government didn't apologize until 1990.)

3. *Part b.* Write the first *Language Focus* sentence on the board and ask a volunteer for the reason for their answer. Guide students in their use of language as they give reasons for their answers.

(Continued on page 107.)

> **Language Focus:**
>
> ***Expressing Opinions***
>
> ▪ We think the first statement is false because . . .
> ▪ We believe the second statement is ___ because . . .

8. Give Examples

a. Pairwork. Decide if the following statements are true or false. Then give details and examples to support or refute each statement. Write your ideas on a chart like this:

	True	False	Details/Examples
1. Japanese Americans helped direct Japanese war planes to important targets in the United States.			
2. People of Japanese ancestry were cheated when they had to leave their homes and businesses quickly.			
3. The internment camps were comfortable places in which to live.			
4. Immediately after the war, the U.S. government apologized to the Japanese who had been forced into camps.			

b. Share ideas with your classmates.

9. Listen

a. Classwork. You are going to hear some information about the internment of Japanese Americans during World War II. Before you listen to the tape, read the questions below. Then listen for answers to the questions and take notes on another piece of paper.

1. According to this passage, rumors that Japanese Americans were helping the enemy led to mistreatment of Japanese Americans. What examples does the passage give?

2. Japanese Americans suffered heavy losses when they were forced to leave their homes and businesses quickly. What example does the passage give?

b. Compare ideas with your classmates.

10. Journal Writing

a. On your own. Why do you think racism exists? As you write your ideas in your journal, think about racism against Japanese Americans before and during the Second World War. Think also of examples of racism you have read or heard about. Explore your answer to the question as you write in your journal.

b. Get together with your classmates and share ideas from your journal writing.

11. Preview

a. Classwork. Read the title of the poem on page 108. What do you already know about Executive Order 9066? Based on the title, what do you think the poem is about?

b. The narrator of this poem is a Japanese American teenager. How do you think Executive Order 9066 might have affected her? Share ideas with your classmates.

12. Shared Reading

Groupwork. Read this poem aloud in different ways. For example, you might take turns reading a sentence aloud.

Language Focus:

Speculating about Past Events

- She might have been forced to move to an internment camp.
- She might have ——.

Activity 9: Listen

1. *Part a.* Ask volunteers to read the instructions and the two questions. Ask students what they already know about the topics.

Then tell them to listen for information and to make notes on a separate piece of paper.

2. Play the tape as many times as needed. (*Answers:* (1) mistreatment: moved to relocation camps with only 48 hours notice. Camps surrounded by barbed wire, patrolled by armed soldiers; families in crowded barracks. (2) heavy losses: A vegetable farmer sold a $100,000 business for $5,000.)

Activity 10: Journal Writing

1. Before the students begin to write, explore with them the question of why racism exists. Remind them about the barriers in Dr. Hugo's zoo. Ask, *When people have racist feelings or policies, do they really know the people of the other race well?* Remind students of the examples of racism they read about in Unit 2 (*Who's Hu?* and the story of the Underground Railroad). Invite your students to give other examples, and accept all ideas offered.

2. *Part b.* Give students ample time to think and write about the topic. Then have students work in groups to share the ideas from their journal writing.

Activity 11: Preview

1. *Part a.* Have a student read the title of the poem aloud. Ask for information about Executive Order 9066 from your students, and elicit their ideas about the topic of the poem.

2. Write the first sentence from the *Language Focus* box on the board. List other modals for speculating: *may have, could have, must have* (when you're fairly certain). Guide students' use of the language as they speculate about the narrator. For example: Her family could have

(*Continued on page 108.*)

Activity 11: Preview *(continued)*

lost their business. She might have felt frightened. Her friends must have missed her.

Activity 12: Shared Reading

Have students read the poem silently. Then let them work in groups to experiment with different ways of reading. Encourage them, for example, to try emphasizing different words in the poem or alternating a single voice with two or three voices. If possible, tape the finished readings and play all the readings for the class.

IN RESPONSE TO EXECUTIVE ORDER 9066:
ALL AMERICANS OF JAPANESE DESCENT MUST REPORT TO RELOCATION CENTERS

Dear Sirs:
Of course I'll come. I've packed my galoshes[1] and three packets of tomato seeds. Denise calls them "love apples." My father says where we're going they won't grow.

I am a fourteen-year-old girl with bad spelling and a messy room. If it helps any, I will tell you I have always felt funny using chopsticks and my favorite food is hot dogs.
My best friend is a white girl named Denise — we look at boys together. She sat in front of me all through grade school because of our names: O'Connor, Ozawa. I know the back of Denise's head very well.

I tell her she's going bald. She tells me I copy on tests.
We're best friends.

I saw Denise today in Geography class.
She was sitting on the other side of the room.
"You're trying to start a war," she said, "giving secrets away to the Enemy. Why can't you keep your big mouth shut?"

I didn't know what to say.
I gave her a packet of tomato seeds and asked her to plant them for me, told her when the first tomato ripened she'd miss me.

Dwight Okita

[1]**galoshes**   waterproof overshoes

▲▲▲

About the Author

Dwight Okita was born in 1958. He now lives in Chicago where he writes poems and makes videos.

13. **Share Ideas**

a. Groupwork. What is your reaction to the poem? Share ideas with the people in your group. Here are some other questions you can discuss.

1. What information does the narrator of the poem give about herself?
   List what you know about her.
2. How is the narrator similar to and different from her classmates?
3. How does Denise's behavior towards the narrator change?
   Why do you think this happens?
4. What does this poem say to you about barriers?

b. Share ideas from your discussion with your classmates.

 **14.** **Write**

On your own. Write a diary entry from the point of view of the narrator of the poem. Choose one specific day in the narrator's life. Then tell what happened on this day and describe your (the narrator's) reaction.

Diary/Date

Activity 13: Share Ideas

1. *Part a.* Have students continue to work with the same groups to share ideas about the questions. Ask volunteers to read the questions aloud. Groups should select one member to take notes during their discussion.

2. *Part b.* Explore with the whole class some of the ironies of the poem. Ask, *What is the tone of the first sentence? When would you say this?* (In response to an invitation.) What is the literal meaning of the narrator's father's statement about love apples in the first stanza? The symbolic meaning? How might Denise have been feeling that day in Geography class? Will she miss the narrator?

3. Draw students' attention to the biographical information about Dwight Okita. Ask them, *Could Okita have spent time in an internment camp?* (No. He was born after the end of the war.) Ask students to think about how Okita could have written this poem. Elicit that he must have gotten information reading or hearing accounts of people who were forced to leave their homes, and from his own memories of his friendships as a teenager. Ask students' opinion of empathy as a way of crossing barriers of time, place, and point of view. *How is it possible to understand the feelings of someone from another time or place?*

Activity 14: Write

1. Tell students that like the poet Dwight Okita, they can write from another's point of view by drawing on their own experiences as teenagers as well as what they have learned about internment camps.

2. Brainstorm possible approaches: an ordinary day at school, the day the narrator's family leaves for the camps, a special day, such as the narrator's birthday or a family holiday celebrated in the camp.

Ask a volunteer to read the introduction. Elicit from volunteers the two kinds of information that they will be reading in the unit. Then have students skim the unit quickly and find the page on which the article about the New York program appears and the pages where the teenagers' suggestions appear. Give them a few minutes to scan the material and look at the illustrations. Ask students: *Which information interests you most? Why?*

Activity 1: Brainstorm

Review brainstorming with students. Tell them to call out ideas without worrying about correctness. Then write the words *racial barriers* on the board. Ask students to take a few minutes to think about the term. Have one or two volunteers go to the board to write down ideas as students call them out. Accept all ideas without judgement.

Activity 2: Preview

1. *Part a.* To introduce the activity, ask students what team activities they have participated in (for example, sports, school, religious, or community activities). Write some examples on the board. Ask students to tell about a friendship they made and one lesson they learned about working with people during the activity.

2. Have a student read the instruction line. Ask students to share their own experiences when they talk about whether a game can bring cultures together. Circulate and participate as groups talk about the question.

3. *Part b.* Introduce some information about Hasidic culture. The Hasidim belong to a sect that began in Poland in the eighteenth century. They are conservative, and retain customs and clothing different from mainstream culture.

4. Have volunteers read the instructions and the questions. Encourage students to speculate about the possibilities and to make notes about their ideas. Elicit and write some ideas on the board.

(Continued on page 111.)

Chapter 4: Breaking Down Racial Barriers

*W*hat can be done to break down the barriers between people of different races and cultures? In this chapter, you will read about a program in New York that is bringing together students from different cultural backgrounds. You will also find out what teenagers from around the United States have to say about breaking down racial barriers.

> ***Study Strategy:***
> ***Brainstorming***
> See page 163.

1. **Brainstorm**

Classwork. What comes to mind when you hear the words *racial barriers*? Write your ideas on the board.

2. **Preview**

> ***Study Strategy:***
> ***Previewing***
> See page 167.

a. Pairwork. Read the title and the first sentence of the magazine article on page 111. What is your answer to the question at the beginning of the article? Why?

b. The magazine article on page 111 is about the Peace Games, which bring teenagers together to play basketball. The teenagers, who are from different cultures and communities, must get along and work together to win a basketball game. Before you read the article, think of possible answers to the questions below.

1. Why were the Peace Games started?
2. What is the purpose of the Peace Games?
3. What effects have the Peace Games had?

3. **Read**

As you read the article, look for answers to the questions from Activity 2.

▲▲▲

Aiming for Peace

Can a simple game of hoops[1] bring together two totally different cultures and communities?

People in Brooklyn, New York, think so. And they have some results to prove it.

For years, Hasidic Jews and African-Americans have lived side by side with one another in the Crown Heights section of Brooklyn. But they have never bothered to learn much about one another.

In 1991, violent riots[2] broke out after a young African-American was killed by a Hasidic driver. Soon after, a Hasidic man was stabbed to death.[3]

The two groups became bitter enemies. That's when community leaders started CURE, a program to bring together teens from both groups. CURE stands for Communication, Understanding, Respect, and Education.

A central part of CURE is the Peace Games. In the Peace Games, Hasidic and African-American teens meet on the basketball court. The teams consist of youths from both communities. To win a game, these teens must learn how to play together and get along.

"Before, we would just say Hasidic people were different without trying to understand why," says Sean Joe, 24. "It was surprising to find out we had things in common—like basketball, music, and a love of good food."

At first, Yudi Simon had his doubts. He and his father had been attacked by a

[1] **hoops**	basketball
[2] **riots**	violent disorder by a large group of people
[3] **stabbed**	
to death	killed with a knife

▲▲▲

Have students read silently. Remind them to look for answers to the preview questions as they read the article. Circulate to assist students as they work.

Activity 4: Review

1. *Part a.* After students work in pairs, have them compare the speculations that are on the board from *Activity 2* with the information in the article.

2. *Part b.* Have volunteers report the effects of the program, and write them in a tree diagram on the board. (The teenagers have painted a mural together, planted trees together, and have started an interracial rap group; the violence has stopped.)

On another section of the board, write the three sentence frames from the *Language Focus* box. Ask volunteers to use information from the tree diagram to talk about the effects of the basketball program. Encourage them to use the patterns from the *Language Focus* box.

Activity 5: Design

1. *Part a.* List the sentence frames on the board, on the side. Ask students to complete the sentences. For example: In order to play basketball, you have to *trust your team members*.

2. *Part b.* On the board, write some of the examples students offered in *Activity 2*. Ask, *How did these activities bring people together?* Guide students' use of the language for cause and effect. For example: *As a result of tutoring for my church program, I met a lot more people in my community. A street fair is a good way to bring people together because they can enjoy each other's foods and music.*

3. Circulate and participate in groups' discussions.

4. *Part c.* Write ideas on the board as groups share them with the class. Then ask students to identify one idea that they like and explain why they like it.

group of Crown Heights youths during the riots. His father had been stabbed in the leg. So Yudi, 16, wasn't sure what to expect.

"As soon as I started to play, though, I saw how effective basketball was," he says. "In order to play basketball, you have to trust your teammates. You need to use teamwork. These are the same skills you need in order to get along."

Since the first basketball games were played, the groups have gotten together to paint a mural, plant trees, and even form an interracial rap group.

The results have been good. The violence has stopped. And Yudi says he meets kids from the program all the time.

"You see someone you know from playing basketball, and you go say hello and talk," he says. "That never happened here before."

Scott Brodeur

Language Focus:

Relating Cause and Effect

- One effect of the Peace Games was that the teenagers learned more about each other.
- The Peace Games resulted in . . .
- Because of the Peace Games, . . .
- Due to the Peace Games, . . .

4. Review

a. Pairwork. Share answers to the questions from Activity 2.

b. Classwork. What effects did the Peace Games have? List your ideas in a tree diagram on the board.

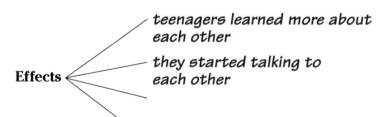

Effects — teenagers learned more about each other
— they started talking to each other

5. Design

a. Classwork. Why is basketball a good way to break down barriers between people? List your ideas on the board.

In order to play basketball, you have to _____.

If you want to win a basketball game, you must _____.

Basketball is a good way to bring people together because _____.

b. Groupwork. Basketball is one way to break down barriers. In your group, think of another way to bring together people from different cultures. Then tell why you think it is a good way to bring people together.

c. Share your group's idea with the class.

6. Preview

a. Classwork. Look over the reading on pages 111–112. Who are the writers? What is their purpose in writing?

b. Classwork. Here is one student's answer to the question, *What can individuals do to bring about greater understanding between different racial and ethnic groups?* What suggestions does this student make?

> People should start being educated about other races at an early age so that when they come in contact with these people later they will act kindly toward them. Younger people should be brought up to believe that all races are equal. World geography classes should deal more than they do now with races. Foreign history courses should also be available. These courses would give kids an understanding of other cultures so when they meet people from these cultures they know how to react. People should also be educated about the great mistakes prejudice has caused in history. Example: The Holocaust.
>
> *Eighth-grader*
> *Laramie Jr. High School*
> *Laramie, Wy.*

Language Focus:

Reporting Another Person's Ideas

- This student says that schools should teach children about different races.
- This student suggests that . . ..
- According to the student from Laramie, ...

7. Jigsaw Reading

a. Groupwork. Each person in your group can choose a different answer to read. As you read, look for the student's suggestions. List them on another piece of paper.

Activity 6: Preview

1. *Part a.* Give students a few minutes to scan the readings and to find the writers. Elicit the answers from volunteers. (*Answers:* The writers are middle and high school students. They are writing in answer to the question, What can individuals do to bring about greater understanding between different racial and ethnic groups?)

2. *Part b.* Have a student read the instructions. Then ask the class to silently read the paragraph. Find out what students already know about the Holocaust. If they don't know the term, explain that it refers to the systematic genocide of minorities, especially Jews, in Europe under the Nazis.

3. Write the sentences from the *Language Focus* box on the board. Note that a sentence follows each reporting clause or phrase. Have students produce more examples by reporting their ideas from the previous exercise, for example, Melanie suggests that we have an International Day at our school every year. According to one group, schools should teach more foreign languages.

Then ask, *What does this student suggest?* Guide students in using the language for reporting ideas as they answer. List the suggestions from the paragraph on the board as students report them.

Activity 7: Jigsaw Reading

1. *Part a.* If necessary, introduce the term *jigsaw.* Draw puzzle pieces on the board. Point out that when all the pieces are together, they form a complete picture. Have a volunteer read the instruction line. Tell students that in a jigsaw reading, they will read on their own and take notes. Then they will work with a group and report on their readings.

(Continued on page 114.)

Activity 7: Jigsaw Reading *(continued)*

2. *Part b.* Have students number off around the class, from one to six. Tell them to read the suggestion with the same number and to take notes. Suggest that they use the notes still on the board from *Activity 6* as a model.

3. When students finish, have them form groups of six students and report on their readings. Each student in the group should have read a different suggestion. Encourage them to identify cause and effect as they argue their points.

4. *Part c.* After students have reported in their groups, have the recorder read the list of suggestions aloud. The list should then be passed around the group and students can "vote" by marking with a plus sign the two suggestions they prefer. Students should present reasons for their preferences.

5. Have groups identify the two suggestions that they like best and tell why. Record ideas in note form on the board for students to refer to as they do *Activity 8*.

What can individuals do to bring about greater understanding between different racial and ethnic groups?

1
Have lectures in public schools about understanding different cultures; maybe if someone really knew about someone else's culture then they would know why that person acts different.

11th-grader
Middletown High School
Middletown, R.I.

2
Expose children at an early age to different racial and ethnic groups. All through a child's elementary years and high school years, other cultures must be taught in school. If someone is referring to another racial or ethnic group in a negative way tell them how you feel about it. Remaining silent only allows them to think that you believe the same.

11th-grader
Craig High School
Janesville, Wis.

3
For a greater understanding there should be more ads like the ones on MTV that say 'Paper is to recycle (people aren't).' And make more ads with deeper meaning on how to stop prejudice. For example, The Olympics: A Cartoon Ad: A man from Angola is dribbling the basketball, passes it behind his back, and it's picked up by a Chinese who spins it on his finger. Then he passes it to a man from Lithuania, who dribbles between his legs than alleyoops it to Scottie Pippen, who hammers a dunk. He breaks the backboard, and everything is black, and the basketball is sitting there and has a picture of the World on it.

Eighth-grader / Laramie Jr. High School / Laramie, Wyoming

4

I think that individuals need to start getting more involved with the people around them. Learn how to be friendly and get out and meet people. Big, small, fat and tall. It shouldn't matter. These days, kids just need to learn to be open! Kids also need the encouragment of their parents. That right there might be what is really holding the whole process back.

11th-grader
Meridian Independent
School District
Meridian, Texas

5

We can intermix; people who need public housing can also live in the suburbs so the city won't be known as the only place where all the black, Hispanic, and other races live. We should also have groups that encourage people to be proud of who they are. We should encourage people to at least try to like a racial group they dislike for one day.

Seventh-grader / Visitation Academy / St. Louis, Missouri

6

Make sure more classes and areas are racially mixed. Teach children about prejudice at an earlier age and make it clear to them that it is not good. Stop teaching prejudice at home. Learn to settle any disputes without violence and insults.

Eighth-grader • Placerita Jr. High School • Newhall, California

b. Groupwork. Take turns reporting the suggestions. Choose one person in your group to record all of the suggestions.

c. Groupwork. Look over the list of suggestions. Put a plus sign (+) next to the two suggestions you like best. Tell why you think they are good ideas. Then report your group's ideas to the class.

8. Write a Letter

What can your school do to bring about greater understanding between different racial and ethnic groups? Write a letter to your school principal with your suggestions.

Activity 8: Write a Letter

1. On the board, write the school principal's full name, and the address of your school. Model for students how to format a formal letter with an inside address. In diagram form, show the parts of a business letter.

2. Have students work individually or in groups to write their letters. Refer students to the Writers Guide on page 171 to help them get started. Encourage them to spend time collecting ideas, quickwriting, conferring with a partner, etc., before writing a first draft.

Circulate and encourage them to support their ideas by explaining cause and effect. They can also report ideas from the articles they have just read.

3. Help students revise their letters. You may want to put one or two anonymous examples on the overhead projector in order to talk about mechanics (for example, paragraph indentations, proper margins, capital letters). When letters are revised successfully (they need not be perfect) send the letters to your school principal. Invite the principal to respond to the letters either in writing or by visiting the class and talking to your students about their ideas.

Read and discuss the activities with the class. Have each student select an activity. Students can work individually, in pairs, or in groups. When students complete their projects, have them present their work to the class.

Activity Menu

1. Why Build Barriers?

Research a barrier built by people. Find out why it was built and what purpose it served or serves. Collect pictures to show your classmates and tell them what you learned.

2. Take Photographs

Take photographs of different kinds of barriers in your area. Display your pictures with captions identifying the purpose of each barrier.

3. Professor Hugo's Zoo

Imagine Professor Hugo's zoo the following year. What happens when he brings the zoo to Earth? In writing, tell your story of the zoo.

4. Two Points of View

Think of a disagreement you had with another person. Describe the disagreement from your point of view. Then put yourself in the other person's shoes and describe his or her point of view.

5. Set a Goal

Think of something you hope to accomplish in the future. Picture yourself reaching your goal and describe the picture you see in your mind.

6. Write a Diary Entry

What was life like in the internment camps? Look for descriptions of living conditions in one of the camps. Based on the information you collect, write a diary entry from the point of view of someone living in the camp.

7. Overcoming Obstacles

Look for biographical information about Langston Hughes or Sandra Cisneros. Find out about an obstacle they faced and what they accomplished in spite of this obstacle.

As I Grew Older

by Langston Hughes

It was a long time ago.
I have almost forgotten my dream.
But it was there then,
In front of me,
Bright like a sun—
My dream.

And then the wall rose,
Rose slowly,
Slowly,
Between me and my dream.
Rose slowly, slowly,
Dimming,
Hiding,
The light of my dream.
Rose until it touched the sky—
The wall.

Shadow.
I am black.

I lie down in the shadow.
No longer the light of my dream before me,
Above me.
Only the thick wall.
Only the shadow.

My hands!
My dark hands!
Break through the wall!
Find my dream!
Help me to shatter this darkness,
To smash this night,
To break this shadow
Into a thousand lights of sun,
Into a thousand whirling dreams
Of sun!

Those Who Don't
by Sandra Cisneros

Those who don't know any better come into our neighborhood scared. They think we're dangerous. They think we will attack them with shiny knives. They are stupid people who are lost and got here by mistake.

But we aren't afraid. We know the guy with the crooked eye is Davey the Baby's brother, and the tall one next to him in the straw brim,[1] that's Rosa's Eddie V. and the big one that looks like a dumb grown man, he's Fat Boy, though he's not fat anymore nor a boy.

All brown all around, we are safe. But watch us drive into a neighborhood of another color and our knees go shakity-shake and our car windows get rolled up tight and our eyes look straight. Yeah. That is how it goes and goes.

[1] **brim** hat

As I Grew Older

1. Have students look up some information about Hughes in an encyclopedia, or tell them that Hughes (1902–1967) was an African American writer who wrote poetry, fiction, nonfiction, and autobiography. He was prominent in the Harlem Renaissance of the 1920s, when African American artists of all kinds were especially productive.

2. Have students work in small groups and take turns reading sections of the poem to each other. Circulate and encourage students to think about the emotions expressed in each stanza (e.g. frustration, despair, or determination), and to read expressively. Have groups read for the class and compare the readings.

3. *Optional:* Ask groups to write a story to serve as an example of the experience described in the poem. Ask them to consider the following questions: *What was the person's dream? What barriers overshadowed it? How is the person breaking through the barriers to recover the dream?* Ask groups to share their stories with the whole class.

Those Who Don't

1. Write the first sentence from stanza one and stanza two on the board. Ask students what question each of these paragraphs will answer. (Probably, *Why are they scared?* and *Why aren't we afraid?*) Have students work in groups of three to brainstorm and come up with several sentences to complete each of the two paragraphs. Ask volunteers to read their predicted paragraphs.

2. In their groups, have students read the poem to each other. Have groups that wish to do so give dramatic readings for the whole class.

3. Ask students, *What kind of barriers is Cisneros writing about?*

4. *Optional:* Ask students to compare the way the poems by Cisneros and Hughes look on the page. Then ask them to write a prose poem in the style of Cisneros.

Unit 4:

CROSSING BRIDGES

119

Activity 1: Share a Poem

1. *Part a.* Elicit students' ideas about the origin of the painting and the design of the bridge.

2. *Part b.* Read the poem aloud in English and ask students to guess the original language. If there is a Vietnamese speaker in the class, ask this student to read it in both Vietnamese and English.

3. Encourage students to speculate about the girl's destination and reason for leaving. Discuss various possibilities.

Chapter 1: Bridge Designs

1. **Share a Poem**

a. Classwork. Look at the bridge in the painting. Which part of the world do you think the painting is from? Is the bridge design similar to any bridges you have seen before?

b. Read the poem. Where do you think the young woman was going? Why?

Nàng thì dặm khách xa-xăm,	Far, far away she was going
Bạc phan cầu giá,	Across frost-covered bridges
đen rầm ngàn mây	Toward an unknown land

Nguyễn Du from The Tale of Kieu, *1813*

▲▲▲

2. Journal Writing

Think about a bridge you often use or one that you remember well. Write about it in your journal. Draw a sketch of the bridge and describe it in as much detail as you can.

3. Construct an Arch

Materials: *for each team, 1 sheet of graph paper, 2 sheets of construction paper, scissors, two large hardcover textbooks of equal size, 2 sheets of 8.5 × 11 inch paper*

Pairwork. Look at the bridge in the picture. What is its basic design? Your task is to design an arch with shapes you will cut from paper. Follow the instructions on pages 122–123.

Activity 2: Journal Writing

1. Before asking students to write, brainstorm ideas with the class. Talk about local bridges and about bridges students used in other places that they have lived. Ask: *What did the bridge look like? What was it made of? What did it cross? When did you use it?*

2. When students finish writing and sketching their bridges, have them work in pairs or small groups to compare and discuss their bridges.

Activity 3: Construct an Arch

> **Materials:**
> ─────────────────────
> For each team: 1 sheet of graph paper, 2 sheets of construction paper, scissors, two large hardcover textbooks of equal size, two sheets of 8½ × 11 inch paper

1. Direct students' attention to the picture of the Roman arch bridge. Ask, *What is its basic design?* Elicit that the curved shape of the arch is its basic design. (The curve on top is filled in to make a flat roadbed.)

2. Have students choose partners. Distribute the materials. Then have volunteers read the instructions for steps 1 and 2. Circulate as students complete the first two steps.

3. Have a student read step 3 and the hint. Circulate as the teams work. Encourage them to move the shapes around to guess the function of each shape. If teams are unable to figure out how many of each shape they will need, give them the additional hint that they will need 10 of the first shape (A), 2 of the second shape (B), and one of the third shape (C). Refer to the finished design only if necessary.

4. Once each team decides how many of each shape to cut out, have them read and complete steps 4 and 5. After all teams have completed step 5, ask teams to report the process they went through to plan their designs.

(Continued on page 122.)

Activity 3: Construct an Arch (continued)

5. Step 6, parts a and b. Have volunteers read the instructions for Step 6. Then have students carry out parts a and b. Elicit the results. (The flat beam design buckles under the weight of the paper clip, but the arch design does not.)

6. Step 6, part c. Ask students to speculate about why the arch design is stronger. Accept all answers. If students do not come up with an explanation, you may want to bring in simple books on bridge design or explain with a diagram that in the arch design, the weight of the load is distributed along the arch, and then transmitted into the ground.

7. Step 7. Tell students to read over the steps for *Activity 3*, and the notes that they took for Step 5. Have them list the basic steps that they took. Write some connecting words on the board and remind students to connect the parts of their report with transitional expressions like these:

First, next, after that, finally;

When/After/As soon as we _____, we _____.

8. Give students an opportunity to share their reports, either by reading aloud to the class or by posting on a bulletin board.

Step 1: Make a sketch of the basic design.

Step 2: Look at the shapes below. Draw the same three shapes on your sheet of graph paper. Cut them out. These shapes are the patterns for making your basic arch blocks.

Hint:

You will need only one of shape C

Step 3: You will need a total of 13 blocks. Decide how many blocks from each shape you will need to make an arch design. Place your graph paper patterns on the construction paper and use a pencil to outline enough blocks to lay out your arch.

Step 4: Cut your blocks out of the construction paper. Arrange them on a flat surface in the shape of an arch.

Step 5: Discuss each of these questions with your partner. Take notes on your answers:

a. How did you plan your design?

b. How did you decide how many of each shape you needed?

Step 6: Compare an arch bridge design with a simple flat beam design.

a. Set up two hardcover texbooks of the same size on a flat surface about eight inches apart. Place a flat sheet of plain 8.5 x 11 inch paper (not construction paper) across the two ends. Place a paper clip in the center of the paper. Observe what happens.

b. Bend the paper in the shape of an arch and fix it between the two books. Brace the ends of the paper against the book bindings, as shown in the illustration. Tape a paper clip to the center of the paper arch. Observe what happens.

c. Compare the strength of the two designs. Which one is stronger? Why?

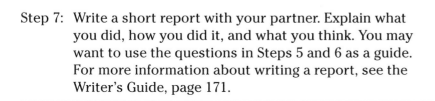

Step 7: Write a short report with your partner. Explain what you did, how you did it, and what you think. You may want to use the questions in Steps 5 and 6 as a guide. For more information about writing a report, see the Writer's Guide, page 171.

First, we made a sketch of the basic design. Next...

Activity 4: Identify

1. *Part a.* After students consider the four bridge designs, have them work with partners or in small groups to exchange ideas. Then ask the whole class to pool their ideas. (*Possible answers:* The cantilever is different from the rigid beam in that each end of the cantilever bridge is supported independently. There is a space in the middle of the bridge between the two cantilevers. The suspension differs from the arch in that the arch is rigid, whereas the cables of a suspension bridge hang freely from the supporting towers.)

2. *Part b.* Have students discuss the bridge designs with a partner. Elicit answers.

3. *Optional:* Have students reread their journal entries for *Activity 1* and look at their sketches. Ask, *What do you think is the basic design of the bridge that you wrote about?* Have volunteers sketch on the board the bridge that they wrote about and describe it briefly to the class.

4. Identify

a. On your own. You have already considered two types of basic bridge design: the **arch** and the **simple beam**. The drawings below illustrate two more complex bridge designs. How are they different from the simple forms?

cantilever ▼

suspension ▲

b. Look at these photographs and drawings. Identify the type of bridge design for each. Compare your answers with those of a classmate.

Old London Bridge, c. 1750 ▶

FLUVIUS

South warke

▲ Quebec Bridge

◀ Vermont covered bridge

Bridges over a Peruvian River, c. 1752 ▶

Activity 5: Write

1. *Part a.* Ask a volunteer to read the instructions. Then give students a few minutes to read the caption and look at the photograph of the Brooklyn Bridge. Ask other students the questions, and elicit any other information students might already have about the bridge. Students should recognize from the previous activity that the Brooklyn Bridge is a suspension bridge.

2. *Language Focus.* Ask students, *What else would you like to know about this bridge?* Brainstorm questions about the bridge, and write them on the board.

Who built it?

Where is it?

What does the bridge connect?

Point out or elicit the different word order for questions about the subject (no change from sentence word order) and questions about the verb (helping verb or a form of <u>be</u> precedes the subject).

3. Ask students to read the facts. Brainstorm questions based on this information and add them to the list on the board. Have several students model asking and answering questions. Then have students work in pairs for additional practice. Circulate as students practice and guide their formation of *wh-* questions.

4. *Optional:* Have students look up information about questions not answered in the information box.

(Continued on page 127.)

The Brooklyn Bridge, completed 1883

<table>
<tr><td>5.</td><td>**Write**</td></tr>
</table>

a. Classwork. Discuss the bridge in this photograph. What does the information in the box tell you about it? What is its basic design?

b. Write a short description of the Brooklyn Bridge based on the photograph and the facts in the box. Add more information from other sources if you want to.

Facts About the Brooklyn Bridge

Location: East River between Brooklyn and Manhattan in New York City

Length: main span 1,595 ft. (486 m.)

Materials: steel, concrete

Dates of Construction: 1869–83

Chief Engineers: John A. Roebling and Washington Roebling

Language Focus:

Getting Information

Using *Wh-* questions.

When did construction of the Brooklyn Bridge begin?

5. *Part b.* Brainstorm some possible audiences for the writing (e.g., a personal friend, a tourist visiting the bridge, an historical account). Ask them to select details appropriate for their audience.

6. When students finish writing, put several anonymous examples on the overhead and have a discussion about the information that was included. Point out or elicit any problems with grammar or mechanics. Then have students revise their paragraphs.

1. Have a volunteer read the introduction. Ask students to think about the poems they have read so far and to give examples of common things with symbolic meaning (for example, waves in Saigyo's poem, *The Waves of Matsuyama* or the road in the woods in Frost's poem, *The Road Not Taken*).

2. Brainstorm with students some symbolic bridges that people have to cross in their lifetimes, and write ideas on the board (for example, moving, graduating, starting a new job, getting married).

Activity 1: Brainstorm

Ask a volunteer to read the instructions and the three examples. Point out that we often use the *-ing* form of the verb (the gerund) when we want to name an activity. Have students work in groups to brainstorm and make their lists.

Activity 2: Quickwrite

1. *Part a.* Review quickwriting with students. Tell them to write for five minutes without stopping. The goal of quickwriting is to capture ideas, so they should not think about correctness at this point. Tell them that if they get stuck they can write a key phrase such as *crossing bridges* until the next thought comes to them.

2. Model quickwriting on the board by writing some ideas about a time when you faced a change. Then use paper and pencil to continue quickwriting along with your students.

3. *Part b.* Circulate and join in as students talk about their experiences. Encourage students to ask each other questions and to explain their experiences in detail before they fill out the chart on a separate piece of paper.

Chapter 2: Facing Change

*B*ecause bridges make it possible to move from one place to another, they often symbolize change. Sometimes people have to leave a place or make a change in their lives whether they want to or not. In this chapter, you will think and read about facing these kinds of changes.

◇1. Brainstorm

Groupwork. Think of some changes you have already faced in your life. What other changes do you think you will face in the future? List your ideas on another piece of paper.

Examples: moving to a new place to live

having a new brother or sister

going to a new school

> **Study Strategy:**
> **Brainstorming**
> See page 164.

◇2. Quickwrite

a. On your own. Think about a time when you had to leave a place or start something new. Quickwrite for five minutes about your experience.

b. Pairwork. Read your quickwriting aloud to a partner. Invite your partner to ask questions about the details. Then work with your partner to make notes on the right side of an experience chart like this.

What happened?	
How did you feel about it then?	
How do you feel about it now?	

c. Groupwork. Get together with another pair. Tell your partner's story.

▲▲▲

3. Preview

Classwork. The story you are going to read was written by Ernest Hemingway. The photographs below give you some ideas about the author's life. What do they tell you about him? Discuss each item before you read the story. What can you conclude about Ernest Hemingway? What kind of person was he? What did he write about?

A Pictorial Biography of Ernest Hemingway (1899-1961)

THE SUN ALSO RISES

Daily Press
Bloody Civil War Breaks Out in S...
Fascis... Republica... Governm...

Activity 3: Preview

1. Have a student read the instructions. Give students time to look over the pictures; answer any questions that they might have.

2. Review the language for making speculations about the past. On the board, write

He might have lived in _____

He could have been a _____

He must have _____

3. Ask volunteers to complete the sentences on the board by identifying a picture and making speculations based on it. For example:

That's the Eiffel tower. He might have lived in Paris.

He's using crutches. He must have been wounded.

4. Have students work with partners to make speculations. Then have the whole class pool ideas. Elicit their conclusions about Hemingway and his work.

Activity 4: Shared Reading

1. Draw students' attention to the picture. Ask them to guess who the characters are and what is happening. You may want to read the story aloud the first time as students listen.

2. Draw a story map on the board and elicit the setting, characters, conflict, and action of the story. (*Answers:* <u>Where and When</u>—Spain, Ebro River, Easter Sunday during the Spanish Civil War. <u>Who</u>—an old man of 76 from a nearby village and a younger man, probably a soldier. <u>Conflict</u>—The younger man wants the old man to cross the river to escape danger. <u>Action</u>—The two talk, the young man tries to persuade the old man to leave. The old man won't go, and the younger man gives up.)

3. *Optional:* For the second reading, have students work in pairs and read paragraphs of the story to each other.

4. Shared Reading

THE OLD MAN AT THE BRIDGE
by Ernest Hemingway

An old man with steel rimmed spectacles[1] and very dusty clothes sat by the side of the road. There was a pontoon bridge across the river and carts, trucks, and men, women and children were crossing it. The mule-drawn carts staggered[2] up the steep bank from the bridge with soldiers helping push against the spokes of the wheels. The trucks ground up and away heading out of it all and the peasants[3] plodded along in the ankle deep dust. But the old man sat there without moving. He was too tired to go any farther.

"Where do you come from?" I asked him.

"From San Carlos,[4]" he said, and smiled.

That was his native town and so it gave him pleasure to mention it and he smiled.

"I was taking care of animals," he explained.

"Oh," I said, not quite understanding.

"Yes," he said, "I stayed, you see, taking care of animals. I was the last one to leave the town of San Carlos."

He did not look like a shepherd nor a herdsman and I looked at his black dusty clothes and his gray dusty face and his steel rimmed spectacles and said, "What animals were they?"

"Various animals," he said, and shook his head. "I had to leave them."

I was watching the bridge and the African looking country of the Ebro Delta[5] and

[1]**spectacles**   eyeglasses
[2]**staggered**   walked with great difficulty
[3]**peasants**   poor farmers or farm workers
[4]**San Carlos**   coastal town in eastern Spain
[5]**Ebro Delta**   an area of flat, rich land near the mouth of the Ebro River in eastern Spain

wondering how long it would be before we would see the enemy, and listening all the while for the first noises that would signal that ever mysterious event called contact,[6] and the old man still sat there.

"What animals were they?" I asked.

"There were three animals altogether," he explained. "There were two goats and a cat and then there were four pairs of pigeons."

"And you had to leave them?" I asked.

"Yes. Because of the artillery.[7] The captain told me to go because of the artillery."

"And you have no family?" I asked, watching the far end of the bridge where a few last carts were hurrying down the slope of the bank.

"No," he said, "only the animals I stated. The cat, of course, will be all right. A cat can look out for itself, but I cannot think what will become of the others."

"What politics have you?[8]" I asked.

"I am without politics," he said. "I am seventy-six years old. I have come twelve kilometers now and I think now I can go no further."

"This is not a good place to stop," I said. "If you can make it, there are trucks up the road where it forks for Tortosa."

"I will wait a while," he said, "and then I will go. Where do the trucks go?"

"Towards Barcelona," I told him.

"I know no one in that direction," he said. "But thank you very much. Thank you again very much."

He looked at me very blankly and tiredly, then said, having to share his worry with some one, "The cat will be all right, I am sure. There is no need to be unquiet about the cat. But the others. Now what do you think about the others?"

"Why they'll probably come through it all right."

"You think so?"

"Why not?" I said, watching the far bank where now there were no carts.

"But what will they do under the artillery when I was told to leave because of the artillery?"

"Did you leave the dove[9] cage unlocked?" I asked.

"Yes."

"Then they'll fly."

"Yes, certainly they'll fly. But the others. It's better not to think about the others," he said.

"If you are rested I would go," I urged. "Get up and try to walk now."

"Thank you," he said and got to his feet, swayed from side to side and then sat down backwards in the dust.

"I was taking care of animals," he said dully, but no longer to me. "I was only taking care of animals."

There was nothing to do about him. It was Easter Sunday[10] and the Fascists[11] were advancing toward the Ebro. It was a gray overcast day with a low ceiling[12] so their planes were not up.

That and the fact that cats know how to look after themselves was all the good luck that old man would ever have.

[6]**artillery**	large, heavy guns
[7]**contact**	in war, the first exchange of fire
[8]**What politics have you?**	What political system do you believe in?
[9]**dove**	a family of birds, including pigeons; also a symbol for peace
[10]**Easter Sunday**	a Christian holiday that celebrates renewal of life
[11]**Fascists**	in Europe during the 1930's and 1940's, any political group that supported a right wing military dictatorship
[12]**a low ceiling**	cloudy conditions that make it difficult for airplane pilots to see the ground

Activity 5: Locate

Optional: After students locate the places on their own, sketch an outline of the map on the board, and have volunteers label it with the places.

Activity 6: Retell

1. With the class, discuss possible places to break the story, but let pairs decide how they want to divide the narrative. After pairs of students retell the story and share their ideas about the questions, have them join other pairs to compare ideas. Answers will vary. (*Some possible answers:* (1) He had to leave his home town. He had to leave creatures to which he had emotional attachments and responsibility. (2) He worried about what would happen to the animals. (3) He didn't know anyone in Barcelona. (4) He stayed by the river.)

Activity 7: Interpret

1. *Part a.* Draw students' attention to the picture again, and ask volunteers to describe the situation. Ask, *What is going to happen soon?* (a battle; bombardment by Fascist aircraft) Ask for students' ideas about how the young man and the old man were feeling while they were talking.

2. Have a student read the instructions. Then ask volunteers to read the examples in the speech and thought bubbles. Have them experiment with emotional and flat readings, and ask the class to give feedback about which readings sound more realistic.

(*Continued on page 133.*)

5. Locate

On your own. Find the places in the story on this map of eastern Spain.

6. Retell

Pairwork. Divide the story into two parts. Then take turns retelling each part. Discuss these questions with your partner.

What change did the old man have to face?

What did he worry about most?

Why didn't he want to go to Barcelona?

What did he do in the end?

7. Interpret

a. Pairwork. Read the whole story again. Then look at the lines of dialogue on the left side of the chart on the next page. Read what each character said on the left, then write what you think the character was *really* thinking. You might want to write more than one possible thought for each line of dialogue.

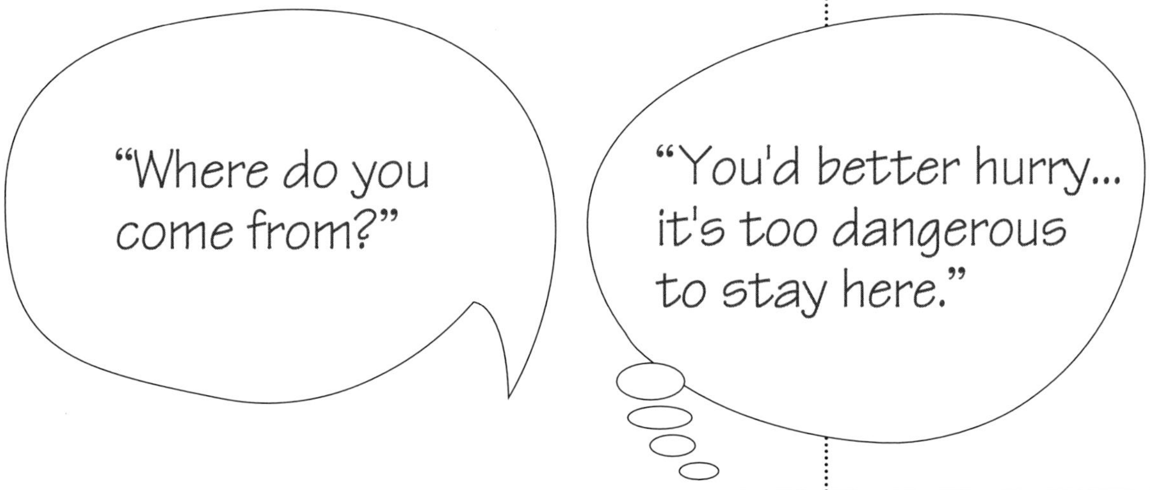

"Where do you come from?"
"You'd better hurry... it's too dangerous to stay here."

What they said	What they were thinking
Narrator: Where do you come from?	*You'd better hurry...*
Old Man: From San Carlos. I was taking care of animals.	
Narrator: Oh.	
Narrator: This is not a good place to stop.	
Old Man: I will wait a while, and then I will go.	
Narrator: If you are rested I would go. Get up and try to walk now.	
Old Man: I was taking care of animals. I was only taking care of animals.	

b. Get together with another pair. Compare the right side of your charts and discuss any differences. If you wish, add ideas from your classmates to your own chart.

c. In the same group, prepare to present one set of your "What they were thinking" ideas to the rest of the class. Follow these steps.

Activity 7: Interpret *(continued)*

3. *Part b.* Distribute AM 4/1. Circulate as students work in pairs and small groups. Encourage them to go back to the text for information.

4. *Part c.* Have a volunteer read aloud the instructions for this part. Tell group members to pool their ideas and to decide which to use for the right side of the chart.

(Continued on page 134.)

Activity 7: Interpret *(continued)*

5. *Part d.* Write the sentence from the *Language Focus* Box on the board. Explain that we often use <u>may</u>, <u>might</u>, or <u>could</u> plus the base form of the verb to express what we think will possibly happen in the future. Ask volunteers what might happen to the bridge, the old man, and the animals. Write their ideas on the board as future possibilities.

6. *Optional:* Ask students to imagine that they are the young officer. Tell them to write a diary entry or a letter telling briefly what happened and then speculating about the immediate future, for example, *They might keep the bridge there for a while. The old man may change his mind and cross the river after he rests.*

> **Language Focus:**
> ### *Expressing Future Possibility*
> The goats may get caught.

1. Decide on two members of the group to role play the conversation between the old man and the narrator. These two characters should sit on chairs facing each other and read lines from the left side of the chart. Be sure to pause after each line.

2. The other two members will stand behind the main characters and read the "What they were thinking" lines aloud.

3. Rehearse your presentation two or three times before presenting it to the class.

d. Classwork. Discuss what you think might happen to the bridge, the old man, and the animals in the story. Offer some ideas and listen to those of your classmates. Then write down your own ideas.

8. Share Ideas

Groupwork. What did the narrator do when the old man decided not to move on? Was it the right thing to do? What would you have done? Choose the action you would have taken. Explain your choice to the group.

I would have...

a. left the old man alone

b. forced the old man to move across the bridge

c. helped the old man go back to get the goats

d. waited for the old man to rest, then tried to persuade him again

e. (your own idea) _____

9. Journal Writing

a. On your own. How did you feel about the two characters in the story? What do you think the author feels? Support your opinions by referring to parts of the story.

b. How did you like the story? Explain your reaction.

Language Focus

Past Conjecture

I would have tried harder.

Activity 8: Share Ideas

1. Have a volunteer read the last paragraph of the story aloud. Then ask, *What did the narrator do when the old man decided not to move on?* Ask for students' ideas about whether the narrator acted properly. Then have students read aloud the choices.

2. Write the example sentence from the *Language Focus* box on the board. Label the grammatical elements: would have + past participle.

3. Have students work in groups to discuss their choices. Remind them about the ideas they talked about in *Activity 6*, which can serve as a basis for their decisions. Tell them to give reasons for their decisions. For example:

I would have waited for the old man to rest, and then tried to persuade him again. He might have changed his mind when he felt better.

Guide their use of language for speculating about past events.

Activity 9: Journal Writing

1. Before students write, ask for their ideas about the questions. Ask students: *What kind of person is the young officer? Does he feel empathy for the old man?* Have them find places in the text that show the officer's awareness of the old man's feelings and situation, for example "He was too tired to go any farther." (Para. 1)

2. Circulate as students write. Encourage them to support their opinions with material from the text. After students write in their journals, have them read their entries aloud to a partner.

Draw students' attention to the art. Ask students: *What are some of the differences between childhood and adulthood? What responsibilities and privileges do children have? What responsibilities and privileges do adults have?* Accept all answers. Then have a volunteer read the paragraph and the discussion question. Elicit students' ideas about the importance of "coming of age" ceremonies.

Activity 1: Explore

1. *Part a.* Read the instruction. Then ask volunteers to describe the pictures. If students have experienced a coming of age ceremony, ask them to tell about their experiences.

2. *Optional:* If feasible, bring in music from some of these ceremonies, such as "Las Mananitas," or "Pomp and Circumstance" and play it for your students.

(Continued on page 137.)

Chapter 3: Transitions

*M*any cultures have special ceremonies that mark the change between childhood and adulthood. These "coming of age" ceremonies form a kind of bridge, over which young people must pass to become adult members of their community. Do you think these bridges are important and necessary?

1. Explore

a. Classwork. Look at the examples of coming of age ceremonies in different cultures throughout this unit. About how old are the young people? What are they doing? How do you think they feel? Share ideas and experiences with your classmates.

b. Groupwork. Describe what happens in a typical coming of age ceremony in your culture or another one you know about. Here are some questions to think about.

> How do people dress?
>
> Who performs the ceremony?
>
> What does the young person have to do?
>
> How do people celebrate?
>
> What kinds of food do they eat?

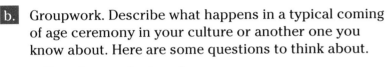

2. Journal Writing

On your own. Write about a ceremony or party you have had. It can be your own coming of age ceremony or any other important moment that marked a change in your life. Describe what happened and how you felt.

Activity 1: Explore *(continued)*

3. *Part b.* After students work in groups, have them form larger groups. Ask students to report on another student's ceremony or party.

Activity 2: Journal Writing

When students finish writing, have them share their journal entries with a partner.

Activity 3: Listen

1. To prepare for the listening, ask students: *What are some symbols of adult status in the United States?* Write ideas on the board. Ask students to look at some of the personal belongings that they carry. Have them work with partners to analyze which items indicate adult status. You may want to participate with some of your own items. Pool ideas and add to the list on the board. (*Possible items:* driver's license or car keys, a bill, a <u>To Do</u> list, cosmetics.)

2. Have students look over the cluster diagram before they listen. Then ask, *What information do you need to complete the diagram?* Elicit ways a graduation ceremony is like other coming of age ceremonies and ask for examples of religious ceremonies.

3. Play the tape while students listen without writing. Then play the tape again while students listen and complete the diagram. Replay as needed. On the board, write two headings: (1) Ways it is like other coming of age ceremonies, (2) Examples. Have volunteers supply information from the listening.

4. *Part a.* Have students use their notes in the cluster diagram as an outline as they talk. Model this first by using the upper part of the cluster diagram, which is still on the board.

5. *Part b.* Have a student read the instructions. Tell students to create a new category for their own ceremony if necessary. The new category should be on the same level as Graduation and Religious Ceremonies in the cluster diagram.

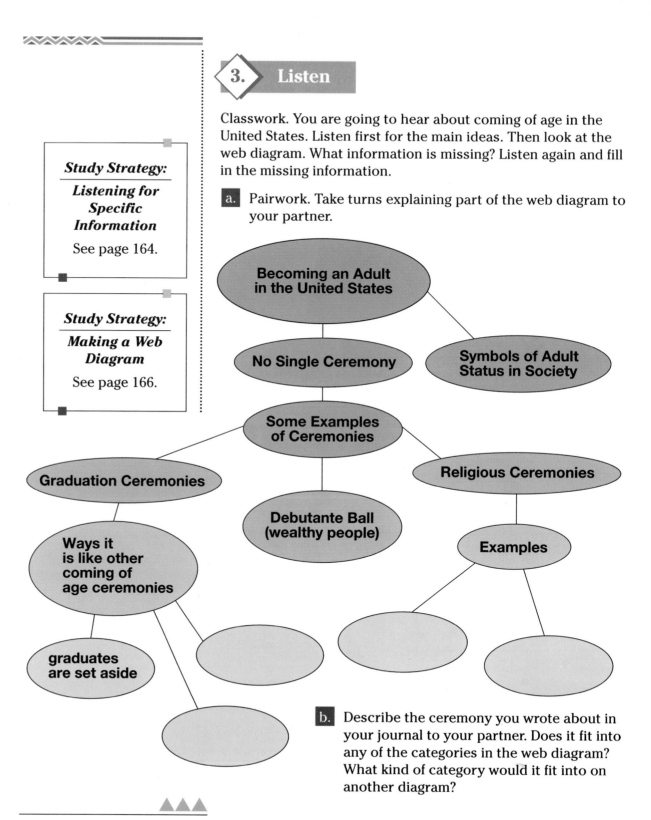

3. Listen

Classwork. You are going to hear about coming of age in the United States. Listen first for the main ideas. Then look at the web diagram. What information is missing? Listen again and fill in the missing information.

a. Pairwork. Take turns explaining part of the web diagram to your partner.

Study Strategy:
Listening for Specific Information
See page 164.

Study Strategy:
Making a Web Diagram
See page 166.

Becoming an Adult in the United States

No Single Ceremony

Symbols of Adult Status in Society

Some Examples of Ceremonies

Graduation Ceremonies

Religious Ceremonies

Debutante Ball (wealthy people)

Ways it is like other coming of age ceremonies

Examples

graduates are set aside

b. Describe the ceremony you wrote about in your journal to your partner. Does it fit into any of the categories in the web diagram? What kind of category would it fit into on another diagram?

4. **Shared Reading**

4. **Shared Reading**

As you read this article, think about how the author feels as she writes about coming of age in her culture. Whose personal experience does she use as an example?

"I Felt Like a Queen"
by Suzanne Flores

Can you imagine planning your next birthday party for almost a year in advance, then, when your birthday arrives, wearing a long gown, dancing all night to a live orchestra,[1] and celebrating for two days? Many Mexican girls do just that on their fifteenth birthday, their *quince años.*[2]

An invitation to a *quince años* is an honor; it means not only getting all dressed up and having a great time, but also taking part in a ceremony that welcomes a girl into the adult world. In a way, it might be compared to the "coming out" party that some families have in the United States. Here, only rather rich "society" people have such parties, but in Mexico, both rich and poor families might have a *quince años*, hoping that it will improve the girl's chances of making an advantageous marriage.[3] A Mexican family might have to spend as much for this birthday as for a girl's wedding. If the family cannot afford it, they ask for help from godmothers and godfathers.[4] For instance, if you are asked to be the cake godmother, you bring the cake. When a Mexican *señorita* descends the stairs to the strains of *"Las Mañanitas"* and the flash of camera bulbs, then dances the "Blue Danube" with her father, there is no doubt she has come of age. From now on, she will change from a young girl in knee socks and braids to a young woman in high heels and make-up, and more than just her clothes will be different: The way she is treated will change, too. People will no longer see her as a little

[1]**live orchestra**	a real orchestra present at the party, not recorded beforehand
[2]***quince años***	fifteenth birthday, also called *quincenera*
[3]**an advantageous marriage**	a marriage that will improve one's social and economic position
[4]**godmother and godfather**	special adults in a child's life; sponsors at a Christian baptism

Activity 4: Shared Reading

1. Have students look at the picture and speculate about where this ceremony is taking place and what is being celebrated. Then ask a student to read the first paragraph aloud.

2. Have students stay with their partners from *Activity 4* and take turns reading the article aloud to each other. To give students a purpose for reading, ask them to find examples of the way life changed for the girl after her quince años party. When students finish reading, make a class list of the changes students discovered in their reading.

girl who can play games and help with the chores but as a person getting ready to become a wife and mother who will soon have adult responsibilities. This party recognizes that important step in life.

The *quince años* party happens mostly in smaller cities and towns, where tradition remains strong. It is part of the traditional view that a girl, in contrast to a boy, will not go to college or have a job but will soon marry and have children. This is her "graduation" ceremony—it says that she is ready to start dating and looking for a husband.

My Mexican mother-in-law still vividly[5] remembers her *quince años*, although it happened many years ago:

[5]**vividly**   in full detail

"Shortly after my fourteenth birthday, everyone began asking if we were going to have a *quince años*. Of course we were! We began by looking at gown patterns for me and all my cousins, right down to the youngest, since we all wanted to dress up. Everyone loved the planning and the excitement that began to build as we set the date for the Mass[6] at church, saw the seamstress, searched for our gentlemen dancing partners, and rehearsed the waltz with them. We did not rent a ballroom but decided to have the party in the patio of my house. The neighbors all helped to clean and decorate it, knowing that this party was for everyone.

"Finally, it was the morning of my birthday, bringing with it the first surprise of the day. Imagine waking up to live orchestra music and being the center of everyone's attention: I felt like a queen surrounded by all her subjects.[7] My uncle played in an orchestra and brought eight of his friends to serenade me with the Mexican birthday song, "*Las Mañanitas.*" Then my parents fed everyone a breakfast of *atole* (a thick, puddinglike drink) and *tamales* (steamed corn bread with a filling of either fruit or spicy meat).

"At noon we all went to church for the Mass of thanks and a beautiful speech by the *padre*[8] about how my parents felt seeing me pass from girlhood to this age so full of hopes and dreams. Then everyone was hugging me, and we were off to the photographer. Back home, I was surrounded by family, friends, and presents. We had more food—consomme,[9] rice, chicken *mole* (a spicy sauce of at least twelve ingredients, including nuts, chilies, chocolate, and spices), *tamales*, and drinks—and then the party began in earnest.[10]

"My father led me out for the first waltz. I danced all night, and the next day the party continued, with big chunks of birthday cake and more surprises in the celebration of my *quince años*. The young man who was my partner for the second dance later became my husband."

from *Faces* Magazine, February, 1988

---

[6]**Mass**   in the Catholic church, the main religious ceremony
[7]**subjects**   people ruled by a king or queen
[8]***padre***   Catholic religious leader; priest
[9]**consomme**   a clear soup; broth of meat or vegetables
[10]**in earnest** in a serious way

Activity 5: Share Ideas

1. Have pairs of students join other pairs to form groups of four or six students. Circulate as students discuss the questions, and participate in the groups. Invite students to elaborate on their answers by asking them further questions.

2. When students have finished sharing their ideas, ask them to report some of their ideas to the class.

Activity 6: Evaluate

1. *Part a.* Have a student read the quotation aloud. Ask students to quickwrite for a few minutes about their reactions to the traditional view of girls' futures. Then have them compare their ideas with a classmate.

2. *Part b.* Draw the chart on the board and ask pairs of students to make a similar chart and to write the modern view in the right hand column. Elicit their ideas and write them in the chart.

3. *Part c.* Ask for students' opinions of the traditional and modern views and make a list on the board of the advantages and disadvantages of each view. Students may enjoy exploring compromise positions that accommodate the advantages of both views. Accept all opinions without judgement.

---

5. Share Ideas

Groupwork. Share ideas about the reading with your classmates. Here are some questions you might think about.

a. What is the purpose of the quince años in Mexican society? Do you think it is important or necessary?

b. How do poor families manage to give their daughters a quince años?

c. Why do you think the quince años happens mostly in smaller cities and towns?

d. Which part of the ceremony do you like best? Which part do you like least? Explain why.

6. Evaluate

a. Pairwork. Read this quotation from the story. What is your personal reaction to this traditional view? Discuss your opinion with your partner.

"It is part of the traditional view that a girl, in contrast to a boy, will not go to college or have a job but will soon marry and have children. This is her 'graduation' ceremony—it says that she is ready to start dating and looking for a husband."

b. Compare the traditional view expressed in the quotation with the modern view. Write your ideas in a chart like this.

Traditional View	Modern View
Girls will not go to college.	
Girls will not get jobs.	
Women are mainly wives and mothers.	

c. Discuss the advantages and disadvantages of both views.

7. Research

a. Pairwork. Find out what older people remember about a traditional coming of age ceremony. Follow these steps:

1. Arrange to interview a relative or older person in your community. Set up a special time and place for the interview.

2. Prepare your questions in advance. Try to find out as many details as you can about the older person's experience.

3. Prepare to take notes or tape record your interview.

4. Write a report based on your interview. Summarize the answers to your questions, and use quotes from the interview to make it interesting. Conclude your report by describing what it was like to interview this person. What did you learn? How did the person feel about it?

b. Classwork. Put your reports together. Add drawings, postcards, or copies of photographs if you can. Publish a class collection of "coming of age" ceremonies in different times and places. For more information about publishing a collection of writing, refer to the Writer's Guide on page 174.

Activity 7: Research

1. *Part a.* Set aside class time over a two- or three-week period for students to plan and work on their projects. Let them know that this is independent work, but that you are available as a resource at each step. Establish a deadline for each step of the project and give students feedback as they complete each step.

2. *Step 1.* Ask students to report about whom they plan to interview, when, and where. To assist students who have not been able to locate a subject, brainstorm with them about people whom they have met through their jobs, church, or school activities. *Steps 2 and 3:* Have students reread the example in "I Felt Like a Queen" and make a list of questions that the article answers. Students can brainstorm additional interview questions in groups. Have them role play using the tape recorder or taking notes. Remind students to ask their subjects for copies of memorabilia such as photographs, postcards, and newspaper clippings which they can use in their reports.

3. *Step 4:* Have students work with a partner or in small groups to develop the first drafts of their report. Encourage them to listen to each others' interview tapes and share information and memorabilia, and to give feedback about what they found most interesting in the material.

4. *Part b.* Make copies of the collection for students to present to the people whom they interviewed.

Have a volunteer read the introduction. Then ask students to take a few minutes to think about an important friendship in their own lives. On the board, write some questions to stimulate thinking, such as, *When did you become friends? What do you like about this person? What activities do you share? If you don't live near each other, how do you stay connected?* Have students quickwrite about their friendships and then share their thoughts with a partner.

Activity 1: List

1. On the board, write the two examples from the *Language Focus* box about forming adjectives from nouns. Note that *-ity* and *-ness* are noun suffixes that indicate a quality or condition. Brainstorm some other examples and write each on the board in two columns labelled *adjective* and *noun.* For example, loyal/loyalty; reliable/reliability; supportive/supportiveness; cheerful/cheerfulness.

2. *Part a.* Have students make their lists of important qualities in a friend. Ask volunteers for a few examples of qualities. Encourage them to name the qualities in the ways shown in the example. Add new qualities to the list on the board.

3. *Part b.* Have students form groups of four to compare and expand their lists. When they have finished, ask several students to add to the list on the board.

4. Ask students which qualities they feel are the most important. Express your own opinion and tell about a time in your own experience when a particular quality was very important. Ask students for examples to illustrate the importance of the qualities that they selected.

Activity 2: Journal Writing

Have a volunteer read the directions. Encourage students to support their ideas with an example, either an incident that actually occurred, or one that they can imagine.

(Continued on page 145.)

Chapter 4: Life Spans

𝒯he span of a bridge is the distance from one side to another. A person's life span is the length of time between birth and death. Relationships between friends and relatives are a lot like bridges. In this chapter, you will read about some of the ways people build new bridges or repair old ones in order to stay connected to the past, the future, and to one another.

1. List

a. Pairwork. What qualities do you think are important in a friend? State each quality two ways.

Example: I think it's important for a friend to be honest. Honesty is an important quality.

List as many qualities as you can:

Our list of important qualities: ___*honesty*___, _____,

_____, _____, _____

b. Get together with another pair. Compare your lists. See if you want to add any more qualities to your list.

Language Focus:

Forming Adjectives from Nouns

generosity—
    generous
honesty—
    honest
importance—
    important

2. Journal Writing

On your own. Choose the one quality from the list you made that you personally feel is *most* important. Write about it in your journal. Give an example situation in which this quality is important.

3. Define

Groupwork. Suggest ways of finishing these sentences. Make as many different sentences as you can. Share your group's sentences with the class.

Friendship is knowing that _____

An example of friendship is when _____

▲▲▲

4. **Share a Song**

Classwork. Read this song aloud.

YOU'VE GOT A FRIEND

by Carole King

When you're down, and troubled
And you need some love and care
And nothin', nothin' is going right
Close your eyes and think of me
And soon I will be there to
Brighten up even your darkest night.
You just call out my name
And you know wherever I am
I'll come runnin' to see you again.
Winter, spring, summer, or fall,
All you have to do is call
And I'll be there. You've got a friend.
If the sky above you
Grows dark and full of clouds
And that ol' north wind begins to blow
Keep your head together
And call my name out loud,
Soon you'll hear me knockin' at your door
You just call out my name
And you know wherever I am
I'll come runnin' to see you again.
Winter, spring, summer, or fall,
All you have to do is call
And I'll be there, yes, I will
Now, ain't[1] it good to know that you've
got a friend

When people can be so cold?
They'll hurt you, yes, and desert[2] you
And take your soul if you let them
Oh, but don't you let them.
You just call out my name
And you know, wherever I am
I'll come runnin' to see you again.
Winter, spring, summer, or fall,
All you have to do is call
And I'll be there, yes, I will
You've got a friend. You've got a friend.
Ain't it good to know you've got a friend?

[1]**ain't** isn't it, in nonstandard English
[2]**desert** abandon, leave cruelly

Carole King (1942-)

Carole King was born in New York City, and began to play the piano at the age of four. As a teenager, she liked to hang out at rock and roll concerts, and started a group of her own. At Queens College, she met Gerry Coffin, with whom she began to write songs and who later became her husband. Together, they wrote some of the most popular songs of the 1960's and 1970's, including "Locomotion," "Will You Still Love Me Tomorrow," and "Up On The Roof."

Activity 3: Define

1. Have students work in groups to share ideas and examples that they wrote about in their journals.

2. Ask a volunteer to read the instructions and the sentence frames. Ask each group to select one person to make notes, and then to talk about ways of finishing the sentences. Suggest that students focus on ideas that came out of their journal writing and discussion.

3. When groups finish sharing ideas, collect their ideas in a list on the board.

Activity 4: Share a Song

1. Direct students' attention to the biographical information about Carole King on page 145, and elicit any other knowledge students may have about her. If possible, bring in a tape of some of King's songs and play some of them for your students. Ask them which of the songs they like and why.

2. Play "You've Got a Friend" as students read along. When you play the song the second time, sing the refrain: *"Winter, spring, summer, or fall . . ."* and encourage students to sing along with you. With the students, read the lyrics aloud several times, or have students work in groups of three and take turns reading the three sections of the song aloud to each other. Then play the tape again and with the class sing along for the whole song.

Activity 5: Share Ideas

1. Ask, *What is Carole King's idea of a friend?* Elicit several interpretations and write them on the board. Ask students to compare King's ideas with their own definitions, which should still be on the board from *Activity 3.*

2. Have students discuss questions *b* and *c* in small groups. Circulate and participate in the discussions. Encourage students to think of examples that they have experienced or observed when they discuss the ways in which friends support each other.

3. *Optional:* Ask students to select two or three lines from the song that they like and find meaningful. Ask them to write in their journals about what these lines mean to them, and which of their friends they associate them with.

Activity 6: Role Play

Brainstorm some situations with the class before students begin to write. Students' journal entries from *Activity 2* may also stimulate their ideas.

Activity 7: Share a Poem

1. Ask students to read the title of the poem by Daisy Zamora and the lines by Li-Tai-Po. Ask students to speculate about the narrator: *What do you think she and her sister have in common? What do you think the narrator wants to happen?* Write students' ideas on the board.

2. Have students listen to the Spanish version. Ask them, *How does the poem make you feel?* Ask them to quickwrite their impressions of the mood that the poem creates, and then to share these impressions with a partner.

3. Pronounce *Danbury, Hamden, Middletown, Hartford,* and *Meriden* for your students. Then have students work in groups of four and take turns reading stanzas of the poem to each other, beginning with the stanza by Li-Tai-Po.

(Continued on page 147.)

---

5. Share Ideas

Classwork. Discuss your reactions to the song with your classmates. Here are some other questions to think about.

a. Does it fit your personal definition of friendship?

b. According to the song, when do friends need each other most?

c. How can a friend "brighten up even your darkest night"?

6. Role Play

Pairwork. Imagine a situation when "nothing is going right." Write out a dialogue in which one friend calls another to ask for help. What would a good friend say or do? Practice your dialogue, then perform it for the class.

7. Share a Poem

This poem was originally written in Spanish by a poet from Nicaragua, Daisy Zamora. Listen to the Spanish version first. Then read the English translation.

Daisy Zamora (1950-)

Daisy Zamora was born in Managua, Nicaragua in 1950. As a young girl, she attended private religious schools and was later trained as a psychologist. However, she is best known as a poet and a painter. She was also active in the political movement that overthrew the dictator Somoza Bebayle in 1979. She now lives with her husband and three children in Managua, where she also teaches and continues to write poetry.

Letter to My Sister Who Lives in a Foreign Land

by Daisy Zamora
tr. Margaret Randall & Elinor Randall

. . . And I was sent south of the village of Wei
—covered with little laurel arbors—
and you to the north of Roku-hoku,
until all we had in common were thoughts
and memories

—"Letter from the Exiled One,"–Li-Tai-Po

I still remember our first games:
parades and paper dolls,
and Teresa, the doll we couldn't stand:
Teresa-are-you-able-to-come-and-set-the-table.

Life doesn't move backwards and I want to know you.
Re-know you.
That is, know you all over again.
Of course there will be things I'll recognize.
I'm interested in your special places,
your friends, so different from mine
who speak another language and follow other paths.

Danbury, Hamden, and Middletown,
Hartford and Meriden. All those places
so familiar to you and to your memory.
In our shared blood I have lived two lives,
many lives.

8. Match

On your own. Find these people, places, and things
in the poem.

a. a Chinese poet

b. the title of a Chinese poem

c. two villages in China

d. a doll

e. four towns in North America

Activity 8: Match

1. Elicit the answers. (*Answers:* (a) Li-Tai-Po,
(b) Letter from the Exiled One, (c) Wei and Roku-hoku, (d) Teresa, (e) Danbury, Hamden,
Middletown, Hartford, and Meriden.)

2. Direct students' attention to the biographical
information about Zamora on page 146. On a map
of New England point out the location of the five
cities (in Connecticut) mentioned in the poem.
Have a volunteer read aloud the lines by Li-Tai-Po.
Ask students to compare the situations in the two
poems.

Activity 9: Share Ideas

1. Ask a volunteer to read the discussion questions. Circulate and participate in the groups' discussions. When students finish talking about the questions, ask them to pick out a part of the poem that talks about a kind of bridge between the two sisters. Ask them to quickwrite about the way this bridge connects them and then to share their ideas with their groups.

2. *Optional:* Have groups compose a letter from Zamora's sister in answer to the poem. They may want to use some of the biographical information about Zamora in composing their letter.

Activity 10: Write

1. *Part a.* Ask a student to read the instructions. Let students know that they will be sharing what they write, as they may be sensitive about sharing very private information or feelings.

Optional: It may help students to quickwrite first about the relationship to generate ideas and memories about shared activities.

2. *Part b.* If possible, groups should include speakers of other languages besides English so that group members will benefit from the reader's explanation of his or her letter.

Activity 11: Preview

1. *Part a.* Compile a class list on the board as students offer ideas. Ask students about the position of older people in a culture that they are familiar with, Ask, *Are older people treated respectfully? What is their place in the family? What is their contribution?*

2. *Part b.* Distribute AM 4/2. Before students begin their discussions, ask them to think about an older person they know well and to quickwrite for five minutes about that person. Ask them to try to recall both positive and negative feelings they have about this person. Then ask a

(Continued on page 149.)

---

9. Share Ideas

Groupwork. What kind of bridge does the poet want to build? Why is it important to her? Share your ideas with the group.

10. Write

a. On your own. Write a letter, note, or poem to a relative or friend who does not live nearby. Remind the person of a memory you both share. Write it in the language you would naturally use to communicate with this person.

b. Groupwork. Share your letter with a small group of classmates. Read it first in the original, then explain it to the group in English.

11. Preview

a. Classwork. Look at the title of the article before you begin to read. What do you think the article is about? Look at the photograph. What kinds of bridges are the people in this picture building?

b. Pairwork. What words come to mind when you think of an older person? Make a list of descriptive words. Which words describe positive qualities? Which describe negative ones? Group your words on a chart like this one.

Positive (+)	Negative (–)	Neutral (neither + nor –)

12. Shared Reading

Across Ages
by Scott Brodeur

What words come to mind when you think of an older person?

If your answers are: mean, cranky[1], helpless, or boring, you are not alone. They are the same words some Philadelphia[2] students used to describe older people.

That was before the students joined Across Ages, a new program. Across Ages pairs youths with older people who act as their mentors.[3] The purpose is to get teenagers and older people to understand and help one another.

"When we first found out we were going to have mentors, we asked how old they would be," says Will Bush. "They told us 40 and older. We thought, man, that's old."

"But when the first meeting was over, nobody wanted the mentors to leave. We were having so much fun."

Mentors meet with students once a week. Together, they talk about school, homework, personal problems, or whatever else comes up. They also go on trips to places like basketball games, museums, and restaurants.

A New Start

Reaching out to someone older has helped Steven Mason find direction in his life. Before Across Ages, he was missing school. He wasn't doing his homework. He didn't have a lot of faith in himself.

Then Steven met his mentor, Earl P. Powell. Now he's getting A's and B's instead of failing.

"When we get together, we go eat somewhere and talk, " says Steven. "We talk about my grades and what I want to be when I grow up. Mr. Powell encourages me to do my best in school. He makes sure I do my homework. He really cares."

Some students have problems at home. Many live with just one parent. Others are exposed to[4] violent crimes as well as drugs and alcohol at a young age. They like the extra attention they get from their mentors.

"When our mentors talk to us, they listen and understand," says Will. Mentors are often easier to talk to than parents or relatives, he says.

[1] **cranky**   easily annoyed or angered
[2] **Philadelphia**   the largest city in Pennsylvania
[3] **mentors**   wise and trusted teachers or counselors
[4] **are exposed to**   come into contact with; forced to see

---

Activity 11: Preview *(continued)*

volunteer to read the instructions. After they write, ask students for examples of positive, negative, and neutral qualities that came to mind as they quickwrote. Write one or two qualities on the board under each column heading.

Activity 12: Shared Reading

1. Ask students to read the first three paragraphs of the article. Then ask them to work with a partner and compare their own ideas about older people with those of the Philadelphia students before the mentor program started. Ask students to predict what kind of activities the teenagers and their mentors would enjoy together.

2. Have pairs combine into groups of four students and take turns reading paragraphs to each other.

3. After students read the article, ask them which shared activities they predicted, and whether any of the "bridges" in the article surprised them. Elicit any qualities that they now might want to add to their lists in *Activity 11*.

4. *Optional:* Ask pairs of students to role play a meeting between a mentor and a teenager that they read about in the article.

"Parents are busy people. Sometimes, they can be too busy to hear everything a child has to say," says Anna Mizell, 68. "But I'm retired. I have plenty of time to listen and help."

Antonio Walker is glad for that.

"Mentors give great advice," he says.

"You can trust them because they have all this experience. They know how it is."

Sam Wyche, 75, is the mentor for Will and Antonio. Sam says he gets as much out of the program as the students.

"I enjoy the kids. I like doing things with them," Sam says. "They're interested in what I have to tell them. That makes me feel good."

Sam got involved for another reason, too. "I hope I'm helping kids who really need it," Sam says. "I wasn't the greatest boy in the world when I was their age. But it's even tougher to grow up now, and I want to help push these kids through it.[5]"

Pat Lewis, 62, agrees with Sam.

"Children can't be children today," Pat says. "There are pressures to get into drugs and to have sex at an early age. It's not even safe for many kids to walk outside after dark anymore."

Pat often tells stories about safer times when she was a kid. Students love to hear her talk about trolley[6] rides and old-fashioned cars.

"You can learn from the stories," says Aaron Taggart, "They're fun to hear."

Pat also encourages students to try new things and to build on their talents.[7] Together, they've worked on arts, crafts, and writing projects.

"So many students are talented," Pat says. "Our job as mentor is to find those talents and to urge them to keep up at it."

Joy Harris loves showing Pat her poems. Pat's poems have been published in books. Joy has been writing since she was 7.

"Mrs. Lewis will be on the other side of the room and stop everything when she sees me,"

Joy says. "It's great to have someone who takes an interest in my work like she does."

But Pat does more than just read Joy's poems. "She tells me my poems are good," Joy says. "She says I have to keep doing it because I have a special talent. I smiled when she said that. It made me feel really great."

A Special Project

One project that helped mentors and students learn about each other was an oral history. Students interviewed the mentors and recorded what the mentors shared about their lives.

Through the oral histories and spending time together, students began to realize something: Older people are regular people too. Even some myths students used to believe are disappearing.

"I used to think older people got tired quickly," says Antonio. "But when Mr. Powell plays basketball with us, and we're dragging tired, he's like, 'Come on, just another couple shots.'"

Finding your own mentor can be helpful to students everywhere, Steven says. "I would tell other kids to find an older person who can be their mentor," he says. "It's fun. And it's great to always have someone there for you."

Steven and the other students have changed since they started in Across Ages. When you ask them to describe older people, the words they use now are: nice, fun, caring, and funny.

"I never thought I'd tell someone I had a friend who was 75 years old," says Antonio. "But now I do."

[5]**push these kids through it**   help them succeed
[6]**trolley**   an electric streetcar
[7]**talents**   natural abilities or skills

13. **Share Ideas**

Groupwork. Discuss the article with the members of your group. Here are some questions to think about.

a. How did the young people in this article change?

b. What did the younger people learn from the older people?

c. What did the older people learn from the younger people?

d. Would you agree to participate in a program like "Across Ages"? Why or why not?

14. **Write**

On your own. Think about the readings and discussions of friendship you have had. Look at the sentences you wrote with your group in #3. Write a longer explanation of what friendship means to you. Write at least one complete paragraph.

Begin by organizing your ideas in the form of a cluster like the one below. You can add to this one or make a completely different cluster of your own.

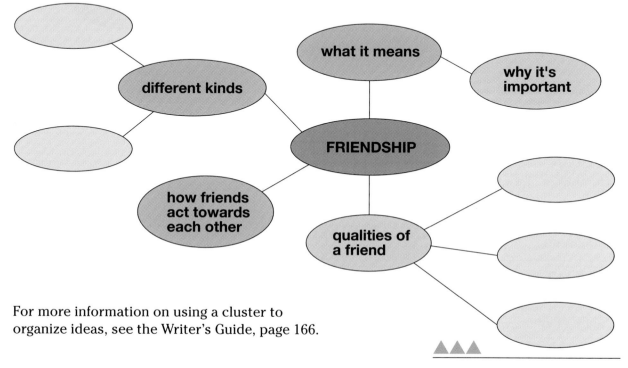

For more information on using a cluster to organize ideas, see the Writer's Guide, page 166.

Activity 13: Share Ideas

1. After groups discuss the questions, ask them to share ideas with the class.

2. *Optional:* To extend the activity, ask students to write a description of an ideal mentor. They may want to consider personal qualities, special talents, gender, and age in their description.

Activity 14: Write

1. Ask students to review their journal writings and the definition sentences that they wrote for *Activity 3.* You may also want to play the tape of the Carole King song again at this point.

2. Give students time to work on their cluster diagrams. Then have them work with a partner. Ask them to explain to their partners what friendship means to them, and to use their diagrams as notes to guide their explanations. Circulate and join in as students explain their ideas. Model responses by asking additional questions and encouraging students to give examples.

3. When students finish their writing, ask them to read their paragraphs to each other in small groups.

Ask students to look at the illustrations on pages 153 and 155 and to predict what the story is about. Then ask a volunteer to read the introduction. Ask for other examples of science fiction that students know about (many will have seen parts of the *Star Wars* and *Star Trek* series). Brainstorm categories of daily life with students (e.g., communication, relationships with people, food, transportation, housing). Ask students to work in small groups and list ways these things have been depicted in science fiction. How might they change in the new millennium?

Activity 1: Research

Distribute AM 4/3. Ask students to note other interesting facts as they do their research, especially information related to the possibility of life on Mars. When they finish their research, combine pairs into groups of four or six students to pool information. Ask what they could not find, and elicit other interesting facts. Compile the additional information that students offer in a chart on the board. (Information: distance from sun: Earth—92.9 million miles, Mars—141.5 million miles; length of year: Earth—365 days, Mars—687 days; number of moons: Earth—1, Mars—2; Average atmospheric temperature: Earth—59°F; Mars— -220°F at the poles, 68°F at the equator; composition of atmosphere: Earth—mainly nitrogen and oxygen with small amounts of carbon dioxide, Mars—mainly carbon dioxide and nitrogen with small amounts of argon and other gases; signs of life: Earth—plants and animals, Mars—no signs of life found by space probes.)

Chapter 5: Bridges Across Time and Space

*S*cience fiction writers build bridges by imagining what life will be like in the future. In this chapter, you will read a selection from *The Martian Chronicles,* in which science fiction writer Ray Bradbury invites readers to look at one vision of the future. How can this kind of imaginary bridge help people build a better world?

Study Strategy:
Taking Notes in a Chart
See page 169.

1. **Research**

Pairwork. Search in an encyclopedia or science dictionary. Find the following facts about Earth and Mars.

	Earth	Mars
Distance from the sun		
Length of year		
Number of moons		
Average atmospheric temperature		
Composition of atmosphere (gases)		
Signs of life		

2. Preview

a. Classwork. Based on what you know about Mars, do you think life could exist there? Share your ideas with your classmates.

b. Groupwork. Imagine intelligent life on Mars or on another planet. Discuss how the alien creatures might look, act, and communicate with outsiders. Make a sketch of your aliens and describe them to the class.

c. On your own. Read this description of *The Martian Chronicles*, a science fiction novel written by Ray Bradbury and first published in 1946.

This is the story of the people who, as the first arrivals in a far-off land, failed in their efforts to build a new world in the image of the world they had left. It also tells of a strange, dying race—men and women with eyes like golden coins who wore masks to hide their feelings and could stroke books to bring forth songs.

This is a brilliant and imaginative fantasy that is deeply rooted in reality. It is a prophecy that is made without despair.

This is the work of one of America's finest storytellers. To read Ray Bradbury is to escape in time and space to that world where fancy and irony show people things about themselves they would otherwise fail to see.

d. Classwork. From this description, would you be interested in reading the novel? Why or why not? Explain to your classmates.

Activity 2: Preview

1. *Part a.* Ask volunteers for their ideas about the possibility of life on Mars. Encourage them to relate their speculations to the information on the board from *Activity 1.*

2. *Part b.* Have each group appoint a spokesperson to describe how the alien looks, acts, and communicates. Pass around the pictures for everyone to enjoy.

3. *Parts c* and *d.* Draw students' attention to the illustration and ask whether it attracts them to the book. Have students read the jacket copy silently, and then to select parts of the description that make them want or not want to read the novel. Have students work with partners to read the parts they selected and explain why these sentences make them want or not want to read Bradbury's book.

Activity 3: Read

1. Have students read the title and the first paragraph, and look at the illustration. Then ask them to write one question about the meeting mentioned in the title. Elicit several questions and write them on the board. Ask students to speculate about the answers, such as:

A   I wonder whether the Martian and Tomas will be able to communicate.

B   They might use some kind of sign language.

2. Have students silently read the story through. Ask them to look for information about the questions that they wrote. Then have them work in pairs to read their questions and the answers they found in the text.

3. Have partners read the story aloud to each other. Before they read, ask students, *What did Tomas Gomez and Muhe Ca do to create a bridge between them?* Ask students to look for ways the two were able to connect.

4. After students read to each other, have them join other pairs to pool their ideas about how the two characters were able to forge connections (for example, smiling, waving, and tapping themselves on the chest, looking at each other, talking, learning the other's language, offering a drink).

3.   **Read**

On your own. Read this selection from *The Martian Chronicles.* As you read, try to imagine yourself in the position of the colonist from Earth, Tomas Gomez. How would you feel? What would you do?

August 2002: Night Meeting

It was a long road going into darkness and hills and he held to the wheel, now and again reaching into his lunch bucket and taking out a piece of candy. He had been driving steadily for an hour, with no other car on the road, no light, just the road going under, the hum, the roar, and Mars out there, so quiet. Mars was always quiet, but quieter tonight than any other. The deserts and empty seas swung by him, and the mountains against the stars.

There was smell of Time in the air tonight. He smiled and turned the fancy[1] in his mind. There was a thought. What did Time smell like? Like dust and clocks and people. And if you wondered what Time sounded like it sounded like water running in a dark cave and voices crying and dirt dropping down upon hollow box lids, and rain. And, going further, what did Time look like? Time looked like snow dropping silently into a black room or it looked like a silent film in an ancient theater, one hundred billion faces falling like those New Year balloons, down and down into nothing. And that was how Time smelled and looked and sounded. And tonight—Tomas shoved a hand into the wind outside the truck—tonight you could almost touch Time.

He drove the truck between hills of Time. His neck prickled[2] and he sat up, watching ahead.

He pulled into a little dead Martian town, stopped the engine, and let the silence come in around him. He sat, not breathing, looking out at the white buildings in the moonlight. Uninhabited for centuries. Perfect, faultless, in ruins, yes, but perfect, nevertheless.

---

[1]**fancy**   an interesting or amusing thought
[2]**prickled**   felt a tingling sensation

He started the engine and drove on another mile or more before stopping again, climbing out, carrying his lunch bucket, and walking to a little promontory[3] where he could look back at that dusty city. He felt very good, very much at peace.

Perhaps five minutes later there was a sound. Off in the hills, where the ancient highway curved, there was a motion, a dim light, and then a murmur.[4]

Tomas turned slowly with the coffee cup in his hand.

And out of the hills came a strange thing.

It was a machine like a jade-green insect, a praying mantis,[5] delicately rushing through the cold air, indistinct,[6] countless green diamonds winding over its body, and red jewels that glittered[7] with multifaceted[8] eyes. Its six legs fell upon the ancient highway with the sounds of a sparse rain which dwindled[9] away, and from the back of the machine a Martian with melted gold for eyes looked down at Tomas as if he were looking into a well.

Tomas raised his hand and thought Hello! automatically but did not move his lips, for this was a Martian. But Tomas had swum in blue rivers on Earth, with strangers passing on the road, and eaten in strange houses with strange people, and his weapon had always been his smile. He did not carry a gun. And he did not feel the need of one now, even with the little fear that gathered about his heart at this moment.

The Martian's hands were empty too. For a moment they looked across the cool air at each other.

It was Tomas who moved first.

"Hello!" he called.

"Hello!" called the Martian in his own language.

They did not understand each other.

"Did you say hello?" they both asked.

[3] **promontory**	a high ridge of land	[6] **indistinct**	not clear
[4] **murmur**	a low, continuous sound	[7] **glittered**	shone
[5] **praying mantis**	a large pale green insect with forelimbs often held in a praying position	[8] **multifaceted**	having many parts
		[9] **dwindled**	slowly disappeared

"What did you say?" they said, each in a different tongue. They scowled.[10]

"Who are you?" said Tomas in English.

"What are you doing here?" In Martian; the stranger's lips moved.

"Where are you going?" they said, and looked bewildered.[11]

"I'm Tomas Gomez."

"I'm Muhe Ca."

Neither understood, but they tapped their chests with the words and then it became clear.

And then the Martian laughed. "Wait!" Tomas felt his head touched, but no hand had touched him. "There!" said the Martian in English. "That is better!"

"You learned my language, so quick!"

"Nothing at all."

They looked, embarrassed with a new silence, at the steaming coffee he had in one hand.

"Something different?" said the Martian, eyeing him and the coffee, referring to them both, perhaps.

"May I offer you a drink?" said Tomas.

"Please."

The Martian slid down from his machine.

---

[10]**scowled**   frowned angrily
[11]**bewildered** puzzled

Ray Bradbury (1920-   )

Ray Bradbury was born in 1920 in Waukegan, Illinois. He published his first story for a science fiction magazine in 1940. *The Martian Chronicles* was his second and most well known book. It was produced as a movie in 1960 and as a television miniseries in 1980. His other works of fantasy and science fiction include *The Illustrated Man* and *Fahrenheit 451*, which were also made into motion pictures.

4. Role Play

Pairwork. Act out the conversation between Tomas and the Martian. Remember, one of you will have to speak in a language other than English for part of the conversation.

5. Share Ideas

Groupwork. What's your reaction to the story? Share ideas with the people in your group. Here are some questions to think about.

a. Which part of the story was most interesting?

b. Is it similar to any story you have read or heard before? Please explain.

c. How did you feel after you finished this selection?

d. Most science fiction stories teach readers a lesson. What lesson do you think Ray Bradbury wanted to get across in this part of the novel?

e. Do you want to read more of *The Martian Chronicles*? Why or why not?

6. Analyze

On your own. Reread the second paragraph in the selection. How does the author describe "time"? Group the words and phrases used to describe "time" into three categories:

| TIME | | |
Smells like . . .	Sounds like . . .	Looks like . . .
dust		

Activity 4: Role Play

Optional: Ask students to continue working with the same partners to invent the next part of the story. Then have them form groups with other pairs and compare stories.

Activity 5: Share Ideas

1. Ask volunteers to read the instructions and the five questions.

Circulate and join in as groups share ideas. Encourage them to refer to specific parts of the text to illustrate their ideas.

2. *Optional:* Bring in a copy of *The Martian Chronicles* and read the next part of the encounter between Tomas and Muhe Ca to the class.

Activity 6: Analyze

1. Have a volunteer read the instructions. Distribute AM 4/4, one copy to each pair of students. When students finish the task, write the question and answer from the *Language Focus* box on the board. Then write the three categories. Have students ask and answer questions using the patterns in the *Language Focus* box. Complete the chart as they answer. (*Smells like:* dust, clocks, people. *Sounds like:* water running in a dark cave, voices crying, dirt dropping down upon hollow box lids, rain. *Looks like:* snow dropping silently into a black room, a silent film . . . one hundred billion faces falling . . .)

2. Ask students to choose one of the images and quickwrite about the feelings that it evokes. Have them work in groups and report how they reacted to the images that they chose.

Activity 7: Describe

You may want to bring in pictures, perhaps from collections of fine photographs, to stimulate ideas for concrete sensual images for concepts or emotions. If helpful, suggest using at least two words or phrases about each perception and follow this model:

Time

water running in a dark cave

dust, clocks, and people

voices crying

rain

snow dropping silently

into a black room

Activity 8: Apply

Have magazines and newspapers handy for students to consult as they work. They can clip pictures and headlines that they want to include in their time capsules and publish their lists on a poster or bulletin board.

Activity 9: Write

1. Suggest that students reflect on the items they included in their time capsules. What would they like to change about some of the items? What aspects of life that they reflect could be improved? With the millennium approaching, there are many magazine articles predicting life in the future. If feasible, bring one or two articles to class for students to look over for ideas. Encourage students to have fun with this and to illustrate some of their ideas about what people will wear, what houses will look like, etc.

2. Have students choose one group member to take notes about the ideas they generate in step one. These thoughts can be the basis for the introduction and conclusion of their presentations.

(Continued on page 159.)

> **Language Focus:**
>
> **Describing Perceptions**
>
> ■ What did "time" look like to Tomas?
> ■ It looked like snow . . . .

7. Describe

a. Pairwork. Choose another concept or emotion you can describe in a similar way, such as peace, success, joy, or fear. How does it smell? How does it sound? How does it look? Use your imagination to think of as many descriptive words and phrases as you can.

b. Look over the list of words with your partner. Use some of these words to write a short poem.

8. Apply

Pairwork. Imagine that you have been asked to collect things to place in a time capsule from your city or town that will not be opened for 1000 years. The capsule will be carefully sealed so that nothing inside will age or be destroyed. What do you want the people of the future to know about the way you live? Make a list of the things you would put into the capsule. Here are some ideas for things to include.

> newspaper articles
>
> clothing items
>
> photos

Get together with another pair and exchange lists. Give reasons for your choices.

9. Write

Groupwork. Reflect on the story. How would you like to be able to learn another language so quickly? Think about some other things that might be possible in the future. Work with your group to write a description of an ideal society. Here are some ideas to help you get started.

1. In *The Martian Chronicles,* Ray Bradbury wrote about a group of people who wanted to leave the problems of Earth behind and create a new society on Mars. Suppose you had a chance to build a new society on a different planet. What would it be like? How would it be different from life on Earth? Discuss your ideas with your group.

2. Choose one of these aspects of life in your ideal society to write about. Each member of the group should choose a different topic.

    housing

    transportation

    food

    money

    social life

3. Make a list of your ideas on paper. Discuss them with your classmates before you begin to write.

4. Write a paragraph about your topic. Read it aloud to the group. Ask someone in the group to tell you the main ideas.

5. Ask for suggestions from the group on how to make your paragraph better. See the Writer's Guide (p. 174) for more ideas on revising your first draft.

6. With your group, decide on the best order for putting the paragraphs together. Prepare a presentation of your group's work for the rest of the class.

3. Students will need to work together to write an introduction and conclusion for their group's presentation. Groups can present orally, as a dramatic reading, or publish as poster presentations.

Activity Menu

Read and discuss the activities with the class. Have each student select an activity. Then have students review the work they have completed for the unit and select any tasks that they can build on for the activity that they have chosen. Students can work individually, in pairs, or in groups. When students complete their projects, have them present their work to the class.

Activity Menu

1. Construct a Flat Beam

Place two large hardcover books on their ends, about eight inches apart. What do you predict will happen if you attempt to span the distance with a flat piece of paper? Fold a sheet of 8.5 × 11 inch paper lengthwise every inch or so, making each crease in the opposite direction.

Do you predict that the folded paper will make a stronger or weaker beam? Tell a classmate. Place the folded paper between the two books. Place a paper clip, a coin, and finally a small book on the beam. How much weight will it take? Was your prediction correct?

2. Research a Bridge

Find out as much as you can about a bridge in your city or state or a well-known bridge somewhere else. Find when and why it was built. What kind of bridge is it? What materials were used in it? Is it a bridge for automobiles? for people? for railroad trains? How much is it used? How was it paid for? Use an encyclopedia or books and magazines from the library to help you find facts about your bridge.

Take notes and write a report on your bridge or tell the rest of the class about it.

3. Request Support

During the administration of Franklin D. Roosevelt (1933–1945), a great many bridges, roads, and public buildings were constructed under a special U.S. government program called the Works Progress Administration. This program helped people who were unemployed, and it produced some of the country's finest architecture. The Golden Gate Bridge in San Francisco, for example, was built during this period.

Write a letter to your Senator or Congressman, proposing funding for a construction project in your area. Explain why your community needs this project.

Describe the benefits both present and future and speculate on what might happen if it is not funded.

4. Analyze a Popular Song

Select a popular song about love or friendship. Listen carefully to the words several times. What kind of relationship is it about? What does it say about life? Tell a classmate.

5. Plan a Ceremony

Work with a small group of classmates to plan a ceremony that will mark a transition. For example, it could mark the completion of the course or the end of school year. Decide who you will invite, what will happen during the ceremony, what you will wear, and how you will celebrate. Present your plan to the rest of the class.

6. Write a Poem

Write a poem to someone with whom you have a close relationship. The poem can be long or short, but it should form a "bridge" between you and the person to whom it is addressed. Share your poem with a classmate.

7. Search for an Ideal Mentor

What would you look for in a mentor? What kind of experience and background would your ideal person have? Write a "volunteer opportunity" notice that specifies these qualifications and abilities. Describe special ways you would like a mentor to help you.

8. Communicate Friendship

How can former enemies become friends again? Think of some symbols people use to communicate that they no longer wish to fight. Imagine a situation in which two people are so angry that they refuse to speak to each other. Suggest a way one of them can send a signal to the other that would help end the conflict. Try acting out your situation with a classmate.

Read On

The Eighth Wonder of the World

The Brooklyn Bridge is considered[1] one of the greatest engineering feats of the 19th century. For many years after its completion in 1883, it was the longest suspension bridge in the world, and the first to use steel cables. The bridge, which New Yorkers liked to call "the eighth wonder of the world," spans the East River between the boroughs[2] of Brooklyn and Manhattan in New York City.

The bridge was the master work of John Augustus Roebling, a German immigrant who unfortunately did not live to see its completion. Mr. Roebling died as a result of a construction accident in 1871, only two years after work on the bridge began. His son, Washington Roebling, took over as chief engineer, but soon became very ill from a disease caused by his work on the bridge.

Unable to move from his bed, Washington Roebling directed construction by watching from his apartment window. Several times a day, he sent messages with his wife, Emily Roebling, to and from the construction crews. In the process, Mrs. Roebling learned more and more about bridge construction, and soon began to take responsibility for many of the important decisions herself.

Today, the Brooklyn Bridge is still a vital link[3] in the city's transportation system, and is considered a work of great architectural beauty that has continued to inspire[4] numerous artists, poets, muscians, and writers.

[1] **considered**   thought of
[2] **borough**   part of a city or state
[3] **link**   part of a system
[4] **inspire**   to give creative energy

Poetry of Friendship

by José Marti   /   *tr. by Raúl Nino*

I cultivate a white rose
In June as in January
For a genuine friend,
That gives his unadorned hand

And for the cruelty that plucks
This heart that lives within
I do not cultivate gardenias nor weeds
I cultivate a white rose.

The Eighth Wonder of the World

1.   Draw students' attention to the title and pictures, and elicit their knowledge of the Seven Wonders of the World (the most splendid sculpture and buildings of the ancient world). Have students look up *feat* (an accomplishment requiring courage and skill) and ask them to speculate about why it required courage to plan and build the Brooklyn Bridge.

2.   Ask students to read the piece silently the first time. Then do a class reading, with each student taking one or two sentences. Alternatively, have students work in pairs and take turns reading paragraphs to each other.

3.   Ask students to list the three most interesting facts that they learned in the reading. Ask volunteers for their facts and compile a class list on the board.

4.   *Optional:* There are many books and articles about the Brooklyn Bridge and about the Roebling family. Ask students to work in groups and to write questions about additional information they would like to have about the bridge or about the Roeblings. Bring some materials in and have students look through them for information. Ask groups to share this information with the class when they finish.

Poetry of Friendship

1.   Have students work with partners and take turns reading the poem to each other.

2.   Ask students to select one of the nouns described in the poem (e.g., a white rose, his unadorned hand, the cruelty that plucks this heart) and to quickwrite for several minutes about the phrase. Tell students that they may want to think about the following questions as they write: *Imagine you are looking at the thing you chose right now. What does it look like? What symbolic meaning does it have for you?* Ask students to share their ideas with their partners.

3.   *Optional:* Draw students' attention to the first and last lines of the poem. Invite them to write a poem about friendship using a similar pattern.

APPENDIX A
Guide to Study Strategies

1. Brainstorming

Brainstorming is a good way to collect ideas for writing. It is an especially useful strategy to use with a partner or with a group of people.

To brainstorm a set of ideas, follow these steps :

- Write your topic on a piece of paper. This might be a word, a phrase, or a question.
- Think about your topic and write down every idea that comes to mind. Don't evaluate your ideas. Just think and write quickly.

Example:

Topic: **Important decisions**

> *when to get married*
> *where to live*
> *whether or not to go to college*
> *who to marry*

After brainstorming, reread your list and circle the ideas that interest you.

2. Classifying

Classifying means organizing information into groups or categories. For example, you might classify a list of clothing into two groups:

Example:

(unclassified information)

> coat, boots, bathing suit, sweater, shorts, T-shirt, parka, gloves

(classified information)

Cold Weather Clothing	Hot Weather Clothing
coat	bathing suit
boots	shorts
sweater	T-shirt
parka	
gloves	

3. Listening for Specific Information

Listening for specific information can help you listen carefully and understand what you hear. Before you listen to a lecture or a tape recording, ask yourself the questions below:

- What am I going to hear about? What is the topic?
- What do I already know about the topic?
- What questions do I have about the topic? What do I hope to learn?
- What kinds of information do I expect to hear? Dates? Names? Descriptions?

4. Making a Story Map

Making a story map helps you focus on important information in a story. When you make a story map, look for these main parts of the story:

Characters:	Who are the people in the story?
Setting:	Where does the story take place?
The problem:	What is the central issue?
	What are the characters trying to do?
Important Events:	What happens in the story?

Title: _____

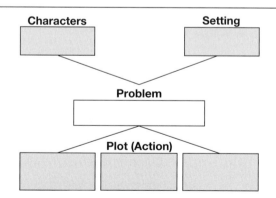

5. Making a Time Line

Making a time line is a way to organize information visually. A time line helps you see the order of events over time. It can also help you find examples of cause and effect.

Example: **Time Line of Spacecraft Exploration**

1957	First artificial Earth satellite First animal in space
1959	First television images of the Earth from space
1961	First human in space First human to orbit the Earth
1963	First woman in space
1965	First space walk
1966	First spacecraft to enter the atmosphere of another planet (Venus) First spacecraft to orbit the Moon First successful soft landing on the Moon
1968	First manned orbit of the Moon
1969	First landing of humans on the Moon

6. Making a Tree Diagram

Making a tree diagram is a useful way to organize your ideas. Before you make a tree diagram, you might want to first list ideas about the topic. Then reread your list of ideas looking for ways to group your information. Write these categories or groups on your tree diagram. Then list ideas in each group.

Example:

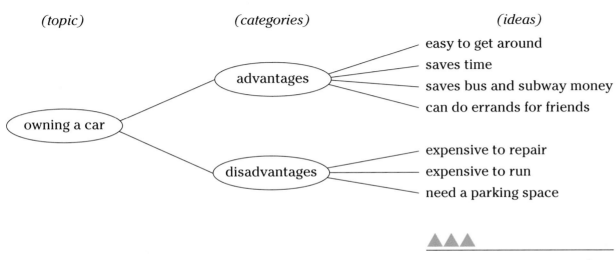

(topic)   *(categories)*   *(ideas)*

owning a car

advantages
- easy to get around
- saves time
- saves bus and subway money
- can do errands for friends

disadvantages
- expensive to repair
- expensive to run
- need a parking space

7. Making a Web Diagram

Making a web diagram or a cluster diagram is a good way to collect ideas before you start to write. Making a web diagram can also help you see connections between big ideas and details.

Follow these steps to make a web diagram:

1. Write your topic in the center of a piece of paper. Circle it.

(**goals**)

2. Think about your topic. What words and ideas come to mind? Write each thought in a smaller circle and connect it by a line to the circle in the center.

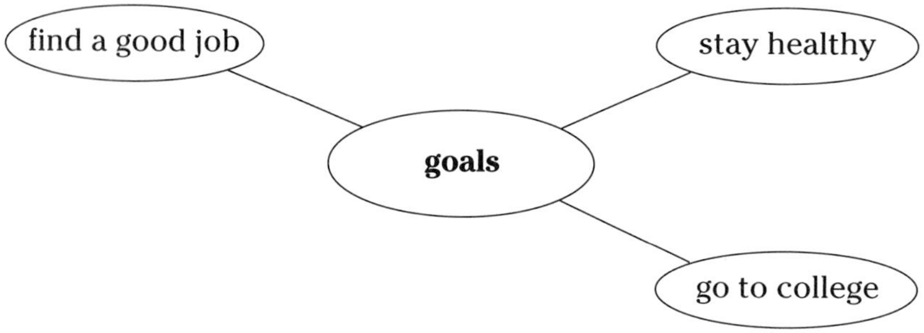

(find a good job)   (stay healthy)

(**goals**)

(go to college)

3. Think about the ideas in the smaller circles. What details come to mind? Write your ideas and connect them to the smaller circles.

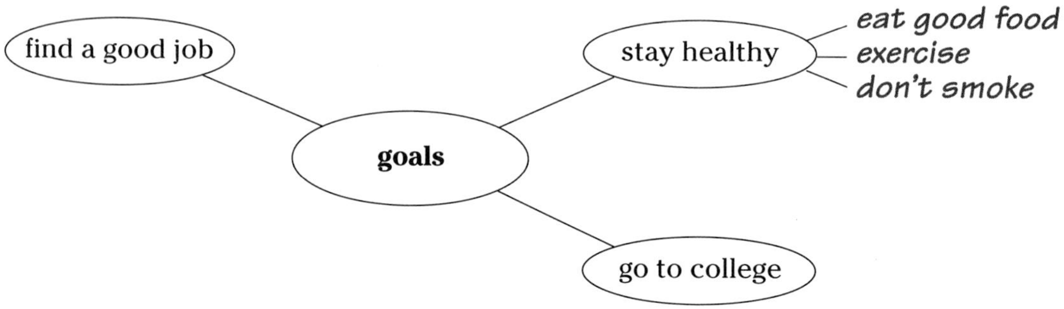

(find a good job)   (stay healthy)— *eat good food*
                                                  exercise
                                                  don't smoke

(**goals**)

(go to college)

8. Predicting

What do you think will happen next in the story? What do you think the outcome will be? When you answer questions like these, you are predicting.

When you predict, you use what you already know about a topic, person, or event. Using what you already know helps you make a logical prediction. Making predictions helps you focus on the material you are studying. You make a prediction and then read to check if your prediction is correct.

 ## 9. Previewing

Previewing is a strategy that can help you understand what you read. The word *preview* means "to look before." To preview an article or story, look over the whole reading before you start to read.

- Look at the title and ask yourself questions about it. What does the title mean to you? What do you think the article or story is about?

- Look at any pictures and predict what the reading is about.

- Recall what you already know about the topic. Think of other things you would like to learn about the topic.

- Read the first paragraph and the last paragraph. Try to figure out the main idea of the reading.

- Set a purpose for reading. Decide what you hope to find out as you read.

10. Quickwriting

Quickwriting, or freewriting, is a useful way to collect ideas for writing. Follow these steps to quickwrite:

1. Choose a topic—something you want to write about.

2. For five to ten minutes, write quickly. Don't worry about grammar or spelling. If you can't think of a word in English, write it in your native language. The important thing is to write without stopping.

3. If you can't think of anything to write, put that down or write the same word over and over again.

4. When you have finished writing, read over your ideas. Circle the ideas that you might want to explore further.

Example:

What is a lake in a storm like? I live near a lake. When it's windy the waves get big, like the waves on the ocean. I can sometimes hear the waves from my house, like some big monster walking on the beach. What else can I say? What else can I say? Waves, waves, waves. What do waves smell like? What do they taste like? If a wave could talk, what would it say? Waves in a storm make me feel uncomfortable—not peaceful . . .

11. Taking Notes in a Chart

Taking notes helps you organize and remember important information. When you take notes, write down the most important information only. To save time and space, write short phrases instead of sentences. The notes in the chart below were made after reading an article about the writer Nicholasa Mohr.

Example:

Nicholasa Mohr

Paragraph	Topic	Details
2	family	<ul><li>parents from Puerto Rico</li><li>lived in New York City</li><li>7 children</li></ul>
3	career as an artist	<ul><li>studied at several art schools</li><li>exhibited her paintings</li><li>did pictures for book jackets</li></ul>
4	career as a writer	<ul><li>wrote novels and short stories</li><li>wrote about Puerto Rican immigrants</li><li>received an honorary Doctor of Letters degree</li></ul>

12. Using Context

Sometimes you can guess the meaning of an unfamiliar word by looking at the context—the other words in the sentence or nearby sentences. While you might not be able to figure out the exact meaning of the word, you may be able to determine its general meaning. This allows you to read without looking up every new word you meet. The examples below show some of the ways you can use context to guess the meaning of new words. The underlined words in the sentences provide context to help you guess the meaning of the boldfaced words.

A definition:

> The **period** of a wave means <u>the time it takes for succeeding waves to pass a fixed point</u>.

A description:

> Near the coast, the pattern of waves becomes more **orderly**—<u>a series of long, evenly spaced ridges</u>.

> Luis Herrera is a **frail** person, only <u>five feet, three inches tall and 115 pounds</u>.

A comparison or contrast:

> In New York, the family lived in a **cramped** apartment, very <u>different</u> from their <u>comfortable house</u> in Haiti.

> Luis Herrera was an **amateur** cyclist for four years, but when he turned sixteen, he became a <u>professional</u>.

A related series of words:

> Harriet Tubman was a <u>strong</u>, **determined** woman.

Cause and effect:

> I was so **absorbed** that <u>I didn't hear footsteps coming up behind me</u>.

Setting:

> While we were <u>on the ship</u>, a <u>wave crashed through</u> the large **hatch**; I got soaking wet and my wife, who was already <u>in bed</u>, was completely drenched.

A synonym:

> Thousands of slaves <u>ran away</u> each year. Some **fled** to get away from cruel owners.

APPENDIX B
Writer's Guide

The Writer's Guide is a series of suggestions that can help you work toward getting your ideas down on paper in finished form, ready for others to read. These suggestions are intended to guide you through some steps that work well for many writers. Use this guide as a menu. As you gain experience, you will learn to select and adapt the steps into a personal writing process that works best for you.

As you begin a writing assignment, start at the top of the diagram and move clockwise around the circle. Ask yourself questions as you go. Remember that the process is not fixed or rigid. Feel free to move back and forth between the steps whenever you need to recycle ideas or revise what you have written.

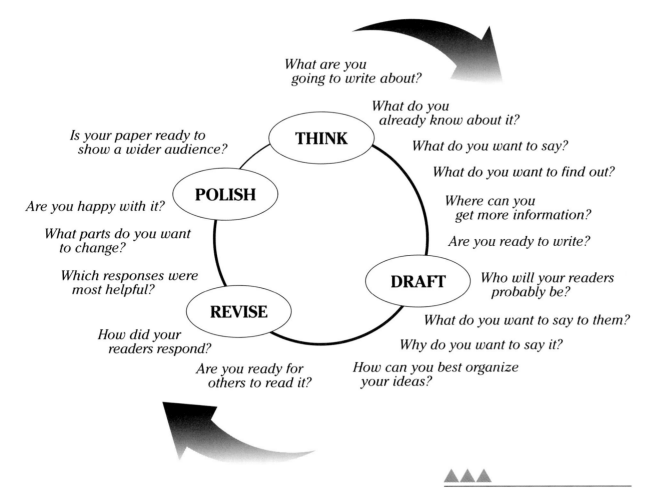

What are you going to write about?

What do you already know about it?

What do you want to say?

What do you want to find out?

Where can you get more information?

Are you ready to write?

THINK

POLISH

DRAFT

REVISE

Is your paper ready to show a wider audience?

Are you happy with it?

What parts do you want to change?

Which responses were most helpful?

How did your readers respond?

Are you ready for others to read it?

Who will your readers probably be?

What do you want to say to them?

Why do you want to say it?

How can you best organize your ideas?

1. Think

Reflect Gather your thoughts about something that happened in the past or on a topic that you have strong feelings about. Take a walk or find a peaceful place where you can relax and concentrate.

Visualize Paint a picture in your mind's eye of something that might happen in another place or time. Add as many details as you can.

Keep a Journal Write down your thoughts and feelings as they happen, or as you think about a specific topic. Journal entries can be as long or as short as you wish, and in any style you choose. You can also use your journal to record some of the other activities listed below.

Quickwrite Quickwriting is a great way to explore your own ideas and experiences related to a topic. Decide about how long you want to spend at it, then concentrate as hard as you can on the topic. Write whatever comes into your head, but don't stop thinking and writing until the time period is up. If you want to continue, take a break before you start again.

Discuss Try out your ideas on a friend. Express your own opinion, but be sure to listen to others, too. The more you talk and listen, the clearer your own ideas will become.

Brainstorm Work with a partner or a small group of classmates to think of ideas related to a topic. Think as hard as you can, then say aloud the words or phrases that come into your mind. One person in your pair or small group can write down the ideas. When the session is over, you can decide which ideas you think are important.

Make a List Lists are especially useful when you are trying to think of a lot of examples of a category, like *walls built by people* or *qualities you look for in a friend*. Since two heads are better than one, it is a good idea to make lists with a friend whenever you can.

Do Research Get more information about your topic by reading or asking other people. Think of some specific questions before you begin. Decide who you can ask or where you can look for the answers. Try checking out the library for books, newspapers, magazines, and encyclopedia articles related to your topic. Take notes on the important things you hear or read.

Focus Your Ideas From all you have thought about, decide on the one main thing you want to say.

▲▲▲

Organize Ideas   Think about ways of relating ideas to each other by making a chart or diagram. It doesn't have to be beautiful, as long as you can understand it and explain it to a classmate. Here are some examples of charts and diagrams used in this book.

Charts

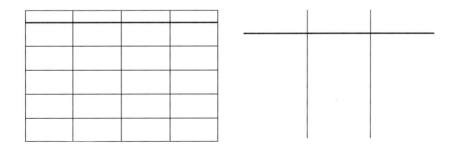

Diagrams

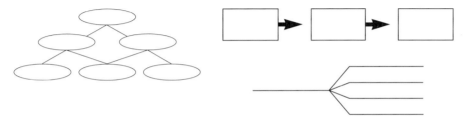

2. Write a First Draft

Have a Purpose   Ask yourself why you are writing. Do you want to describe something or someone? Do you want to express your opinion or convince your reader that something is true? Whatever your purpose is, keep it clearly in mind as you begin to write.

Have a Plan   Look back over everything you have written down so far—lists, quickwriting, journal entries, and notes. You may want to jot down a short outline, or plan. You might also just decide to keep your plan in mind as you sit down to begin your first draft. What are you going to say? Where will you start? How will you finish? Use your plan as a map, to help you move toward your goal. Keep in mind, however, that it is all right to change the plan itself as you explore new directions and discover new ideas.

▲▲▲

Have an Audience in Mind	Who do you expect to read what you write? Choose an audience, either real or imaginary, and keep this group of readers in mind as you write your first draft. Knowing who you are writing for helps you decide on the best ways of saying things. In most cases, your first audience will be your classmates and your teacher. However, you can pretend that your paper or letter will reach other readers (and maybe it really will!)
Get It Down on Paper	Just write! Don't worry about making mistakes. Try to get your ideas down on paper as completely as you can, but don't worry if you get stuck or if some parts seem too long. Keep asking yourself what else your readers might want to know. Stop writing your first draft when you are ready to show it to a small group of classmates and to your teacher.
Invite Responses	Ask your readers to respond to your first draft in one or more of these ways.

- Read your paper aloud. Ask your classmates or your teacher to tell you the most interesting parts. Ask them what else they would like to know.

- Make copies for your readers. Ask them to tell you what they think it is about. Ask yourself if your readers understood what you meant to say.

- Ask one of your classmates to read your paper aloud. Does it sound the way you thought it would? Do you want to change anything? Ask your classmates to show you parts where they were not sure what you meant

3. Revise

Think Again	Read your paper aloud. Ask yourself if there is anything more you want to say, or if there is anything you want to clarify.
Use Responses	Think about your classmates' and your teacher's responses. Which ones were most helpful? The decision to change your writing is yours, so be sure to use only the responses that *you* think will make your paragraph or paper better.
Reorganize	Ask yourself (or a classmate) if there is any better way to organize your ideas. You may want to revise your first plan or rework an earlier chart or diagram.

Write Again (and Again!)	Sit down and rewrite your paper until you are happy with it. Show it to your readers again. This time, ask for specific ways they feel your paper can be improved. Decide which of their ideas you want to include as you revise a second time.

◁ 4. ▷ Polish

Check Grammar	Are your sentences complete? Do your verbs agree with your subjects? Is your use of verb tenses consistent? Ask your teacher if you are not sure.
Check Spelling	Check a dictionary or use a spell check program to be sure your spelling is correct.
Check Punctuation	Proofread your paper to be sure all the periods, commas, and other punctuation marks are in the right places. Check with your teacher if you are not sure.
Check for Smooth Transitions	Read your finished piece aloud one more time. How does it sound? Does it flow smoothly from one idea to the next? Ask your teacher or a classmate for suggestions.

CREDITS

Illustrations — Martucci Studio
Photo Research — Susan Van Etten and
Martucci Studio

Unit 1

xiv Top © David Muench/Tony Stone International; Background © Aaron Chang/The Stock Market. 1 left © Nadia MacKenzie/Tony Stone International, right The Bettmann Archive; 2–3 © Warren Bolster/Tony Stone International; 8 © David Muench/Tony Stone International; 9 The Granger Collection; 12 © Aaron Chang/The Stock Market; 22 The Granger Collection; 23 top The Granger Collection, right The Bettmann Archive; 28 © Mark Kelly/Alaska Stock Images; 29 Courtesy of the Estate of May Swenson; 32 © Nadia MacKenzie/Tony Stone International.

Unit 2

36 © Kurt Knudson; 38 © Stock Imagery; 39 © Rick Rusing/Tony Stone International, right © Chuck Savage/The Stock Market; 40 top © Bob Daemmrich/Stock Boston, bottom © Rick Rusing/Tony Stone International; 41 top © David Hanover/ Tony Stone International; bottom © David Young/Tony Stone International; 53 © Kurt Knudson; 55 top © Frank Herholdt/Tony Stone International, center left Stock Imagery, center right © Diane Padys/FPG, bottom The Stock Market; 58 © Phil Cantor; 60 left © Greg Pease/Tony Stone International, right © Gaby Sommer/The Bettmann Archive; 65 The Granger Collection; 75 © Chuck Savage/The Stock Market; 79 © Courtesy of the Estate of Jacob Lawrence.

Unit 3

80 Top © Bruce Ayres/Tony Stone International, bottom © Bruce Coleman; 81 top © J. McDermott/Tony Stone International, bottom Library of Congress; 82 left © Bruce Ayres/Tony Stone International, right Tony Stone International; 83 top © Bruce Coleman, top right © Susan Van Etten, bottom left © J. Amos/Super Stock, bottom right Susan Van Etten; 92 Heinle & Heinle; 94 © J. McDermott/Tony Stone International; 98 The Bettmann Archive; 99 Library of Congress; 104 © Arthur Grace/Stock Boston; 111 © Danny Clinch.

Unit 4

118 Top © Wide World Photos, bottom © Paul Chesley/Tony Stone Worldwide; 119 background © Myra Miller/Liaison International, top left © Krasner & Trebitz/Liaison International, top right NASA; 121 © Myra Miller/Liaison International; 124 The Granger Collection; 125 top © J. A. Kraulis/Masterfile, center © Larry Ulrich/Tony Stone International, bottom The Granger Collection; 126–127 © Bob Kramer/Stock Boston; 129 top left The Granger Collection, bottom center Wide World Photos, bottom right © Heinle & Heinle; 136 © Paul Chesley/Tony Stone International; 137 top © Bill Arom/Tony Stone International, right © Paul Conklin; 140 © Susan Van Etten; 145 © Krasner & Trebitz/Liaison International; 146 © Kristin Reed; 149 © Bill Aron/Tony Stone International; 152 Both NASA; 153 © Michael Whelan/Bantam Press; 156 The Bettmann Archive; 161 The Bettmann Archive.

𝒯EXT PERMISSIONS

2   "The Waves of Matsuyama" from *Poems of a Mountain Home* by Saigyo, translated by Burton Watson. Copyright © 1991 by Columbia University Press. Reprinted by permission of the publisher.

8   From *The Sea Around Us* by Rachel Carson. Copyright © 1951 by Rachel Carson. Reprinted by permission of Oxford University Press.

20 "Waves of Immigrants" graph from *The Los Angeles Times,* November 11, 1993. Copyright © 1993 by the Los Angeles Times Syndicate. Reprinted by permission.

23 "I was born . . ." by Saverio Rizzo from *The Immigrants Speak: Italian Immigrants Tell Their Story*, by Salvatore LaGumina. Copyright © 1979 by Salvatore LaGumina. Reprinted by permission of the Center for Migration Studies.

25 "Could We Ever Forget" by Ok Kork, translated by George Chigas, from *Cambodia's Lament: A Selection of Cambodian Poetry.* Copyright © 1991 by George Chigas. Reprinted by permission of George Chigas.

26 "Half Cuban" by Monique Rubio from *Hispanic, Female, and Young: An Anthology* edited by Phyllis Tashlik. Copyright © 1994 by Pinata Books, a division of Arte Publico Press-University of Houston. Reprinted by permission.

30 "How Everything Happens (Based on the Study of a Wave)" by May Swenson from *The Complete Poems to Solve.* Copyright © 1993 by The Literary Estate of May Swenson. Reprinted by permission of Macmillan Books for Young Readers, an imprint of Simon & Schuster Children's Publishing Division.

33 "At the Beach" by Kemal Ozer from *This Same Sky* translated by Dionis Riggs. Copyright © 1991 by Kemal Ozer. Reprinted by permission of Dionis Riggs.

35 "The Education of Berenice Belizaire" by Joe Klein from *Newsweek,* Aug. 9, 1993. Copyright © 1993 by *Newsweek,* Inc. All rights reserved. Reprinted by permission.

37 "West Side" from *Hugging the Jukebox* by Naomi Shihab Nye. Copyright © 1982 by Naomi Shihab Nye. Reprinted by permission of Breitenbush Books.

44 "Who's Hu?" by Lensey Namioka from *American Dragons* edited by Lawrence Yep. Copyright © 1980 by Lensey Namioka. Every attempt has been made to find the rights-holder of this article. If located, the rights-holder should contact Heinle & Heinle.

57 "Nicholasa Mohr" from *Speaking for Ourselves* edited by Donald R. Gallo. Copyright © 1994 by Nicholasa Mohr. Reprinted by permission of the author.

63 "The Underground Railroad" by Robert Peterson from *Boys' Life,* February 1993. Copyright © 1993 by Robert Peterson. Reprinted by permission of the author.

67 From *Take a Walk in Their Shoes* by Glennette Tilley Turner. Copyright © 1989 by Glennette Tilley Turner. Used by permission of Cobblehill Books, an affiliate of Dutton Children's Books, a division of Penguin USA, Inc.

73 "The Road Not Taken" by Robert Frost from *Mountain Interval,* 1916, Henry Holt and Co.

75 "Jessica Berg (Graduation)" by Mel Glenn from *Class Dismissed II.* Copyright © 1986 by Mel Glenn. Reprinted by permission of Clarion Books/Houghton Mifflin. All rights reserved.

78 "Footpath" by Stella Ngatho from *Poems of East Africa* edited by D. Cook and D. Rubadiri. Copyright © 1974. Every attempt has been made to find the rights-holder of this article. If located, the rights-holder should contact Heinle & Heinle.

79 "Harriet Tubman" from *Honey I Love* by Eloise Greenfield. Copyright © 1978 by Eloise Greenfield. Reprinted by permission of HarperCollins and Eloise Greenfield.

86 "Zoo" by Edward D. Hoch from *Young Extraterrestrials* edited by Martin Greenberg and Charles Waugh. Copyright © 1958 by King-Size Publications. Copyright © 1984 by Nightfall, Inc. Every attempt has been made to find the rights-holder of this article. If located, the rights-holder should contact Heinle & Heinle.

TAPESCRIPT BOOK 3

Unit One: Making Waves

Chapter 2, page 13, Activity 3.

Listen as a surfer describes his experience riding waves near Waimea, Hawaii. Check things on your list from #2 that are the same as or similar to things the surfer says. Which things were different?

You could see this set coming from way outside. When you're in that situation there's this little voice inside you that's probably just a vital instinct talking saying, "okay, you better paddle for the horizon," and then you get this other voice saying, "okay, you want a big wave, here it is." So fortunately my survival instinct voice didn't talk the other one out of sitting in the line-up waiting, waiting for the big one. So on about the fifth one I just took some strokes and hopped to my feet. I just kind of held on and there was a southeast wind that fortunately kind of kept my surfboard glued to my feet so it felt like a magic carpet ride. I just had this floating sensation, it was so smooth. I could have taken one of the worst wipeouts of my life, but it turned out to be one of the best rides. It was just a great feeling.

Chapter 2, pages 17–19, Activity 9.

Listen and read along.

Earth Shaker, Wave Maker
The Myth of Poseidon

SCENE 1

BARD: This story I will tell, of the all-powerful Poseidon, blue-haired lord of the sea, before whom all mortals tremble. You have heard many tales of his anger, his jealousy, his vengeance—how he stirs up a raging sea, how he shakes the earth when it pleases him— but listeners— this is not a night for such fearful tales. Observe the dazzling stars, feel the gentle sea breeze. Tonight I will please you with a much more delightful story of the mighty Poseidon's gentler side; of his courtship of the delicate and beautiful Queen Amphritite. How did it begin?

POSEIDON: She has stolen my heart. I can think of nothing else. Observe, Dolphin! I am weak. I am no longer able to frighten sailors or terrify land dwellers. I must marry Amphritite!

DOLPHIN: But my Lord, she is terrified of you. She has run away.

POSEIDON: She dares to flee mighty Poseidon? If she is within my watery realm, Dolphin, find her! Bring her here immediately!

DOLPHIN: I'm sorry, my lord. She has fled to the mountains, to the realm of Atlas for protection. He has granted her refuge in a lonely cave, with only birds for companions. She cannot be forced to do anything against her will, but perhaps she can be persuaded.

POSEIDON: Then go to her, Dolphin. You are a creature of both water and air. Tell her of the glittering beauty of this undersea world. Tell her I will share this beautiful golden palace, and all of my power with her.

DOLPHIN: But, my lord. It is you and your power she fears.

POSEIDON: Then convince her! Tell her of my incredible wealth, but not only that. Impress her with my generosity and deep respect for all creatures of the sea. After all, it is only outsiders who enrage me.

DOLPHIN: As you wish. But I can make no promises. She has a mind of her own, as you well know.

SCENE 2

BARD: And so the faithful Dolphin traveled to the realm of Atlas, ruler of a distant, mountainous region on earth. There he found Amphritite hiding in a dark cave, far from the wind and waves. At first, she refused to see him. Only when he shed giant salt tears did she agree to hear what he had to say.

AMPHRITITE: An interesting offer, Dolphin, but I can't imagine living with Poseidon. He's violent, unpredictable, and unreasonable. Look at the way he terrifies innocent sailors. Besides that, he's so ugly! That terrible scowl, and that awful blue hair . . .

DOLPHIN: Beneath his harsh appearance, my lady, there lies a heart of gold. I beg you to listen to one who knows him well. To all of us who live in his realm, he is a wise and gentle ruler. He would never harm the tiniest crab nor cross the majestic whale. His golden palace is beautiful beyond words. All of this he would share with you.

AMPHRITITE: Why is it then, gentle Dolphin, that he shakes the earth and causes the sea to rage, causing untold agony to so many unfortunate mortals?

DOLPHIN: Well, he does have a temper, but his anger is only unleashed against those who fail to honor and treat him fairly.

AMPHRITITE: Dolphin, I believe you are honest and intelligent. Do you think . . .

DOLPHIN: I *know* he is very much in love with you. He mourns because you will not even give him a chance.

AMPHRITITE: This cave *is* getting depressing. Did you say a golden palace?

DOLPHIN: Just come with me and see, my lady. I'll give you a ride on my back. If you don't like him, you will not be forced to stay.

AMPHRITITE: Promise?

DOLPHIN: Promise. You have my word.

BARD: And the loyal Dolphin sped back to Poseidon's realm of the sea with the lovely Amphritite on his back. When he saw her, Poseidon had to stop himself from shaking the earth for joy. With the Dolphin's wise counsel, he persuaded her to become his queen. In time, Amphritite gave birth to a child whose name was Triton. Thereafter, Poseidon was contented to remain in the calm depths of the ocean, occasionally sending Triton to the surface on a golden sea horse to blow up a storm or calm the waves with a mighty blast on his shell.

And with Triton was born an era of peace and prosperity for Greece, in which sailors and land dwellers need not fear Poseidon's wrath as long as they remember to honor him. As for the Dolphin, the sea god did not forget him. Look up at the sky. Poseidon named the constellation "Delphinus" in eternal gratitude, and so that we mortals might be reminded of the creature's intelligence and loyalty.

Chapter 3, page 22, Activity 4 and page 24, Activity 5.

You will hear two stories told by immigrants to America. As you listen to each story, take notes.

Story A

My dear family,

The passage was certainly full of novelty and excitement; I had never imagined that such a huge ship could be tossed about by the waves in such a frightening manner.

Many times I could not walk so much as four or five feet without using two hands to prevent myself from falling. This has strengthened me remarkably. Of the whole 180 passengers probably but 10 were not seasick, and I was fortunate enough to be among them. On one occasion a huge wave crashed through the large hatch; I was soaking wet and my wife, who was already in bed, was thoroughly drenched. Although I held up well throughout the trip, at that moment I thought we would be drowned. We didn't experience anything of special note: eight women gave birth during the voyage without assistance from a doctor or nurse. Of these newborn, two died along with two other children and an old woman. Thus five died. When we came to New Orleans, we sailed up the Mississippi by steamboat to St. Louis.

Hendrik Berendregt, 1846

Story B

I was born in the town of Cimigliono, in the province of Catanzaro, Italy, which I left at the age of sixteen in 1903.

After nineteen days of partly rough seas in an insect laden and decrepit Spanish merchant ship, we sighted the Statue of Liberty and the New York City skyscrapers. We landed at Ellis Island where we had to pass medical examinations, since many immigrants were rejected and were returned to their native land.

From the ferry boat I looked at the magnitude of New York buildings and the extensive harbor and everything seemed gorgeous to me. We had no chance to visit, however, as we rushed to Grand Central Station to proceed to our destination. At Albany we changed trains and after four more hours we arrived at a small station with a few small houses around it

"To the mine," ordered my guardian to the man with the carriage alongside the station. We jumped in and, as we sat inside, he snapped the whip and put the horse at a trot. To the mine? I asked myself, it must be the village name. The carriage came to a stop between two shanties and we descended. My guardian gave the coachman a dollar and, as he left, we entered a worn, semidark room, used as a food and liquor store for the miners.

That was my introduction to the mining town of Talcumville. The town I had imagined to be a beautiful place caused my heart to shrink with disappointment. My home was a dirty shanty in the camp. I thought destiny had transported me to the wrong place, but I decided to adapt myself to the circumstances of the present and hope for a better future.

Saverio Rizzo

Unit Two: Choosing Paths

Chapter 2, page 60, Activity 5.

Listen to the report, and take notes in a chart.

In Columbia, there exists a huge interest in all competitive sports, but there is one that really moves the crowd—the bicycle races. These are amazing things to watch. When you get involved in this world, you will be able to differentiate between a good and a poor bicycle racer. But among all the big names that appear on the scene, there is one that stands out from all the rest—Luis Herrera. He is the most important cyclist of the last decade.

This man is a hero in my country because he is the one with the most victories in Europe. Luis was born in Fusagazuga, and his parents were gardeners on their farm. In his early years, Luis started to help his parents gathering and delivering flowers. He used a bicycle as a vehicle. When he finished with his daily tasks, he would ride to the highest mountains around his home town.

By the age of 13, he participated in his first race. After that moment, he was an amateur cyclist. The next four years were completely full of victories and awards. He turned professional when he was 17.

Luis is a frail person, only five feet, three inches tall and 115 pounds. This set him at a big disadvantage on flat terrain, but at a big advantage on mountainous terrain. The Spanish and French were surprised when Luis won the title of "King of the Mountains" in the Tour de France and the Tour de Spain. Besides these events, he won several foreign championships and much spotlight on the international stage. Three years ago, he gave up because of his age, and he decided to become a businessman. All of the money that Luis accumulated during his career as a cyclist was the basis for a new opportunity. Luis now has more than ten cyclist schools and several factories that produce all of the parts of the bicycle with accessories. He is also a most important flower exporter.

Luis Herrera is an intelligent man. His ambitions do not stop here: He is planning to widen his activities in the flower market. This is a consequence of all the suffering that his family experienced when they were poor people. Luis is and always will be for a lot of Colombian people an example of the principle that if you want to be something in life, you have to work for it. Also you should try to be a good person even though you think that you are reaching the highest mountain.

Chapter 3, pages 67–70, Activity 5.

Listen to the play. Imagine that you are one of the characters in this play. Think about the choices this person makes.

**The Douglass "Station"
of the Underground Railroad
by Glennette Tilley Turner**

FIRST NARRATOR: It is late one night in early November, sometime after the 1850 **Fugitive Slave Act** has become law. Harriet Tubman and a party of eight fugitive slaves have just arrived outside the Douglass home in Rochester, New York.

SECOND NARRATOR: Harriet Tubman goes from a wooded area to the back door, trying to stay in the shadows of the house. Her knock is so quiet it can hardly be heard.

FIRST NARRATOR: One of Douglass' sons looks out the window and whispers:

FIRST SON: It's Moses.

SECOND NARRATOR: Frederick Douglass turns the lamplight off and goes to the door— just barely opening it.

FREDERICK DOUGLASS: Come in, Moses.

FIRST NARRATOR: Harriet Tubman steps inside, and whispers . . .

HARRIET TUBMAN: I have eight. I had them wait in the woods 'til I knew it was safe to come in.

FREDERICK DOUGLASS: One of my sons is the **lookout.** He let us know you were nearby and that **the coast is clear.**

ANNA DOUGLASS: Welcome, Harriet. Have them come in.

SECOND NARRATOR: Harriet Tubman signals to her company of slaves. One at a time they approach the house just as she had done.

FIRST NARRATOR: Douglass barely opens the door and admits the slaves. Once they are inside, they gather near the fireplace to warm themselves after their long journey. Some are barefooted; others are wearing summer-weight clothes.

FREDERICK DOUGLASS: Congratulations. Moses has brought you to the doorstep of freedom. The land of Canada is just across the lake. You'll be there by this time tomorrow night.

ANNA DOUGLASS: Meanwhile, here's food and some blankets so you can eat and then rest.

FIRST NARRATOR: She gestures to an iron pot in the fireplace and blankets in the corner.

FREDERICK DOUGLASS: I know from experience what it's like to escape. You really can't relax until you get to the Promised Land.

SECOND NARRATOR:	The Douglass' second son appears at the door with a huge ladle and dishes up stew for everyone. In the meantime the first son has gone to take his turn as the lookout.
ANNA DOUGLASS:	How was your trip?
HARRIET TUBMAN:	We had lots of close calls, but made it safely this far. Main thing was trying to race the snow. Didn't want that to catch us. Can't take the chance of leaving **tracks.**
FREDERICK DOUGLASS:	Which route did you take this time?
HARRIET TUBMAN:	Eastern Shore to Wilmington in Delaware. Some of the young ones got scared when they heard the slave catchers' dogs. We had to wade in water so the dogs would lose our scent.
FREDERICK DOUGLASS:	It must have been a relief to reach Thomas Garrett's house in Wilmington, wasn't it?
HARRIET TUBMAN:	Yes, he gave us dry clothes and we slept a while. He had a former friend take us to Philadelphia in a wagon with a false bottom.
FREDERICK DOUGLASS:	Where William Still met you—right?
HARRIET TUBMAN:	Yes. Excuse me, Frederick, but what's the plan for us going from here to Canada?
FREDERICK DOUGLASS:	I've arranged for a friend to get you and your party on the morning train. You'll have to board before daylight, so you won't be seen. Hope you don't mind having to travel in the baggage car. It's geting harder and harder to cross the border.
HARRIET TUBMAN:	Let me stop you, Frederick. I thank you for what you're planning, but I won't feel safe 'til we get on the Canadian side. Can you possibly get somebody to take us across the lake tonight? All of a sudden I had this strange feeling the slave catchers are on our trail.
ANNA DOUGLASS:	Can't you wait until morning? As tired as you all are, a good night's sleep would do you some good.
HARRIET TUBMAN:	Thank you, Anna. I am bone tired and the others are too, but I can't chance waiting. Morning may be too late.
FREDERICK DOUGLASS:	What makes you so sure slave catchers are trailing you?
HARRIET TUBMAN:	There's a $40,000 reward on my head and lots of people want to cash in. I don't know what gave me this feeling, but my **hunches** have been right too many times before to ignore them.
FIRST NARRATOR:	Douglass' second son has made an inconspicuous exit while his parents talked with Harriet Tubman. That son now reappears and announces,
SECOND SON:	Excuse me for interrupting, but my brother and I have arranged to take you across the lake.
HARRIET TUBMAN:	Oh, thank you. You certainly raised your sons well. Thank you all!
SECOND NARRATOR:	Harriet gathers her things and wakens the fugitives in her group.
HARRIET TUBMAN:	Hurry now. It's time to go.
FREDERICK DOUGLASS:	Have a safe journey, Moses.
ANNA DOUGLASS:	God be with you.
FIRST SON:	The coast is clear. Let's go.
FIRST NARRATOR:	Harriet and the fugitives walk in the shadows as the Douglass' first son leads the way to the shores of Lake Ontario.

SECOND NARRATOR:	There the second son is waiting to help them into a boat and they all set out for the Canadian shore.

Unit Three: Breaking Down Barriers

Chapter 1, page 91, Activity 10.

Listen to the first part of Scene 1 and read along.

The Zoo

A Reader's Theater based on the story by Edward Hoch

SCENE 1

FIRST NARRATOR:	It's daybreak in August, sometime in the distant future. Outside the city of Chicago, a line of people is forming in a large parking area.
SECOND NARRATOR:	Suddenly a large spaceship appears above the crowd of people.
FIRST EARTH PERSON:	There it is. There's Professor Hugo's Zoo.
SECOND EARTH PERSON:	What do you think he brought this year?
FIRST EARTH PERSON:	I can't imagine. Did you see the zoo last year?
SECOND EARTH PERSON:	With the three-legged creatures from Mars? They were terrifying!
FIRST NARRATOR:	The spaceship slowly descends to Earth and lands in the parking area.
SECOND NARRATOR:	The sides of the spaceship slide up to reveal barred cages.

Chapter 3, page 98, Activity 1.

The article on pages 100–101 and 103–104 deals with the treatment of Japanese Americans before and during the Second World War. According to the articles, racism against Japanese Americans had a long history in the United States. Listen for the examples of racism in this paragraph from the reading. List them on another piece of paper.

Racism against the Japanese had a long history here. The *Issei,* those born in Japan but living in the United States, were not allowed to own land. Nor were they permitted to become American citizens, no matter how long they lived here. They, and their American-born children, called *Nisei,* were **stoned** in the streets. Many restaurants refused to serve them, barbers would not cut their hair, homeowners would not sell or rent to them. Hand painted signs announced JAPS KEEP MOVING—THIS IS A WHITE MAN'S NEIGHBORHOOD.

Chapter 3, page 106, Activity 9.

You are going to hear some information about the internment of Japanese Americans during World War II. Before you listen, read the questions on pages 106 and 107. Then listen for answers to the questions and take notes.

At the start of World War II, some 120,000 Japanese Americans lived on the West Coast of the United States. At least two thirds of these people were American-born citizens, known as Nisei.

After the surprise attack by Japan on Pearl Harbor, many people living on the West Coast believed rumors that Japanese Americans were involved in sabotage and aiding the enemy. Although completely false, the rumors quickly led to widespread mistreatment of Japanese Americans. Public officials demanded that the federal government move Japanese Americans away from the West Coast.

On February 19, 1942, President Roosevelt gave in to public pressure and issued an executive order allowing the army to move Japanese Americans to "relocation camps" inland from the coast. Posted notices gave Japanese Americans 48 hours to sell their homes, businesses, and personal belongings. As a result, many Japanese Americans suffered heavy losses. One vegetable farmer, for example, was forced to sell his business that was worth over $100,000 for only $5,000.

The relocation camps proved to be little better than prisons. Most of the camps were located in isolated desert areas. They were surrounded by barbed wire and patrolled by armed troops. Families were crowded into small wooden barracks covered with tar paper.

Despite their mistreatment, the Japanese Americans remained loyal to the United States. Nearly 20,000 men volunteered to fight in the armed forces. Many served in the famed 442nd Regiment, which suffered heavy casualities while winning many medals for courage.

Americans now realize that the treatment of Japanese Americans during World War II was unfair and unnecessary. In 1988 the Senate voted to give an apology and a tax-free payment of $20,000 to each of the 60,000 surviving Nisei. While this action could not change the past, it did show a recognition that the past actions had been wrong.

Unit Four: Crossing Bridges

Chapter 3, page 138, Activity 3.

You are going to hear about coming of age in the United States. Listen first for the main ideas. Then look at the web diagram. What information is missing? Listen again and fill in the missing information.

In the United States, there is no single ceremony that marks the change from childhood to adulthood. In some ways the ceremony of graduation resembles a coming of age ceremony. The graduates are set aside as a group, wear special clothes—their caps and gowns—and receive diplomas and advice from older people telling them about their new responsibilities as adults. Among some very wealthy people a debutante

ball marks the "coming out" of the young girl into society and proclaims her readiness for marriage. Confirmation in a church and the bar mitzvah and bat mitzvah are coming of age ceremonies in some American religious communities. In the United States, most of us agree the independence of one kind or another is an important aspect of adulthood, but we may not agree on the most important symbol of adult status. A diploma, a wedding ring, a driver's license, our first paycheck, and voting for the first time are some of the many markers of becoming an adult in the United States.

Chapter 3, page 147, Activity 7.

This poem was originally written in Spanish by a poet from Nicaragua, Daisy Zamora. Listen to the Spanish version first. Then read the English translation.

**Carta a una hermana
que vive en un país lejano**

> . . .Y fui enviado al sur de la villa de Wei
> tapizada de bosquecillos de laureles y tú al
> norte de Roku-hoku,
> hasta tener en común, solamente,
> pensamientos y recuerdos.
> —"Carta del Desterrado" Li-Tai-Po

Todavía recuerdo nuestros primeros juegos:
Las muñecas de papel y los desfiles.
Y a Teresa, la muñeca que nos caía mal:
Teresa-pone-la-mesa.

La vida no retrocede y deseo conocerte.
Re-conocerte.
Es decir, volver a conocerte.
Habrá, sin embargo, cosas tuyas que conserves.
Me interesa saber de tus lugares,
tus amigos, tan extraños a los míos
que hablan en otra lengua y buscan otros caminos.

Danbury, Hamden y Middletown,
Hartford y Meriden. Todos lugares
tan famliares a ti y a tus recuerdos.
A través de la sangre he vivido dos vidas,
múltiples vidas.